THE AMERICAN ALMANAC OF FINANCE: FROM THE GOLD STANDARD TO DIGITAL CURRENCIES

First edition. May 23, 2023.

ISBN: 979-8223526650

AF715581

Written by Peter Alexander Abbott.

The American Almanac of Finance

Peter Alexander Abbott
2023 Edition

Auteur: Peter Alexander Abbott
Coverdesign: Maxwell Stillwater
ISBN: See cover

An investment in knowledge pays the best interest.

Benjamin Franklin

1 Introduction

From the bold strokes of its inception to the intricate patterns of today's complex financial ecosystem, this book invites you to traverse the historical pathways that have led to our current financial landscape and glance into the potential futures that lie ahead.

It is a rich narrative that explores the systems, institutions, successes, and crises that have shaped the nation's financial character. As you turn the pages, you will witness the transformative power of economic ingenuity, the resilience in times of upheaval, and the lessons that each era has engraved upon the stone of our financial history.

This book is crafted not just to be informative, but also engaging. It is woven with narratives that bring life to events, making the seemingly complex labyrinth of finance approachable and captivating. We will discuss the prominent figures who stood at the helm in times of challenge and progress, and discover the decisions that have echoed across the decades to shape the present. From the birth of the US Dollar to the dynamic forces of Silicon Valley, each page presents a story waiting to be explored.

Uniquely, this book is designed in a manner that allows you to open any page, start anywhere. Each chapter, each section, has been meticulously constructed as a self-contained exploration of its subject. This is a nod to the interconnected yet autonomous nature of the many facets of finance.

Whether you delve into the emergence of the stock market or the advent of cryptocurrencies, you'll find each area distinctly explored, providing clarity on its relevance and implications.

The Great Depression, the Dot Com Bubble, up to the Gamestop Saga, are dissected, offering valuable insights on the events that precipitated them, their impact, and the recovery.

Through understanding these cycles, we gain a sense of perspective and an awareness of patterns that arm us for future challenges.

Just as significantly, we will discuss the emerging financial trends that are currently molding the American and global economic landscape. The rise of ESG investing, the ever-evolving fintech sector, and the dynamic dance between Wall Street and Silicon Valley are all probed, providing you with a grasp of the forces shaping our world today and tomorrow.

Our financial history, full of triumphs and failures, crises and recoveries, is a testament to the ingenuity, resourcefulness, and resilience inherent in the American economic spirit.

2 The Golden Beginnings

2.1 The Birth of the US Dollar

In a land filled with towering mountains, roaring rivers, and expansive plains, a new world was taking shape. The year was 1775, and the American Revolution had begun to crackle and pop. The colonies, strung out across the Eastern seaboard, had been living under the economic rule of the British Empire. A mix of British pounds, Spanish milled dollars, and an assortment of other currencies sloshed around in the colonial economic stew. Yet, this volatile mix of currencies offered little stability to the fledgling nation. A new form of money was needed - one that was distinctly American.

Enter the US dollar, a nascent idea that held the promise of economic unity and sovereignty. The Continental Congress, an assembly of delegates from the colonies, imagined a currency that would define a nation. It would be the root system from which the mighty oak of American finance would eventually grow. But this newborn currency didn't have an easy start in life. It was backed by nothing but faith and hope - and in those turbulent times, those commodities were in short supply. In its early years, the Continental currency was victim to severe inflation, leading to its rapid depreciation. It reached a point where people remarked, "not worth a Continental," demonstrating the currency's frail beginnings. Yet, amidst the tumult, America's financial architects didn't falter. Alexander Hamilton, the first US Secretary of the Treasury, championed the establishment of a national bank and a bimetallic standard (silver and gold) to bolster the American currency. His forward-thinking strategies set the stage for the future evolution of the US dollar, providing it a concrete foundation upon which to build.

Fast-forward to the early 19th century, the US dollar began to wield influence on the world stage. The Coinage Act of 1792 had formally established the US dollar and defined its value in terms of silver and gold. By pegging the dollar to these precious metals, the United States offered a predictable standard that other nations could trust. This was a game-changing moment, not just for America, but for the world. Into the 20th century, the US dollar's influence expanded exponentially. With the passage of the Federal Reserve Act in 1913, a central bank was created to regulate the supply of money, providing a cushion against financial panics and economic crises. In the aftermath of World Wars and economic upheaval, the US dollar emerged as a key player in global finance, eventually becoming the world's leading reserve currency. Today, the greenback, as it is often affectionately called, serves as a symbol of American economic might. It is the backbone of American finance, fueling a complex, vibrant economy that powers a nation of more than 330 million people. Yet, its history is a saga of resilience, determination, and adaptability, echoing the broader story of America itself. This is a tale not just of dollars and cents, but of vision, courage, and the ceaseless march of progress.

2.2 The First and Second Banks

The United States in the early 1800s was a country in rapid transition. As the dust settled after the American Revolution, the US dollar was beginning to find its footing, and the nation was starting to explore the promise of a new, cohesive monetary system. In the streets of New York, Philadelphia, and Boston, the whisperings of a new age could be heard. It was a time of optimism and enterprise. The notion of American exceptionalism started to gain ground as a young nation envisioned its future.

Hamilton's dream of a national bank had materialized into the First Bank of the United States, instituted in 1791. Despite controversy over its establishment, it played a crucial role in providing financial stability and fostering economic growth. The US dollar's circulation increased, and it began to evolve into a more robust and reliable medium of exchange.

The path of the US dollar was not always smooth. The charter for the First Bank was not renewed in 1811, leading to a period of economic instability. The War of 1812 further strained the young nation's finances, underscoring the need for a robust banking system to support the currency. Recognizing this need, the Second Bank of the United States was established in 1816. This renewed national banking presence provided a steadying hand on the American monetary system. The US dollar began to solidify its role, moving from an experiment towards an established keystone of American financial life. Yet, while these new financial institutions worked to stabilize the American currency, they also faced challenges and controversies. The debate over the role of a central bank in a democratic society, the struggle between state and federal powers over monetary policy, and the battle against corruption and mismanagement all roared in the background.

These early years of the US dollar were a trial by fire, shaping its identity and resilience. They also provided invaluable lessons that would inform the design of future American financial systems, laying the groundwork for the era of the Gold Standard that was soon to come. Despite the turbulence of its inception and early evolution, the US dollar pressed onward.

As a young nation rapidly expanding its borders and wrestling with the challenges of a diverse and growing economy, the United States was also grappling with the complexities of managing a unified currency.

The concept of a single, national currency was still relatively new. Many European nations had long been under the control of monarchs who minted their own coins, while others were formed of a patchwork of smaller states, each with its own distinct currency. The US was treading new territory - it was a republic, born of a revolution, and its currency was a reflection of that unique heritage. Yet, navigating this new path wasn't easy. Throughout the early 19th century, a host of issues arose that put pressure on the fledgling US dollar. The nation was rapidly industrializing, and with that came a need for capital. This demand drove speculation, leading to numerous financial panics, like the Panic of 1819 and the Panic of 1837.

Banks were popping up across the country, each issuing its own banknotes that were meant to be redeemable for US dollars. But, with little regulation, the reliability of these notes varied wildly. In fact, the period earned the name "Free Banking Era," a somewhat chaotic time when anyone could start a bank and issue their own currency. This disorderly financial environment brought inconsistency and uncertainty. A dollar bill from a bank in New York might not be accepted in Illinois or might only be worth a fraction of its face value. Not to mention, counterfeit bills were rampant, further undermining trust in the financial system.

Yet, amidst this cacophony of competing currencies, the US dollar held its ground. It was still the currency backed by the federal government, the unit of account for taxes and public debts. This gave it a stability that many banknotes lacked and served to underscore its central role in the American economy. Through the mid-19th century, the struggle to maintain and manage a unified currency continued. Despite the challenges, the very fact that the United States maintained a single currency through this period of intense growth and transformation was remarkable.

Every financial panic, every failed bank, every counterfeit bill was a lesson learned. They were the raw materials that shaped the evolution of American finance. Each hurdle overcome made the system stronger, more resilient, more prepared for the future.

It's important to remember that the story of the US dollar isn't just a series of facts and figures. It's a human story. It's a story of visionaries and swindlers, of hardworking individuals saving for their future, of businesses striving for growth, and of a nation seeking its path.

The First Bank was a public-private enterprise, with 20% of the capital owned by the federal government and the remaining 80% owned by private investors.

A prominent example of the First Bank's impact was its role in handling the federal government's debts incurred during the Revolutionary War. It provided a means to manage and ultimately pay off these obligations in a structured manner. The bank helped to regulate the nation's money supply, contributing to a more stable economic environment.

The First Bank also faced significant opposition. Critics like Thomas Jefferson were deeply suspicious of centralized financial power and feared that the bank served the interests of the wealthy elite at the expense of ordinary citizens. When its 20-year charter expired in 1811, the bank was not reauthorized due to political opposition.

One notable incident involving the Second Bank was the "Bank War" of the 1830s. President Andrew Jackson, who viewed the bank as a symbol of elite corruption, vetoed the renewal of its charter and removed federal deposits, severely weakening the institution. This act marked a pivotal moment in the history of American banking and reflected the continuing controversy surrounding the concept of a national bank. With the demise of the Second Bank, the United States entered a period known as the "Free Banking Era" (1837-1864). During this time, any group could start a bank and issue notes, provided they met certain requirements. This led to a massive proliferation of banks and banknotes, with over 10,000 different kinds of notes in circulation by 1860.

2.3 The Gold Standard

By the mid-19th century, it became clear that a more regulated banking system was necessary to ensure economic stability. This realization eventually led to the National Banking Acts of 1863 and 1864, establishing a system of national banks and providing for a uniform national currency. These shifts in American banking weren't merely a matter of dollars and cents. They were a reflection of broader struggles — over power, governance, and the nature of American democracy itself.

Through every bank charter and every issued banknote, the story of American finance was being written, setting the stage for the modern system we know today. As the banking system grew and evolved through the 19th century, so too did the underpinnings of the American financial system. At the heart of this evolution was a system that sought to imbue the currency with a tangible value, an objective standard against which the US dollar could be measured. This was the Gold Standard, a system that fundamentally transformed the role of the US dollar and the nature of American finance.

But what exactly was the Gold Standard? Simply put, it was a monetary system where a country's currency or paper money had a value directly linked to gold. Under this system, the government guaranteed the conversion of currency into certain amounts of gold and vice versa. In essence, if you had a dollar bill, it was as good as gold—quite literally. The US, though it had been using gold and silver to back its currency since the Coinage Act of 1792, formally adopted a version of the Gold Standard in 1873. This move marked the beginning of what is known as the classical Gold Standard era, which lasted until the outbreak of World War I in 1914.

The Coinage Act of 1873, sometimes pejoratively referred to as the "Crime of 1873," discontinued the minting of silver dollars and established gold as the sole standard for the dollar. This move had profound implications for the American financial system and the economy at large.

For one, it brought a certain stability to the financial system. By tying the dollar to the value of gold, the government sought to rein in inflation and keep the money supply in check. For another, it sought to inspire trust in the American currency, both at home and abroad. If every dollar was as good as gold, then the credibility of the US dollar was as secure as the gold reserves that backed it.

The adoption of the Gold Standard was not without controversy. In fact, it sparked one of the most heated debates in American financial history. The fervor of the debate surrounding the Gold Standard highlighted just how much was at stake. On one side of the debate were the so-called "gold bugs," who championed the Gold Standard as a bulwark against inflation and financial instability. They pointed to the simplicity and elegance of a system in which every dollar was backed by a fixed amount of gold. This faction included many of the nation's bankers and industrialists, who saw in the Gold Standard a safeguard for their investments and a check on the government's ability to manipulate the currency.

On the other side of the debate were the "silverites" and the "greenbackers," who argued that the Gold Standard was unduly restrictive and favored the wealthy at the expense of the common people. They contended that by tying the currency to gold, the government was limiting the supply of money and thus constraining economic growth. This group included many farmers and laborers, who often found themselves at the mercy of deflationary pressures under the Gold Standard.

One of the most notable events of this debate was the presidential election of 1896, when the Democratic candidate William Jennings Bryan gave his famous "Cross of Gold" speech. Bryan passionately argued for bimetallism, a system using both gold and silver as a basis for the US dollar, as a way to inflate the currency and relieve debt-ridden farmers and laborers. Although Bryan ultimately lost the election to William McKinley, a staunch gold supporter, the election underscored just how divisive the issue of the Gold Standard had become. Despite the controversy, the Gold Standard remained in place, and the US dollar became an increasingly dominant force in the global economy. By the early 20th century, the US was a rising industrial power, and the dollar was widely viewed as a reliable, stable currency. This was not just due to the backing of gold but also to the growing strength of the American economy and the soundness of its financial institutions.

The Gold Standard was not without its problems. One of the inherent issues was that it limited the flexibility of the monetary policy. Since the money supply was tied to the amount of gold, it was difficult for the government to respond to economic downturns by adjusting the money supply. This rigidity would eventually contribute to the severity of the Great Depression in the 1930s. Another issue was that the system depended on the ability of governments to defend their gold reserves. If investors lost confidence in a government's ability to convert its currency into gold, they might demand conversion en masse, depleting the country's gold reserves and sparking a financial crisis. The rigidity of the Gold Standard, while providing stability, also gave rise to significant challenges. When a country's economy needed to expand or contract in response to economic conditions, the fixed supply of gold could be a constraint. For example, during times of economic growth, more currency was needed to represent the increasing amount of goods and services being traded.

If gold supply could not keep pace with economic growth, the result could be deflation, where the general level of prices would decrease. In America, this issue was particularly acute during the westward expansion and the rapid industrialization of the late 19th and early 20th centuries. The economy was growing at a tremendous pace, but the money supply, constrained by the gold reserves, struggled to keep up. This disparity led to numerous financial crises, including the Panics of 1873, 1893, and 1907.

To understand these crises, consider the Panic of 1893. This was a severe economic depression triggered by a run on the gold supply, overbuilding, and risky financing practices in the railroad industry, which led to a series of bank failures. In an attempt to alleviate the crisis, the U.S. government had to inject money into the economy, but its ability to do so was limited by the Gold Standard. This restriction contributed to the depth and duration of the depression. Similarly, during times of economic downturn, the Gold Standard made it difficult for the government to implement measures that could alleviate the situation. When the economy contracts, an increase in the money supply can help stimulate economic activity by making money cheaper and easier to borrow.

Under the Gold Standard, the money supply was tied to gold reserves and could not be increased at will.

These problems were not theoretical; they had real-world consequences. In 1907, a financial panic led to a severe recession, again highlighting the weaknesses of the Gold Standard. Many banks and businesses failed, and the unemployment rate spiked. The Panic of 1907 was so severe that it led to significant reforms in the banking sector, including the creation of the Federal Reserve System, which we will discuss in a later chapter. The Gold Standard also had implications for international trade. Because each country set its own value of gold, exchange rates could fluctuate if countries revalued their currency. This uncertainty could create volatility in international markets and discourage trade. Furthermore, countries with larger gold reserves had an advantage, as they could potentially manipulate their currency to their benefit.

It's clear that while the Gold Standard provided a measure of stability and trust in the U.S. dollar, it also presented significant challenges. The tension between these benefits and drawbacks was a defining feature of the late 19th and early 20th centuries in American finance. This tension, in many ways, set the stage for the eventual transition away from the Gold Standard and towards the modern financial system we know today.

2.4 The Panic of 1907

To fully grasp the complexities and influence of the Panic of 1907 on the American financial landscape, we must first understand the broader economic climate leading up to this historic financial crisis. It's important to remember that the backdrop to this event was a rapidly transforming nation. The United States was in the midst of its Industrial Revolution, a time of feverish growth, significant social change, and burgeoning economic disparities. The early 1900s saw a wave of speculative investing, both in new industries and in the stock market. The country was transitioning from a largely agrarian economy to a more industrialized one. Advances in technology, communication, and transportation were swiftly reshaping industries and markets. The railroad industry, in particular, was booming, offering tantalizing investment opportunities. Yet this rapid industrial growth also created a volatile economic environment. Business cycles were extreme, with periods of rapid expansion followed by sharp contractions.

In 1906, an earthquake devastated San Francisco, one of the most significant financial centers of the West. The rebuilding efforts required massive amounts of cash, much of which was covered by European insurance companies. This led to a substantial amount of gold flowing from Europe to the US, causing money to tighten in London and exacerbating existing economic tensions. 1907 proved to be a turbulent year, marked by an economic downturn and a contraction in the availability of credit. Tensions reached a boiling point in October 1907, when F. Augustus Heinze's attempt to corner the market on United Copper Company stock failed spectacularly. Heinze, along with his notorious associate Charles W. Morse, had conspired to manipulate the price of the company's shares. When their scheme unraveled, it led to a run on the banks associated with Heinze, triggering a cascade of bank failures.

The runs spread quickly across New York City, leading to a general loss of confidence in the financial system. Trust companies, the forerunners of today's investment banks, were hit especially hard. They had been engaging in increasingly risky investment behaviors and were less regulated than traditional banks. As the runs continued, even healthy institutions were threatened as they faced unprecedented demands for cash.

The Panic of 1907 marked a critical moment in American financial history. Not only did it expose the vulnerabilities inherent in the financial system, but it also revealed the limitations of the country's ability to respond effectively to such crises. Under the Gold Standard, the money supply was inflexible, and there was no central banking authority to act as a lender of last resort and inject liquidity into the system during times of crisis.

This monumental event in financial history was not just a crisis but also an inflection point that marked a shift in the understanding of the need for financial reform and central banking. The severity of the Panic underscored the need for an institution that could provide stability and oversight, leading to the creation of the Federal Reserve System in 1913. Before we explore the formation and impact of the Federal Reserve, it's worth spending some time understanding the key players and the significant events during the Panic of 1907. It's through these details that we can truly appreciate the severity of the crisis and its lasting impact on American finance.

As mentioned earlier, the Panic began with a failed attempt to corner the market on United Copper Company stock. At the heart of this scheme were F. Augustus Heinze and Charles W. Morse. Both were influential figures in the financial world, with intricate networks of banks and trust companies. When their plot was revealed, the ensuing scandal was enough to initiate a loss of confidence in the entities they controlled, sparking bank runs and a subsequent credit crunch. The situation quickly spiraled out of control. As bank runs spread across New York City, the Knickerbocker Trust Company, one of the city's largest trust companies, found itself in the crosshairs. On October 22, 1907, customers started to withdraw their deposits en masse from the Knickerbocker, precipitating its collapse and further exacerbating public fear. Within a few days, the panic had spread to other trust companies. The Trust Company of America, another large institution, became the next significant target. Panic-stricken depositors lined up in the streets, eager to withdraw their savings before it was too late. It was a race against the clock, a true financial pandemonium.

Amid this chaos, one figure emerged as an unlikely hero: John Pierpont Morgan, better known as J.P. Morgan. At this time, Morgan was a titan of American finance, controlling a vast empire of banking and industrial interests. Recognizing the dire situation and the lack of a central institution to manage the crisis, he took it upon himself to steer the economy away from total collapse. Morgan, along with a group of influential financiers, convened at his library in New York City to formulate a plan. They worked tirelessly to assess the solvency of the endangered Trust Company of America and other institutions, aiming to prevent further bank failures. Morgan even managed to convince other bankers to pledge their own money to support the faltering Trust Company of America, staving off its collapse.

Despite Morgan's efforts, the panic did not immediately subside. The stock market continued to plummet, and credit was still severely strained. In a move that displayed both his power and his understanding of the critical situation, Morgan convinced the leading New York banks to pool their resources into a fund that could be used to make loans to financial institutions in need. This action helped restore some level of confidence and stability in the banking system. Morgan's intervention was instrumental in curtailing the Panic of 1907, but it also highlighted a glaring problem. It was clear that the United States, one of the world's largest and fastest-growing economies, could not rely on private financiers to manage financial crises. The need for a central banking institution, a lender of last resort that could provide stability during financial turbulence, was now more apparent than ever.

The impact of the Panic of 1907 went far beyond the immediate financial crisis. It triggered a national and even international reevaluation of banking practices and financial regulations. The lessons learned from the panic sparked a series of reforms, including increased oversight of banking activities, tighter restrictions on speculative investments, and, most importantly, the creation of the Federal Reserve System.

As we turn our attention to the establishment of the Federal Reserve, it's crucial to understand how deeply the Panic of 1907 influenced this development. This crisis laid bare the weaknesses of a decentralized banking system and the Gold Standard, propelling the United States towards an era of centralized banking and more flexible monetary policy. The birth of the Federal Reserve marked a significant evolution in American finance, shaping the course of the nation's financial trajectory throughout the 20th century and beyond.

2.5 The Birth of the Federal Reserve

The establishment of the Federal Reserve System was a defining moment in American financial history. It marked a significant departure from the earlier laissez-faire approach to banking and finance, ushering in an era of increased oversight and regulation. The experience of the Panic of 1907 played a central role in prompting this change, highlighting the need for a more resilient and flexible financial system. The idea of a central bank wasn't new in 1913. The U.S. had previously experimented with central banking with the First and Second Banks of the United States.

Both institutions were controversial and faced fierce political opposition, which led to their eventual demise. Still, the idea of a central bank persisted, spurred on by the economic turbulence and financial panics of the late 19th and early 20th centuries.

In the wake of the Panic of 1907, reform became an urgent priority. Various proposals were considered over the next few years, culminating in the passage of the Federal Reserve Act in 1913. This act established the Federal Reserve System, which included twelve regional Federal Reserve Banks and a central governing board, later known as the Federal Reserve Board. The structure of the Federal Reserve System was a compromise between those who wanted a centralized system under the control of the federal government and those who preferred a decentralized system controlled by private banks. The twelve Federal Reserve Banks were distributed across the country, serving as the operating arms of the system, while the Federal Reserve Board, appointed by the President, provided overall direction.

One of the primary functions of the Federal Reserve System was to provide elasticity to the money supply, a feature critically missing during the Panic of 1907. The Federal Reserve could adjust the money supply according to the needs of the economy, enabling it to contract or expand as required. This flexibility was a radical departure from the constraints of the Gold Standard, where the money supply was rigidly linked to gold reserves. The Federal Reserve was also tasked with acting as a lender of last resort, providing banks with liquidity in times of financial stress. This function was crucial in preventing bank runs, which had been a significant factor in previous financial panics. By providing this safety net, the Federal Reserve aimed to stabilize the banking system and instill confidence among depositors.

In addition to these responsibilities, the Federal Reserve also played a significant role in supervising and regulating banks. It established standards for bank operations, examined banks to ensure compliance, and enforced applicable laws and regulations. This supervisory role was intended to prevent the kinds of risky and speculative behaviors that had contributed to financial instability in the past. The creation of the Federal Reserve represented a significant shift in American finance. For the first time, the U.S. had a centralized banking authority with the power to manage the money supply, provide liquidity during financial crises, and oversee the operations of banks. While the Federal Reserve has undergone numerous changes and faced many challenges since its inception, it has remained at the heart of American finance, playing a pivotal role in shaping the country's economic trajectory throughout the 20th century and into the 21st.

As we explore the history and evolution of American finance, it's essential to understand the far-reaching impact of the Federal Reserve. The institution has been instrumental in navigating various economic crises, from the Great Depression to the Financial Crisis of 2008. In the face of these challenges, the Federal Reserve has adapted and evolved, becoming an increasingly important player in the global financial system.

Yet the creation of the Federal Reserve was not without controversy. The institution has faced criticism and debate from its inception, with questions about its effectiveness, its influence over the economy, and its level of transparency. These debates continue to shape discussions about the role of central banking and monetary policy in today's economy.

A tangible example of the Federal Reserve's role can be seen in its response to the Great Depression, a catastrophic economic event that defined the 1930s. The stock market crash of 1929 and the subsequent economic downturn were pivotal moments that tested the Federal Reserve's ability to manage a crisis. When the stock market crashed in October 1929, it set off a chain of events that plunged the United States into the deepest and longest-lasting economic downturn in its history. Millions of people lost their jobs, and thousands of banks failed. The economy contracted sharply, and deflation set in, making debts harder to repay and contributing to a downward spiral of economic activity.

The Federal Reserve, under the leadership of the Federal Reserve Bank of New York and its president, Benjamin Strong, initially responded to the crash by injecting liquidity into the banking system. This was a direct application of its role as a lender of last resort.

When Strong died in 1928, just before the crash, the Federal Reserve lost its most influential leader and was left without clear direction. As the Depression worsened in the early 1930s, the

Federal Reserve made a series of policy errors. Misjudging the severity of the situation, it allowed the money supply to shrink significantly, which was exactly the opposite of what was needed to combat the deflationary pressures in the economy. The Federal Reserve also failed to prevent a wave of bank failures in the early 1930s, further deepening the economic crisis.

2.6 The Great Depression

The Great Depression was a testing time for the Federal Reserve and exposed significant flaws in its management of monetary policy. The institution's failures during this period became a focal point for economic scholars in the decades that followed, most notably Milton Friedman and Anna Schwartz, who argued in their book "A Monetary History of the United States" that the Federal Reserve's errors had significantly contributed to the severity and duration of the Great Depression. These criticisms eventually led to significant changes in the Federal Reserve's policies and operational procedures. The institution became much more proactive in managing the money supply and combating inflation. Furthermore, the Federal Reserve took on an expanded role in managing the overall economy, with an increased focus on maintaining full employment and stable prices.

The lessons learned from the Great Depression still resonate in the Federal Reserve's actions today. For instance, during the financial crisis of 2008, the Federal Reserve, under the leadership of Chairman Ben Bernanke, took decisive action to stabilize the financial system. Recognizing the mistakes made during the Great Depression, the Federal Reserve acted quickly and aggressively to inject liquidity into the financial system and prevent a complete economic meltdown. The role of the Federal Reserve has undeniably evolved over time, expanding and adapting in response to changing economic conditions and lessons learned from past crises. Yet, its core functions – controlling the money supply, regulating and supervising banks, and acting as a lender of last resort – have remained consistent throughout its history.

The evolution of American finance, is not only a story of institutions and policies but also of innovations and revolutions. As we transition into the modern era, we'll explore how developments such as the end of the Gold Standard, the rise of digital currencies, and the emergence of green, sustainable finance have continued to reshape the financial landscape.

While we've touched upon the mistakes the Federal Reserve made during the Great Depression and its significant shifts in policy since then, we've yet to discuss an essential concept that has steered the institution's decision-making - the "dual mandate". The dual mandate refers to the Federal Reserve's statutory objectives of maximum employment and stable prices, set forth by the Congress in the Federal Reserve Act. The dual mandate is a core part of the Federal Reserve's monetary policy framework and has guided its response to economic changes and crises. By striving for maximum employment, the Federal Reserve seeks to ensure that anyone in the country who wants to work has a job. This doesn't mean zero unemployment, as there's always some level of unemployment due to factors like job transitions and mismatches in skills. But it implies striving for the lowest possible level of unemployment that is consistent with stable prices.

The second part of the dual mandate, stable prices, means maintaining a low and steady rate of inflation. This is crucial as high and volatile inflation can disrupt economic activity and cause uncertainty, making it difficult for households and businesses to plan for the future. The Federal Reserve has explicitly defined price stability as a longer-run goal of 2% inflation, a target shared by many other central banks worldwide. Balancing the two objectives of the dual mandate can be challenging, as they can sometimes be at odds with each other. For example, reducing unemployment might require the Federal Reserve to lower interest rates to stimulate economic activity, but doing so could lead to higher inflation. Conversely, to curb high inflation, the Federal Reserve might need to raise interest rates, which could slow down the economy and increase unemployment.

Navigating these trade-offs requires a deep understanding of economic conditions and a careful analysis of economic data. The Federal Reserve employs a large staff of economists who provide research and analysis to inform the decision-making of the Federal Open Market Committee (FOMC), the body responsible for setting monetary policy. The FOMC meets eight times a year to assess the state of the economy, review the outlook for inflation and employment, and decide on the appropriate stance of monetary policy. Over the years, the FOMC has used a variety of policy tools to fulfill its dual mandate. The most well-known of these is the federal funds rate, the interest rate at which banks lend to each other overnight. By raising or lowering the federal funds rate, the FOMC can influence other interest rates in the economy, affecting borrowing costs for households and businesses and thereby influencing spending and investment decisions.

In addition to the federal funds rate, the FOMC has also used other tools to influence monetary conditions, particularly in response to the financial crisis of 2008. These include large-scale asset purchases, often referred to as "quantitative easing", and forward guidance about the future path of the federal funds rate. These unconventional policy tools have allowed the Federal Reserve to provide additional monetary stimulus even when the federal funds rate is near zero, a situation often referred to as the "zero lower bound". The Federal Reserve's pursuit of its dual mandate has played a crucial role in shaping the trajectory of the U.S. economy over the years. By adjusting monetary policy in response to changes in inflation and unemployment, the Federal Reserve has helped to stabilize the economy, smooth out economic cycles, and promote sustained economic growth.

Despite the critical role that the Federal Reserve plays in managing the U.S. economy, its actions are often the subject of intense debate and scrutiny. Questions about the effectiveness of its policies, the transparency of its decision-making process, and the broader impact of its actions on income distribution and financial stability are all part of the ongoing discourse about the role and functioning of the Federal Reserve. The evolution of the Federal Reserve's monetary policy tools provides a fascinating glimpse into the changing dynamics of the American financial system. After the financial crisis of 2008, the Federal Reserve, along with other central banks worldwide, found itself in uncharted territory. The severity of the crisis necessitated a significant policy response, and with interest rates already at or near zero, the conventional tool of cutting rates was largely exhausted.

This led to the development and implementation of what have now come to be known as 'unconventional monetary policies'. One such policy, as briefly mentioned before, is quantitative easing (QE). In essence, QE involves the large-scale purchase of financial assets, such as government bonds and mortgage-backed securities, by the central bank. The aim of QE is to inject money directly into the economy, in an attempt to stimulate spending and investment. The Federal Reserve first embarked on QE in late 2008. Over the next several years, it carried out several rounds of QE, buying trillions of dollars' worth of financial assets. This massive influx of money helped to lower longer-term interest rates, providing a much-needed boost to the economy. QE had a profound effect on the financial landscape. By buying up vast quantities of bonds, the Federal Reserve became a significant player in financial markets. The extra liquidity provided by QE helped to boost asset prices, from stocks to houses, benefiting those who owned these assets.

But QE wasn't without controversy. Critics argued that it risked stoking inflation and creating asset bubbles. Others contended that QE exacerbated income inequality by predominantly benefiting the wealthy, who were more likely to own the assets whose prices were being boosted.

Another unconventional policy tool employed by the Federal Reserve was forward guidance. This involved making explicit statements about the likely future path of interest rates. The idea behind forward guidance is to influence expectations. If people believe that interest rates will stay low for a long time, they're more likely to borrow and spend, providing a stimulus to the economy.

The Federal Reserve started using forward guidance in earnest during the financial crisis. By promising to keep interest rates low for an extended period, it aimed to provide additional assurance to markets, helping to reduce uncertainty and boost confidence.

Like QE, forward guidance also came with its challenges. Communicating about future policy intentions in a clear and credible way is no easy task. Once expectations have been set, changing course can be tricky, as it risks upsetting markets and damaging credibility.

Both QE and forward guidance marked a significant departure from the traditional monetary policy toolkit. They reflected a willingness on the part of the Federal Reserve to innovate and adapt in the face of extraordinary economic challenges. As we move forward in our exploration of American finance, it's essential to understand that the story is not only about institutions and policies but also about the people who have shaped them. Throughout its history, the Federal Reserve has been guided by a diverse array of leaders, each of whom has left their mark on the institution. From the early days of William McChesney Martin, who served as Chairman for nearly two decades and coined the famous phrase about the Fed's job being "to take away the punch bowl just as the party gets going," to Paul Volcker, who tamed the high inflation of the 1970s and early 80s with a bold and controversial policy of high interest rates; from Alan Greenspan, who presided over the Fed during the long economic expansion of the 1990s but was later criticized for his handling of the housing bubble, to Ben Bernanke and Janet Yellen, who led the Fed's response to the financial crisis and its aftermath - these individuals, along with many others, have played a crucial role in shaping the Federal Reserve and, by extension, the American financial system.

The Federal Reserve's history, marked by a series of successes and failures, innovations and controversies, has been instrumental in molding the American economy and its financial structures. But this story is far from over. As we progress through the annals of American financial history, we'll find that the complexities of this evolving landscape only continue to grow. The end of the Gold Standard, the rise of digital currencies, the challenges of financial regulation, and the advent of sustainable finance - these are all pieces of the jigsaw puzzle that continues to shape and redefine American finance.

3 The Stock Market Emergence

The thrilling saga of the American stock market, an extraordinary entity that has powered economic growth, precipitated financial meltdowns, and, through it all, shaped the nation's economic destiny. It's a grand stage where fortunes have been made and lost, where the dreams of countless individuals and corporations have been realized or shattered. This narrative is as much a reflection of human ambition and emotion as it is a chronicle of financial ingenuity and innovation.

We begin with the "Early Stock Market," exploring its rudimentary beginnings in the late 18th century when stock certificates for businesses such as banks and insurance companies were sold to investors in coffee houses and on the street. The chaotic trading scene on Wall Street during these early years was a far cry from today's organized exchanges, but it was where the foundations were laid, setting the stage for an institution that would become synonymous with American capitalism. "The Roaring Twenties" then transports us to an era of unprecedented economic prosperity and exuberance. It was a time when the American stock market captured the imagination of the nation, with stock prices soaring to dizzying heights and ordinary people becoming investors. Yet this period was also characterized by excesses and speculative frenzies, which, as we'll see, sowed the seeds of a devastating downfall.

We'll discuss the darkest hours of the American financial system. a catastrophic event sent shockwaves around the globe and ushered in the Great Depression. We'll examine the fateful events that led to the crash and the human and economic toll it wrought. We then move to the aftermath of the crash in "The Securities and Exchange Commission." Born out of the ashes of the 1929 crash, the SEC was established to restore investor confidence and maintain fair, orderly, and efficient markets. This pivotal development marked the beginning of a new era of financial regulation that profoundly changed the way the stock market operates.

Finally, we'll explore the incredible transformation of the stock market in the late 20th and early 21st centuries. Technological innovations, financial engineering, evolving market structures, the rise of institutional investors, high-frequency trading, and the democratization of investing – these and other developments have reshaped the landscape of the stock market, presenting new opportunities and challenges.

3.1 Early Stock Market

We find ourselves standing beneath the shade of a Buttonwood tree in 1792. It was under this tree that 24 brokers gathered, braving the wilderness of uncharted financial landscapes, to sign what is now known as the Buttonwood Agreement. This agreement, simple yet profound, laid the groundwork for the New York Stock Exchange and brought order to the hitherto chaotic trading practices. Trading in these nascent days was an exhilarating spectacle, rife with speculation and promise. Conducted in coffee houses and bustling streets, the buying and selling of government bonds and banking stocks underpinned the new financial order.

This was no utopian marketplace; insider trading and market manipulation were all too common, thriving in the absence of regulations.

Still, in the face of these challenges, the early stock market began to show signs of growth.

The narrative of progress was primarily driven by the robust expansion of the American economy, the emergence of joint-stock companies, and a growing perception of the stock market as a crucial source of capital for burgeoning businesses. The 19th century bore witness to a series of booms and busts, showcasing the stock market's inherent volatility. Episodes like the Panic of 1837 and the Panic of 1857 served as stark reminders of the risks involved in stock trading.

Each crisis also served to highlight the resilience of the stock market and its ability to recover and thrive.

As the United States transitioned from an agrarian society to an industrial powerhouse, the role of the stock market evolved accordingly. It became a pivotal tool for mobilizing capital, enabling businesses to fund expansive projects that defined the era – railroads, telegraph lines, factories, and mines. In essence, the stock market's contribution was instrumental in driving the U.S. to the forefront of global industrialization. The emergence of the early American stock market represented a significant shift in the way businesses and government entities raised funds. While banking stocks and government bonds were the main financial instruments traded, the range of companies listed on these early exchanges was steadily expanding. The market was finding its feet, and with each step, it was becoming an increasingly critical component of the broader American economy.

The informal gatherings of brokers in coffee houses gradually transitioned into more structured trading sessions, often held outdoors in good weather.

These outdoor sessions presented challenges. Traders had to contend with the noise and hustle of busy streets, and inclement weather often disrupted proceedings. As a result, in 1817, the New York Stock & Exchange Board was formed and indoor locations were established, providing a more consistent and professional environment for trading. Yet, as the stock market began to organize and expand, it remained largely unchecked. Manipulation of stocks by unscrupulous individuals and insider trading was a rampant issue, leading to an unstable trading environment. These practices were emblematic of a market that was still finding its regulatory footing. Indeed, the lack of oversight and transparency created an environment ripe for speculation, often leading to sudden booms and busts.

These market crashes, like the Panic of 1837 and the Panic of 1857, served as grim reminders of the market's fragility. The Panic of 1837, triggered by a bubble in land prices, and the Panic of 1857, precipitated by the downfall of the Ohio Life Insurance and Trust Company, were severe economic downturns that highlighted the inherent volatility of the market. Yet, they also showcased the market's resilience. Despite the significant financial and societal damage they caused, the market managed to rebound each time, demonstrating its fundamental strength.

While the early stock market was characterized by volatility and uncertainty, it also witnessed significant innovation and growth. The establishment of telegraph lines in the mid-19th century revolutionized communication, enabling quicker and more efficient exchange of information. This technological advancement had a profound impact on the stock market, as it allowed for real-time communication of prices and trades, bolstering the market's speed and efficiency.

The early American stock market was not just a mirror reflecting the economic conditions of its time. It was a dynamic and integral part of the country's economic development. As the United States evolved from an agrarian society to an industrialized nation, the stock market played a pivotal role in facilitating this transformation. By mobilizing capital for businesses, particularly in sectors such as railroads, telegraph, and manufacturing, it enabled large-scale projects that drove industrialization and economic growth. The early stock market, therefore, was a key actor in the American economic narrative.

It was not just a stage where financial transactions occurred but an arena where the dreams of a nation were traded. From the tentative trades under the Buttonwood tree to the establishment of the New York Stock & Exchange Board, these early steps in the evolution of the American stock market set the course for the complex financial entity we know today.

As the 19th century came to a close, the American stock market was steadily maturing. While still not the titan of global finance it would become, the market had nevertheless become a prominent feature of the American economic landscape. It had weathered numerous financial storms, including the Panics of 1837 and 1857, and emerged from each crisis stronger and more resilient.

The stock market, once a small gathering of brokers trading beneath a Buttonwood tree, had evolved into an influential and sophisticated financial entity.

The transition from the 19th to the 20th century was marked by significant advances in technology and communication. The telegraph had revolutionized the speed and efficiency of trade, allowing real-time communication of prices and transactions. Furthermore, the advent of the telephone towards the end of the 19th century provided an additional boon to the market, allowing even more efficient communication between traders. This swift exchange of information fueled the stock market's growth, facilitating a rapid increase in the volume and frequency of transactions. Yet, even as the stock market grew in size and sophistication, it remained a high-risk environment. The lack of comprehensive regulation and oversight meant that unscrupulous practices such as insider trading and market manipulation continued to plague the market. These issues underscored the need for improved regulatory measures, a need that would become increasingly apparent as the American economy entered the 20th century.

As the calendar pages turned to the 1920s, a new chapter in the history of the American stock market was about to be written. The post-World War I era ushered in a period of unprecedented economic growth and prosperity, an era that would come to be known as the Roaring Twenties. This was a time of exuberance, both socially and economically, and the stock market was not immune to this wave of optimism. The Roaring Twenties marked a period of extraordinary growth for the stock market. With the war over, industry was booming, and American citizens found themselves with increased disposable income. Many turned to the stock market as a means to grow their wealth, leading to a surge in investment. The optimism was infectious; stocks seemed only to rise, further fueling the euphoria and drawing in new waves of investors eager to participate in what seemed to be a never-ending bull market.

This period of intense speculation was, in part, driven by the introduction of buying on margin – a practice that allowed investors to purchase stocks with borrowed money. The potential for significant returns lured many into the market, amplifying the level of speculation and further inflating stock prices.

With these monumental gains also came substantial risk. The market was now vulnerable to any perturbation that could undermine investor confidence, potentially triggering a large-scale sell-off.

Thus, the stage was set for a complex interplay of events and factors that would come to define this era in American financial history. The Roaring Twenties, with its remarkable boom and subsequent bust, would serve as a stark reminder of the cyclical nature of financial markets. It would underscore the perils of unchecked speculation and illuminate the need for improved market oversight and regulation. Yet, even amidst the turbulence, the resilience and adaptability of the American stock market would continue to shine through, pointing towards the dawn of a new era.

3.2 The Roaring Twenties

As the decade of the 1920s began, America stood at the precipice of an era marked by extraordinary change and evolution. The nation was shaking off the ravages of World War I and stepping into a period of peace and prosperity. Optimism filled the air, and the economy, fueled by innovation and an abundance of consumer goods, was taking off. The stock market, not to be left behind, embraced this buoyant spirit, marking the dawn of an era known as the Roaring Twenties. It was a unique period in the American financial history that witnessed a flurry of activity in the stock market. Stocks were on a seemingly unstoppable upward trajectory, and the idea of the 'permanent bull market' began to take hold in the collective psyche. The allure of easy money drew in millions of new investors, many of them ordinary citizens who had never before participated in stock trading. These new market participants, armed with optimism and the promise of quick profits, propelled the market to dizzying heights.

The optimism of the era was spurred in large part by the widespread adoption of buying on margin. This practice allowed investors to purchase stocks with a small down payment, typically around 10-20% of the stock's value, while borrowing the remainder. As stock prices rose, investors could sell at a profit before repaying their loans. It was a system that, while profitable in a rising market, was incredibly risky.

Simultaneously, the business landscape of America was transforming. The advent of mass production techniques, especially in the automobile and consumer goods industries, led to an unprecedented increase in productivity. Companies like Ford and General Electric were churning out products at a remarkable pace, capturing the imagination of investors and contributing to a surge in corporate profits.

This industrial boom translated into rising stock prices, further fueling the bullish sentiment in the market.

The feverish speculation that characterized the Roaring Twenties wasn't just confined to Wall Street. The real estate market, particularly in Florida, was also in the throes of a speculative frenzy. Tales of overnight riches lured investors into the market, inflating a real estate bubble that would eventually burst in 1926. With the stock market reaching new highs, a sense of invincibility permeated the air. Yet, beneath the surface, the foundations were starting to crack. The speculative frenzy, fueled by margin buying and excessive optimism, had inflated a bubble that was growing increasingly unstable. Warning signs began to appear, such as the collapse of the Florida real estate bubble, but the euphoria of the Roaring Twenties drowned out the voices of caution. The stage was being set for a dramatic shift, one that would end the decade on a note vastly different from how it had begun. As the Roaring Twenties continued, the stock market rose with an almost relentless fervor. Between 1925 and 1929, stock prices more than quadrupled, and the Dow Jones Industrial Average rose from 63 points in August 1921 to a peak of 381 points in September 1929. The spectacle of seemingly unlimited gains turned Wall Street into a national fascination. Newspapers and radio broadcasts disseminated market news to the public, further fueling the fervor for stock trading. More and more people, irrespective of their financial background, began to speculate in stocks.

The stock market had become a symbol of prosperity and opportunity. It was, for many, a ticket to the American dream. Buying stocks on margin allowed everyday people to participate in the financial market and potentially make substantial profits. Even those with limited means could now invest in Wall Street, buying stock for just a fraction of its price and paying the rest later when the stock was sold. This democratization of the stock market was a double-edged sword; it expanded the base of investors, but it also exposed more people to the inherent risks of market speculation.

On the sidelines of the financial frenzy, President Calvin Coolidge's administration embraced a laissez-faire approach towards the economy. Coolidge believed that business was the engine of America's prosperity, and he encouraged an environment of low regulation and low taxes. This political climate further stimulated the economy and, in turn, the stock market. Yet, for all the optimism and prosperity of the Roaring Twenties, there were growing concerns among some financial observers. Critics argued that the stock market's meteoric rise was fueled by speculation rather than underlying economic fundamentals. Some economists and business leaders voiced concerns over the high levels of consumer and corporate debt and the skyrocketing valuations of stocks, which they felt were unsustainable.

Despite these warnings, most Americans, caught up in the excitement of the bull market, turned a deaf ear to the cautionary voices. It seemed that nothing could halt the heady ascent of the stock market.

But as the decade wore on, the strains of the overextended financial system would start to show, and the Roaring Twenties were headed for a dramatic conclusion.

In the midst of the Roaring Twenties, new industries were being born, transforming the economic landscape. The automobile industry, led by figures like Henry Ford, was revolutionizing transportation. Radio corporations such as RCA were connecting Americans like never before. These innovations were seen as harbingers of a new era, and their stocks were some of the hottest on the market. The excitement surrounding these sectors drove their stock prices to staggering heights, adding fuel to the speculative fire.

Not all was well beneath the surface. While the stock market was booming, the agricultural sector was in a severe depression. Crop prices had fallen dramatically after World War I, and farmers were grappling with high levels of debt. Additionally, income inequality was growing, with the wealthiest 1% of Americans earning more than a third of all income. These issues pointed to deep-seated imbalances in the economy. The Roaring Twenties, it seemed, were not roaring for everyone. As the decade neared its end, the cracks in the veneer of prosperity were becoming increasingly apparent. The bull market, with its frenzied speculation and inflated stock prices, was on a collision course with reality.

In the heady days of the late 1920s, optimism remained the dominant sentiment. The relentless upward march of the stock market seemed to encapsulate the spirit of the age. A new generation of investors, flush with the confidence of seemingly endless prosperity, believed they were invincible. They had not lived through a major financial downturn, and their experiences had conditioned them to believe that the market's rise was unstoppable. It was an intoxicating belief, one that would come with a steep price.

Yet, behind this facade of unending prosperity, there were economic tremors that hinted at the impending financial earthquake. Agricultural distress continued to plague the rural parts of America. Many small farmers, unable to compete with larger agricultural businesses, were driven into bankruptcy. Despite the stock market's exuberance, these farmers saw little of the prosperity that city-dwellers were enjoying. Meanwhile, the gap between the rich and the poor continued to widen. While the wealthiest Americans accumulated vast fortunes, a significant portion of the population struggled to make ends meet. The top 1% of the population owned roughly 40% of the nation's wealth, the highest it had been in decades. This level of inequality contributed to an unstable economic foundation.

Despite these warning signs, the party continued on Wall Street. The newly introduced concept of buying on margin allowed for rampant speculation, enabling even those with modest means to partake in the stock market's spectacular rise.

This system of buying on margin was like a house built on sand; it relied on the continued rise of stock prices. If prices fell dramatically, those who had bought on margin would be unable to repay their loans, leading to a cascade of selling that could trigger a market crash.

As the Roaring Twenties neared its conclusion, the American stock market was a powder keg waiting to explode. Overvaluation, rampant speculation, and economic inequality had created an environment ripe for disaster. And in the fall of 1929, the spark that ignited the powder keg finally arrived. The Stock Market Crash of 1929 marked a dramatic end to the Roaring Twenties, sending shockwaves through the American and global economies. It was a financial tsunami of catastrophic proportions that would usher in a decade of economic struggle and reshape the landscape of American finance. The Roaring Twenties, with all its glitter and glamour, was about to give way to the somber reality of the Great Depression.

3.3 Stock Market Crash of 1929

The fall of 1929 would go down in history as one of the darkest periods of American finance. The stock market, which had been the symbol of the nation's prosperity throughout the Roaring Twenties, was about to take a plunge that would shake the foundations of the American economy. The Stock Market Crash of 1929 was not just a sudden collapse; it was a cataclysmic event that signaled the end of an era and the beginning of a decade-long economic struggle. On October 24, 1929, a day that would be known as Black Thursday, the U.S. stock market began to show signs of distress. In a sudden and unforeseen shift, stock prices started to drop precipitously. Panic quickly set in among investors, triggering a massive sell-off. Within hours, a record 12.9 million shares were traded on the New York Stock Exchange, a volume so high it overwhelmed the ticker tape system, causing it to lag behind by hours.

The news of Black Thursday spread quickly, causing shockwaves throughout the nation.

A group of leading Wall Street bankers intervened in a bid to stem the tide, purchasing large amounts of stock to restore confidence in the market. Their efforts seemed to work momentarily, as the market rebounded slightly the next day. But the respite was brief.

The following week, the market experienced further tumultuous days—Black Monday and Black Tuesday, on October 28 and 29. On these two fateful days, the stock market collapsed completely. Despite the efforts of the bankers, the market was unable to resist the massive sell-off pressure. On Black Tuesday alone, over 16 million shares were traded, and the Dow Jones Industrial Average fell by 12%. By the end of the trading day, investors had lost $14 billion, an astronomical sum for that era.

The Wall Street Crash of 1929 marked the beginning of a prolonged economic downturn, one that would come to be known as the Great Depression. The crash wasn't just a financial disaster; it was a psychological blow that shattered the unwavering confidence of the Roaring Twenties. The belief in ever-rising stock prices had been irreversibly damaged. The American public, who had once viewed the stock market as a ticket to quick wealth, was now deeply disillusioned.

The reverberations of the Stock Market Crash of 1929 were felt not just in the U.S. but around the world. The collapse of the American stock market sent shockwaves through global financial systems. As American banks called in overseas loans in a desperate attempt to cover their losses, foreign banks found themselves in a precarious position. The economic crisis quickly spread across the Atlantic, plunging Europe into a financial downturn.

The magnitude of the crash was staggering. Between September and November of 1929, the market lost over $30 billion in value – an amount roughly equivalent to the total cost of U.S. participation in World War I. In the months that followed, the downward spiral continued, with the Dow Jones Industrial Average bottoming out in July 1932 at a meager 41.22 points, down 89% from its peak in September 1929. The Stock Market Crash of 1929 left a lasting impact on the American psyche and prompted significant changes in the country's financial regulations. As the dust settled and the nation grappled with the economic aftermath, it became evident that changes were needed to prevent such a catastrophe from occurring again. The crash exposed the weaknesses in the American financial system – rampant speculation, inadequate regulation, and a dangerous level of optimism and greed. These revelations would lead to the introduction of measures designed to safeguard the economy and protect investors, paving the way for the creation of the Securities and Exchange Commission.

The aftermath of the 1929 Stock Market Crash was as devastating as it was wide-reaching. As banks failed, savings were wiped out. For the many who had bought stocks on margin, the crash was catastrophic. They were not only stripped of their investments, but they also owed significant sums to their brokers. Many of these individuals were unable to repay their debts, resulting in personal bankruptcies that further exacerbated the economic downturn. In the wake of the crash, unemployment skyrocketed. As companies buckled under the weight of the economic depression, they were forced to lay off workers. The unemployment rate in the United States rose from around 3% in 1929 to over 25% by 1933, leaving millions of Americans jobless and struggling to make ends meet. For a nation that had reveled in prosperity and optimism merely a few years earlier, the stark reality of the Great Depression was a crushing blow.

While the crash was certainly the trigger, it's important to note that it was not the sole cause of the Great Depression. Underlying economic issues, including the uneven distribution of wealth, high levels of debt, stagnant agricultural prices, and the flawed banking system, all contributed to the severity and length of the depression. The crash was, in many ways, a symptom of these larger systemic issues. On a societal level, the crash and the subsequent depression led to significant changes in how Americans viewed capitalism and their government. Confidence in the free-market system was deeply shaken.

For many, the crash and the ensuing economic depression exposed the dark side of capitalism: its propensity for instability and its inability to protect the most vulnerable members of society. Amid the economic turmoil, Americans began to look towards their government for assistance, marking a major shift in public sentiment. Prior to the crash, the government had typically taken a hands-off approach to the economy, a policy known as laissez-faire. But as the Great Depression deepened, it became clear that a more active government role was needed to restore stability and spur recovery. In response to the public's outcry, President Herbert Hoover, who had assumed office just months before the crash, attempted to combat the depression with various measures, such as the establishment of the Reconstruction Finance Corporation, which aimed to stimulate economic activity by providing loans to banks, railroads, and other businesses.

These measures proved to be too little, too late, and were unable to stem the tide of the economic crisis.

As the smoke cleared from the 1929 Crash, it became painfully evident that the existing financial regulatory framework was grossly inadequate. Without sufficient checks and balances, the market had spiraled into a cycle of speculation that had ended in disaster. The lack of transparency in the financial practices of corporations had allowed for widespread fraud and misinformation. It was clear that the market could not self-regulate and that government intervention was necessary to protect investors and the economy. The devastating aftermath of the crash sparked a nationwide demand for reform.

The public outcry culminated in a series of Senate hearings, known as the Pecora Investigation, led by chief counsel Ferdinand Pecora. These investigations were designed to unravel the causes of the Wall Street Crash and the subsequent economic downturn, as well as to shed light on the corrupt practices and lack of transparency within the banking and securities industry.

The Pecora Investigation laid bare the unsavory practices that had contributed to the crash. The hearings revealed that many bankers had sold worthless stocks and bonds, defrauding their customers and destabilizing the financial system. It was discovered that some corporate executives had taken advantage of inside information to enrich themselves while their unknowing shareholders shouldered the losses. These revelations were met with public outrage and increased the pressure for financial reform. The findings of the Pecora Investigation were instrumental in shaping new regulatory measures. As President Franklin D. Roosevelt took office in 1933, he was tasked with restoring confidence in the American economic system. Roosevelt understood the necessity of a regulatory body that could oversee the securities industry and protect investors from the fraudulent activities that had contributed to the economic disaster. Thus, as part of his New Deal programs aimed at economic recovery, the creation of a new federal regulatory agency was proposed.

In 1933, the Securities Act was passed, mandating greater transparency in financial statements so investors could make informed decisions.

This Act was just the first step in a larger overhaul of the American financial system. The need for continuous oversight was clear, leading to the conception of a permanent regulatory body. The Securities and Exchange Commission (SEC) was established in 1934 with the mission to protect investors; maintain fair, orderly, and efficient markets; and facilitate capital formation. The creation of the SEC marked a significant shift in the regulation of the American financial industry. It reflected a newfound belief that government intervention was necessary to prevent the excesses of unchecked capitalism and to ensure the stability and integrity of the market.

This momentous development, the creation of the Securities and Exchange Commission, symbolized a turning point in the story of American finance. As the nation endeavored to rebuild from the ashes of the 1929 Crash and the Great Depression, the establishment of the SEC represented a critical step towards constructing a more stable and equitable financial system.

3.4 Securities and Exchange Commission

The establishment of the Securities and Exchange Commission (SEC) in 1934 was indeed a turning point in the annals of American finance. For the first time, there was a federal agency tasked with ensuring the fair and transparent functioning of the securities industry.

Initially, the SEC was given the authority to enforce two key pieces of legislation: The Securities Act of 1933, which required comprehensive financial disclosures for publicly traded securities, and the Securities Exchange Act of 1934, which regulated the secondary trading of those securities. The fundamental principle underpinning both of these Acts was that investors should have access to all material facts about an investment prior to buying or selling and that fraudulent activities in the market should be prohibited. Joseph P. Kennedy, a prominent businessman and father of future president John F. Kennedy, was appointed as the first chairman of the SEC. Some found his appointment surprising, given his reputation for ruthless business practices.

President Roosevelt defended his choice by stating, "Set a thief to catch a thief," suggesting that Kennedy's intimate knowledge of the tricks of the trade would enable him to effectively regulate the industry.

The SEC's early years were focused on bringing structure and oversight to a previously unregulated market. The agency quickly moved to register all major securities exchanges, including the New York Stock Exchange, thereby subjecting them to extensive regulations. Companies that wanted to have their securities listed on these exchanges were required to provide detailed information about their operations, including balance sheets, profit and loss statements, and descriptions of their business practices.

In 1940, the SEC's powers were further broadened with the passage of the Investment Company Act and the Investment Advisers Act. These acts were designed to regulate mutual funds and those who provide investment advice, again emphasizing the need for transparency and accountability in all corners of the securities industry.

The new regulatory framework introduced by the SEC fundamentally changed the landscape of American finance. By requiring disclosure of key financial information and providing oversight of brokers, dealers, and exchanges, the SEC helped restore investor confidence in the stock market following the shock of the 1929 crash. The rules and regulations enacted by the SEC meant that the market was no longer a 'wild west' where anything goes, but a regulated marketplace where fairness, transparency, and accountability were the order of the day. While the SEC's immediate mandate was to restore trust in the market following the 1929 crash, it also set out to create an environment conducive to capital formation and economic growth. By protecting the interests of investors and ensuring a fair and transparent market, the SEC sought to encourage more widespread participation in the stock market.

After all, a vibrant and trustworthy stock market is a critical component of a healthy economy, enabling businesses to raise the capital they need to grow and innovate.

Over the years, the SEC has consistently worked to maintain and enhance the integrity and efficiency of the market. The Commission has the power to bring civil enforcement actions against individuals and companies for violations of securities laws, such as insider trading, accounting fraud, and providing false or misleading information about securities and the companies that issue them.

Such enforcement actions are critical to deterring wrongdoing and protecting investors.

Take, for example, the case of Enron, an energy company that had once been hailed as a star of the stock market. In 2001, it was discovered that Enron had been using accounting loopholes to hide debt and inflate profits. The SEC brought charges against Enron and its executives, and the company was eventually forced into bankruptcy. This was a stark reminder of the importance of stringent financial oversight, and the case served to further underscore the SEC's vital role in upholding the integrity of the market.

Another key part of the SEC's mission is to educate investors to ensure that they have the knowledge to make informed decisions. The agency provides a wealth of resources to the public, including the EDGAR database, which allows people to access information that companies are required to disclose, such as their annual and quarterly reports. The SEC also regularly publishes investor alerts and bulletins to inform the public about new types of scams and what to look out for. But the SEC's work does not stop at the U.S. borders. As financial markets have become more global, the SEC has also worked to improve cross-border cooperation among securities regulators. This has involved sharing information and collaborating with foreign counterparts to ensure the enforcement of securities laws, thereby further strengthening investor protection.

Over its nearly a century-long history, the SEC has proven itself to be a dynamic organization, continuously adapting to new challenges and changes in the market. From the early days of radio to the rise of the internet and the complexities of the digital age, the SEC has sought to ensure that regardless of the technology or the state of the market, transparency, fairness, and investor protection remain paramount. In the years following the establishment of the Securities and Exchange Commission, the American stock market began to regain the trust and participation of the public, thanks in large part to the SEC's enforcement of transparency and accountability. Gradually, the landscape of American finance began to stabilize, setting the stage for a new era of growth and innovation.

3.5 Modern Stock Market

While the foundation of the modern stock market was built on the lessons learned from the crash of 1929 and the subsequent establishment of the SEC, it is also a product of continuous evolution, driven by economic cycles, technological advancements, and changes in market structure. It's in this constant flux and adjustment that the market has been able to remain robust and resilient, even in the face of economic downturns and periods of uncertainty. One of the significant developments in the evolution of the stock market was the shift from physical to electronic trading. This transition was a game-changer in terms of the speed and efficiency of transactions. What was once a crowded trading floor full of frantic brokers shouting orders transformed into a network of computers executing trades in microseconds.

Electronic trading has also democratized the stock market, making it more accessible to individual investors regardless of their location. The rise of electronic trading was closely followed by the advent of the internet, which further revolutionized the world of finance. Investors no longer had to rely solely on brokers or financial advisors for information; instead, they could research companies, view real-time stock prices, and execute trades from their personal computers. This development brought an unprecedented level of access and transparency to the stock market.

The modern stock market also saw the introduction of new financial products and instruments. From index funds and exchange-traded funds (ETFs) to derivatives and complex structured products, these innovations have allowed investors to diversify their portfolios and manage risk in more sophisticated ways. Lastly, the role of institutional investors, such as pension funds, insurance companies, and mutual funds, has grown significantly in the modern stock market. These large, professionally managed investment pools wield considerable influence and hold a substantial portion of all publicly traded stocks.

Now that we have traced the arc of the stock market from its fledgling beginnings to the complex, electronic, and global system that we know today, we started with the early days of the American stock market, a time when stocks were viewed with suspicion and the concept of investing was still novel. It was a time of ambitious entrepreneurs and opportunists, shaping an economy on the fly.

During this period, we saw the birth of essential components of today's financial markets, like brokers, public offerings, and the emergence of a national banking system. We discussed the Roaring Twenties, a period of exceptional economic prosperity and innovation. This era saw a stock market boom, fueled by post-war optimism, consumerism, and new technologies. It was during this time that the stock market became a mainstream part of American life, attracting a new class of retail investors.

This boom period wasn't to last. The prosperity of the Roaring Twenties precipitated the catastrophic Stock Market Crash of 1929, leading to widespread financial ruin and marking the start of the Great Depression. This dark period served as a stark reminder of the consequences of unchecked speculation, inadequate regulation, and economic imbalance.

The crash resulted in sweeping reforms, leading to the creation of the Securities and Exchange Commission (SEC). This new regulatory body was charged with restoring and maintaining investor trust by promoting transparency and enforcing laws against fraudulent activities in the marketplace. The SEC's establishment was a watershed moment in the evolution of the American financial system, marking a move toward a more regulated and secure market. Finally, we explored the modern stock market – a globally connected, electronic network of buyers and sellers.

This period was marked by revolutionary technological advancements and the introduction of new financial instruments, which collectively reshaped the world of finance. From the advent of electronic trading to the rise of the internet, we witnessed a shift towards increased speed, efficiency, and accessibility in trading.

Understanding this evolution, the trials and tribulations, the innovations and regulations, is crucial for comprehending the complexities of the financial world we live in today. As we transition into the next chapter - the Great Depression, this understanding becomes even more critical. The Great Depression was not an isolated event; it was a product of the economic and financial decisions that came before it. By comprehending the evolution of the stock market, we can better appreciate the factors that led to the Depression, how the crisis unfolded, and its long-lasting impact on the American financial landscape. The past, as they say, is indeed prologue.

4 The Great Depression

The 1930s were characterized by the most devastating economic downturn in modern history: The Great Depression. This was a period of severe economic contraction, skyrocketing unemployment, and profound social and political change. Its shockwaves were felt not just across the United States but around the world, forever changing our understanding of economics, government's role in stabilizing the economy, and the intricacies of global finance. Beginning with the cataclysmic stock market crash of 1929, the Great Depression lasted an entire decade, leaving an indelible mark on the collective

memory of those who lived through it and shaping the course of the 20th century. It was a time of great hardship, as thousands of banks and businesses failed, millions lost their jobs and savings, and many found themselves without homes, queuing for bread or work. The Wall Street Crash and its aftermath exposed the fragile underbelly of the economic boom of the 1920s, revealing systemic weaknesses that had been hidden beneath the surface of the Roaring Twenties' apparent prosperity.

The term 'depression' was chosen intentionally to describe this period. It was meant to denote something more profound and enduring than a mere 'panic' or 'crisis.' Indeed, the Great Depression was not simply a severe recession; it was an era of sustained economic contraction and slow recovery. Despite the dire economic conditions, the term 'depression' also suggested a way out, a return to normalcy, just as a depressed area of land can be filled in or a depressed mood can lift. But the causes of the Great Depression were complex and multifaceted. The reckless optimism and unregulated speculation of the Roaring Twenties, the structural weaknesses in the American banking system, the inequality in income distribution, the flaws in the international gold standard, and the tightening of U.S.

monetary policy in the late 1920s - all these factors and more played a part. This was not a crisis that could be pinned on a single event or decision. Instead, it was the product of a confluence of conditions and actions that, taken together, set the stage for a catastrophe.

The Great Depression was more than just an economic event; it was a human tragedy on a colossal scale. But it also presented an opportunity for deep structural reforms and led to the reshaping of government policy and the economic landscape. The experience of the Depression left a lasting legacy, influencing economic thinking and policy decisions long after the recovery had taken hold.

The depth and breadth of the Great Depression's impact make it a vital chapter in the story of American finance. It left an indelible mark on American society, with its consequences seeping into every facet of life. Unemployment and poverty became common features of the American landscape, changing the social fabric in profound ways. The depression touched everyone - from farmers in the Midwest, whose crops turned to dust in the relentless grip of the Dust Bowl, to factory workers in Detroit, their dreams of prosperity shattered by the collapse of industry. From Wall Street financiers who had once been revered, now discredited and disgraced, to everyday families forced into bread lines, the Great Depression was a communal experience that transcended economic class and geographical boundaries.

But this dark period also inspired profound change and resilience. People adapted, innovated, and persevered, finding new ways to survive in the face of hardship. Communities banded together, supporting each other in ways both big and small. The stark reality of the Great Depression also sparked a reevaluation of America's economic structures and assumptions, leading to significant shifts in economic policy, banking, and finance.

With this backdrop, we now turn our attention to the root causes of the Great Depression. The causes were numerous and intertwined, each contributing to a situation that spiraled into a full-blown economic disaster. The stock market crash of 1929 is often pointed to as the catalyst, but it was merely the most visible symptom of a much deeper systemic failure. The 1920s had been a time of extraordinary economic growth and financial innovation, but beneath the surface, there were serious economic imbalances. The prosperity of the Roaring Twenties had been unevenly distributed, with the rich getting richer and the poor getting poorer. The agriculture sector, still a significant part of the economy, had been struggling throughout the decade. And the rise of consumer debt, fueled by the new culture of consumerism and easy credit, had created an unsustainable bubble.

As we explore these causes in more detail, we will discover that the Great Depression was not the result of any single factor or event. Rather, it was the product of a perfect storm of economic, political, and societal forces that converged at a particular moment in history. Unpacking these causes is critical to understanding not only the severity of the Depression but also why its impact was so widespread and long-lasting. It also provides valuable insights into the measures that were taken to address the crisis, setting the stage for the monumental economic and financial changes that would follow.

4.1 Causes

Remember, In the early morning light of October 24, 1929, Wall Street awoke to chaos. Just a day prior, the optimism of the Roaring Twenties had hung thick in the air. Traders and investors had reveled in a booming stock market that seemed to promise unlimited prosperity. But on that fateful day, later dubbed "Black Thursday," the dream abruptly came to an end as a wave of selling gripped the stock market, triggering a catastrophic crash. The financial bedrock upon which the prosperity of the 1920s had been built suddenly turned to quicksand, sucking the economy into the depths of the Great Depression.

Although the stock market crash of 1929 is often cited as the start of the Great Depression, it was not so much a cause as a trigger. The crash merely exposed the underlying weaknesses in the economy that had been accumulating during the boom years of the 1920s. To understand the causes of the Great Depression, we need to look beyond the crash itself to these deeper systemic issues. Firstly, there was the problem of income inequality. During the 1920s, the benefits of economic growth were heavily skewed towards the wealthy. The top 1% of households saw their income rise dramatically, while the majority of Americans experienced stagnant or falling wages. This inequality created an unstable economy reliant on high levels of consumer debt to maintain demand. The wealthy, with their disproportionately high incomes, were pouring their money into investments rather than spending it on goods and services. This caused an overproduction crisis, as businesses continued to churn out goods that consumers increasingly couldn't afford.

Secondly, there was the issue of speculation and margin trading. During the Roaring Twenties, investing in the stock market became something of a national pastime. Encouraged by the seemingly endless upward trajectory of the market, many ordinary Americans began investing, often borrowing heavily to do so. This speculation was facilitated by loose lending practices, particularly the widespread use of buying stocks on margin. This meant investors only needed to put down a small fraction of a stock's price upfront, borrowing the rest from their broker. As long as stock prices kept rising, this worked fine, but when the market turned, investors were left with huge debts they could not repay.

Thirdly, the farming sector was in trouble. While cities boomed during the 1920s, the rural economy struggled. Farmers, who made up a large portion of the population, had not shared in the prosperity of the Roaring Twenties. Falling food prices and rising debts left many farmers in dire straits. When the Dust Bowl hit in the 1930s, this underlying weakness in the agricultural sector exacerbated the Depression.

These factors alone were enough to make the U.S. economy vulnerable. But another crucial factor turned this vulnerability into a full-blown crisis: the structure of the financial system, particularly the weakness of the banking sector. During the 1920s, thousands of small banks had proliferated throughout the country, many of which were highly exposed to the struggling agricultural sector. Without a central regulatory authority to oversee them, these banks engaged in risky practices, such as lending to speculators and investing in the stock market. When the stock market crashed, a wave of bank failures followed, which in turn led to a contraction in credit and a further deepening of the economic downturn.

In sum, the causes of the Great Depression were a complex mix of structural weaknesses, economic imbalances, and policy mistakes. They lay not in the events of Black Thursday itself, but in the years leading up to it. It was these underlying conditions that turned a stock market crash into a prolonged depression.

The stock market crash that ignited the Great Depression obliterated substantial sums of wealth. Thousands of investors lost their life savings as major corporations saw their share values plummet. This sudden evaporation of wealth had a chilling effect on consumer confidence and spending, a cornerstone of any economy. Consequently, businesses felt the sting of the shrinking consumer demand. As sales and revenues declined, companies had no choice but to cut costs, often in the form of layoffs. Unemployment skyrocketed in the early years of the Depression. By 1933, around 15 million Americans, or roughly 25% of the workforce, were out of work. The sight of long breadlines and soup kitchens became common in cities across the nation as people struggled to feed their families.

The banking sector, too, felt the tremors of the economic quake. With the rampant bank failures, many people lost their life savings as banks had used those savings for loans and investments that went bad. The subsequent bank runs, driven by panic and a lack of confidence in the banking system, led to even more bank closures. This contraction in the banking sector decreased the money supply, leading to deflation, which only compounded the economic misery. Prices fell, adding further burden on businesses and increasing the real value of debt, squeezing debtors tighter. The agriculture sector, already reeling from the effects of the Dust Bowl - a severe drought that decimated farmland across the Midwest - also faced the wrath of the Depression. Crop prices dropped precipitously, plunging many farmers into bankruptcy and resulting in widespread rural poverty.

While we focus heavily on the economic indicators and the statistical impact, it's critical not to lose sight of the human toll. The economic hardship translated into serious social problems, including malnutrition, homelessness, and a sharp increase in health problems due to inadequate diet and healthcare.

International trade was also severely impacted as countries attempted to protect their economies by imposing tariffs on imported goods, leading to a global decline in trade. This only served to intensify the worldwide depression, a poignant reminder of the interconnectedness of economies.

This maelstrom of economic, financial, and social disaster paints a dire picture of the Great Depression's impact on the American economy.

It also set the stage for an unprecedented government response. A response that would reshape the American economic landscape in ways that still influence how we think about the role of government in the economy today.

4.2 Impact on Economy

It was a time of dramatic change, a juncture at which the American Dream seemed to crumble, leaving families and individuals in a desperate struggle for survival.

The U.S. Gross Domestic Product (GDP), a measure of the nation's overall economic activity, fell precipitously during this time. From its high in 1929, the GDP fell by approximately 30% by 1933. This steep decline mirrored the plummeting stock prices, the surging unemployment rate, and the contracting money supply. It was a stark and distressing depiction of an economy in free fall. Alongside these dismal economic indicators, personal income, expenditure, and investment all nose-dived, contributing to the cycle of contraction and despair. Reduced income meant less spending, and this fall in consumer demand led to lower business investment. After all, why would businesses invest in expanding production when their existing products weren't selling?

The labor market bore some of the most visible scars of the Great Depression. The escalating unemployment rate was not just a statistic; it translated to real human suffering. People lost their jobs in droves, their livelihoods snatched away seemingly overnight. From factory workers to clerks, from bankers to builders, no sector was immune. The loss of jobs meant the loss of incomes, escalating the cycle of reduced spending and reduced demand. Jobs were not the only thing people lost. For many, the Great Depression swept away their homes. Unable to pay their mortgages or rent, countless families lost their homes. Some ended up in shantytowns, ironically named 'Hoovervilles,' after President Herbert Hoover, who was widely blamed for not doing enough to combat the crisis.

The Great Depression did not only trigger a crisis in the labor and housing markets. It also ignited a severe crisis in the banking sector. As mentioned earlier, the early years of the Depression saw widespread bank failures. This was a calamity not just for the banks, but also for ordinary citizens who trusted these institutions with their savings. As banks failed, so too did the faith of the public in the financial system, leading to bank runs, further bank closures, and an overall contraction of credit. The banking crisis, in turn, compounded the economic downturn.

The Depression also left an indelible mark on international trade. The Smoot-Hawley Tariff Act of 1930, aimed at protecting American industries by raising tariffs on imported goods, ended up exacerbating the economic downturn. Other nations responded by imposing tariffs of their own, causing global trade to shrink dramatically. This led to a further decline in production and jobs, adding another layer of complexity to the crisis. The economic impacts of the Great Depression were severe and far-reaching. But as we'll soon explore, they were not the end of the story. These economic trials sparked a series of responses from the U.S. government aimed at ameliorating the economic distress and reforming the financial system to prevent a similar catastrophe in the future. The governmental response would prove pivotal, not just for recovery, but also for the future direction of American economic policy.

Diving further into the ripples created by the Great Depression on the American economy, one cannot overlook the emotional and psychological impact it had on the American public. These were years of desperation and despair, of seeing dreams shattered, and lives upended. This underlying human crisis manifested itself in various forms, leaving its imprint on both the economy and society at large. The declining health of the economy led to a corresponding decline in physical and mental health. As unemployment surged, many Americans found themselves without health insurance, which at the time was often provided by employers. With dwindling income and no insurance, many could not afford medical care, leading to an increase in untreated illnesses. The malnutrition resulting from inadequate food also took a toll on people's health.

The mental health impact of the Great Depression was also profound. The prolonged economic stress led to a significant increase in mental health issues. Suicide rates spiked during the depression years as despair overwhelmed many. This increased burden of disease further strained already struggling families and communities. Furthermore, the Great Depression led to significant changes in family structures and gender roles. With many men out of work, women often had to take on whatever work they could find to support their families, leading to a rise in women entering the workforce. At the same time, the economic strain led to a drop in marriage and birth rates as many felt they could not afford to start or expand a family.

Social unrest also grew during these difficult years. Strikes and labor protests increased as workers sought better wages and working conditions. The economic hardship fueled dissatisfaction with government and big business, leading to a surge in populist sentiment. Internationally, the impact of the Great Depression reached beyond America's borders. The sharp decline in U.S. imports and investments, combined with retaliatory tariffs, led to a global slowdown. Countries dependent on exporting goods to the U.S. or on American investment capital found themselves caught in the economic downdraft. This international dimension of the Great Depression exacerbated political tensions and contributed to the geopolitical instability that would ultimately lead to World War II.

The economy, after all, is not just an abstract concept; it is the sum total of millions of individuals' livelihoods. As such, the Great Depression did not just represent a failure of the financial system or the bursting of an economic bubble. It was a human tragedy on a grand scale. It was a time of hardship and pain, resilience and change.

The sharp decline in industrial production brought about a state of stagnation. Factories, once buzzing with activity, now stood silent, their machines at a standstill. This decline in production not only meant less wealth being generated but also fewer jobs. A positive feedback loop was set into motion: the unemployed could not afford goods, leading to less demand, causing further production cuts, leading to more job losses. imultaneously, the agricultural sector, which had once been the backbone of the American economy, was also on its knees. Farmers were producing more food than could be sold due to reduced consumer purchasing power and international trade barriers. This resulted in an agricultural surplus that ironically coexisted with widespread hunger and malnutrition. Adding to their woes were the devastating dust storms, also known as the Dust Bowl, which ruined farmlands and forced many farming families to abandon their homes in search of work elsewhere.

The banking crisis resulted in a severe credit crunch. Businesses, large and small, found it difficult to access loans for investment, hindering economic recovery. For ordinary citizens, the bank failures not only meant the loss of their savings but also eroded their trust in the financial system, a trust that would take years, even decades, to fully restore.

The fallout from the Great Depression affected not just the industrial and agricultural sectors but also extended to commerce and trade. Retail businesses faced plummeting sales as consumer spending dwindled. Likewise, construction activities, which had once thrived during the boom years, now came to a halt as both demand and financing dried up.

Faced with this unprecedented crisis, it became evident that the market alone would not correct the economic slide. The invisible hand of the market seemed not just invisible but absent. Calls for intervention grew louder, reaching a crescendo during the 1932 Presidential elections.

The incoming administration, led by President Franklin D. Roosevelt, would usher in a new era of economic policy. Under Roosevelt's leadership, the government would no longer be a passive observer of economic affairs. Instead, it would play an active role in managing the economy and safeguarding the welfare of its citizens. The government's response to the Great Depression, a series of initiatives known collectively as the New Deal, marked a significant departure from past policies. The ensuing measures would not only seek to end the economic downturn but also to reform the financial system to prevent future crises.

These proposed reforms and interventions were not without controversy. The economic philosophies underpinning the New Deal represented a fundamental shift in how the government interacted with the economy, stirring fierce debates that continue to resonate even today.

4.3 Government Response & The New Deal

The Great Depression marked a pivotal moment in the relationship between the government and the economy in the United States. It was a time when the laissez-faire economics – the belief that economies function best when markets are left alone and free from government intervention – was being called into question. The catastrophic economic downturn and its widespread social implications prompted calls for the government to step in and take on an active role in reviving the economy. The man who was tasked with this enormous responsibility was President Franklin D. Roosevelt.

When Roosevelt took office in 1933, he did so amid a country reeling from the effects of the deepest and longest-lasting economic downturn in its history. The financial system was in disarray, businesses were failing, unemployment was at an all-time high, and trust in the economy was shattered. The task ahead was daunting, but Roosevelt was determined to restore faith in the American economic system. His strategy for economic recovery and reform came to be known as the New Deal. The New Deal was a series of programs and policies aimed at providing Relief for the unemployed and poor, Recovery of the economy to normal levels, and Reform of the financial system to prevent a repeat depression. This became known as the "Three Rs" of the New Deal. We will explore this deal in greater detail in the following chapter.

In his first 100 days in office, Roosevelt launched a flurry of legislation known as the First New Deal. This legislation was primarily focused on providing immediate relief to suffering Americans and stabilizing the banking system. The Emergency Banking Act, enacted only five days into his presidency, sought to restore public confidence in the banking system by allowing the Treasury Department to inspect the nation's banks. Banks that were deemed sound could reopen, while those that needed help could receive loans. This act was followed by a four-day banking holiday, during which all banks were closed, allowing the legislation to take effect. This swift action helped to restore confidence and prevent further bank runs. The Federal Emergency Relief Act provided direct relief to the unemployed through grants to states for public work projects, while the Civilian Conservation Corps (CCC) and the Public Works Administration (PWA) put unemployed men to work on public infrastructure projects. These measures provided much-needed employment and also resulted in the creation of public works, many of which are still in use today.

Another crucial piece of legislation was the Glass-Steagall Act, which reformed the banking system and established the Federal Deposit Insurance Corporation (FDIC). The FDIC guaranteed individual bank deposits up to a certain amount, restoring confidence in the banking system. The Glass-Steagall Act also separated commercial and investment banking, a reform intended to prevent the kind of risky speculation by banks that had contributed to the stock market crash. While these initial efforts were aimed at providing immediate relief and stabilizing the economy, Roosevelt knew that more fundamental changes were needed to prevent future economic crises. His administration thus embarked on a second wave of reforms, known as the Second New Deal, which focused on providing long-term economic stability and social security. One of the most significant undertakings was the introduction of Social Security.

Before the Great Depression, the provision of support for the elderly, unemployed, and disabled was primarily a local and private matter. But the vast scope of human suffering during the Depression made it clear that a more comprehensive and systematic approach was necessary. The Social Security Act, signed into law in 1935, created a federal safety net for the elderly, unemployed, and others unable to work. Funded by payroll taxes, the program provided retirement pensions, unemployment insurance, and aid to those with disabilities and to families with dependent children. It marked a significant departure from the previous American ethos of individualism and self-reliance and represented a commitment to collective social responsibility.

In addition to these immediate relief efforts, the New Deal also saw efforts to stimulate economic recovery by focusing on the nation's agricultural sector. American farmers had been struggling even before the Depression due to overproduction and falling prices. The Agricultural Adjustment Act (AAA) of 1933 aimed to raise crop prices by paying farmers to reduce production. Though the AAA faced legal challenges and criticisms, it signified an unprecedented level of government involvement in the agricultural economy. The New Deal also included measures to regulate business practices and protect workers' rights. The National Industrial Recovery Act (NIRA) of 1933 established codes of fair practice for industries and guaranteed workers the right to unionize and bargain collectively.

The NIRA was declared unconstitutional by the Supreme Court in 1935, prompting Roosevelt to pursue further labor legislation. This came in the form of the Wagner Act or the National Labor Relations Act of 1935, which reinforced workers' rights to unionize and engage in collective bargaining.

One of the most controversial aspects of Roosevelt's New Deal was his attempt to reform the Supreme Court, often referred to as the "court-packing plan." Frustrated by the Court's opposition to his programs, Roosevelt proposed a bill in 1937 that would allow him to appoint an additional justice for each current justice over the age of

70. This move was widely seen as an attempt to increase the number of justices who would be favorable to his programs.

The plan backfired, with critics accusing Roosevelt of attempting to undermine the judiciary's independence and overreach his executive powers.

Despite this misstep, Roosevelt's New Deal fundamentally reshaped the role of the federal government in American economic life. It marked a shift from a laissez-faire economic policy towards a more interventionist approach, where the government took an active role in managing the economy and ensuring social welfare.

As we continue to explore the government's response to the Great Depression, we'll see that these reforms, while controversial, played a crucial role in revitalizing the American economy and shaping the modern American financial system. They not only provided immediate relief to suffering Americans but also sought to restructure the economy and prevent future crises. While the government worked on multiple fronts to mitigate the effects of the Great Depression, the financial system's stability remained of utmost importance. For decades, America had operated with a banking system characterized by a multitude of small, independent banks, a vestige of a bygone era of localized economies.

These banks' fragile nature had been laid bare by the Depression. The lack of federal insurance had led to the loss of life savings when banks failed, undermining public confidence.

Thus, one of the New Deal's critical measures was to restore faith in the banking system. The first step in this process was the Emergency Banking Act of 1933. Passed just days after Roosevelt took office, this act provided for a four-day nationwide bank holiday, during which time banks would be inspected by Treasury Department officials. Only those deemed solvent were allowed to reopen. This drastic action was aimed at stemming the tide of bank runs by reassuring the public that the banks allowed to reopen were stable and safe.

Roosevelt paired this drastic measure with his first "fireside chat" on the radio, speaking directly to the American people. He explained the measures his administration was taking to tackle the banking crisis and encouraged Americans to trust the banks that passed the government inspections and reopened. These actions helped restore confidence in the banking system, and when the banks reopened after the 'bank holiday,' there was a reversal in the panic – instead of mass withdrawals, many people began to redeposit their money.

The next crucial reform was the Banking Act of 1933, also known as the Glass-Steagall Act. This legislation had two significant components. The first established the Federal Deposit Insurance Corporation (FDIC), which insured individual bank deposits. This measure was designed to further restore public confidence, ensuring that even if a bank failed, its depositors would not lose their money.

The second part of the Glass-Steagall Act was to create a separation between commercial and investment banking. Before the Act, many banks engaged in both activities, using depositors' money to speculate in the stock market. This practice had contributed to the market's instability in the 1920s and the subsequent crash. By forcing a separation, the Act aimed to protect depositors and reduce risk in the financial system.

While these reforms were significant, they were not the end of the government's efforts to reform the banking sector. The Banking Act of 1935 further strengthened federal control over banking. This legislation restructured the Federal Reserve System, centralizing more power in the Federal Reserve Board in Washington, D.C., and giving the Federal Reserve more authority to set national monetary policy.

4.4 Banking Reform

The Glass-Steagall Act, which laid the groundwork for modern banking, was perhaps the most significant outcome of the government's banking reform efforts during the Great Depression.

Understanding the implications of this piece of legislation necessitates looking deeper into the state of the banking system before the Depression.

In the era before Glass-Steagall, commercial banks – those that take deposits and make loans – were often involved in speculative investments. They used the money deposited by their customers to invest in the stock market and underwrite securities. This entanglement of banking and speculation was among the factors that led to the stock market crash of 1929 and the subsequent banking crises. As the stock market plummeted, banks found their investments losing value rapidly. Customers, fearful for their deposits, began a run on the banks, which quickly led to banks being unable to fulfill their obligations and declare bankruptcy. The Glass-Steagall Act brought about a strict separation between commercial and investment banking. This meant that commercial banks were barred from dealing with securities, and investment banks were prohibited from accepting deposits. The goal was to protect depositors' money from the risks associated with stock market speculation, thus reducing the risk of bank failures.

The Act also established the Federal Deposit Insurance Corporation (FDIC), which insured bank deposits up to a certain amount. This was a game-changer in restoring public trust in the banking system. Before the FDIC's establishment, depositors stood to lose their life savings if their bank failed. But with the FDIC, people knew that even if their bank went under, their money was safe. This assurance helped to quell bank runs, stabilize the banking industry, and restore public confidence. In addition to these measures, the Banking Act of 1933 gave the Federal Reserve more power to control credit. The aim was to prevent excessive speculation by limiting the amount of credit available for stock purchases. This increased oversight, along with the separation of commercial and investment banking, was intended to reduce the risk of another stock market crash.

It's worth mentioning that while the Glass-Steagall Act was a crucial step in banking reform, it wasn't the only significant legislative action taken in this sphere during the New Deal era. The Banking Act of 1935 further strengthened the Federal Reserve System and improved the federal government's ability to respond to economic crises. This included changes to the Federal Reserve's structure, improving its capacity to control money supply and lending practices, enhancing its regulatory oversight, and strengthening its role as the lender of last resort for banks.

These banking reforms were part of a broader suite of New Deal initiatives designed to get the American economy back on its feet.

Their significance extends beyond this period: the principles they established – including the separation of commercial and investment banking and the need for federal deposit insurance – have remained key aspects of American banking regulation to this day. They are the foundation upon which our modern banking system is built. And while the financial world has evolved considerably since the 1930s, the importance of having robust regulatory mechanisms to ensure the system's stability has only grown. The reform initiatives, while disruptive to a banking industry accustomed to operating under less oversight, set the stage for a more stable and resilient system, safeguarding the economy from the kind of banking collapse that occurred in the early years of the Great Depression. It also served to restore public confidence, which was essential to stimulate the economy and get America back on its feet.

Reform did not come without controversy or resistance. Critics were quick to point out that the stringent regulations imposed by the Glass-Steagall Act stifled innovation and limited the competitive abilities of American banks on the global stage.

Its supporters emphasized the systemic stability that came with these regulatory measures, arguing that it was a necessary trade-off to avoid another catastrophic economic collapse. The strength of the reforms was put to the test just a few years later. In the late 1930s, the economy took another downturn, often referred to as the "Roosevelt Recession." While this economic contraction was severe, the newly reformed banking sector was able to weather the storm, suggesting that the changes had brought about a degree of resilience.

Meanwhile, the FDIC played a crucial role in maintaining confidence in the banking system during this period. The sight of bank runs and the widespread loss of savings was still fresh in the public memory, and the FDIC's deposit insurance guarantee was a comforting promise that even if their bank failed, customers would not lose their money.

The impact of these reforms extended far beyond the end of the Great Depression. In fact, the regulatory structure that was established during this time remained largely in place for the better part of the century, maintaining a clear separation between commercial and investment banking. This structure has evolved over time, with the boundary between these two types of banking becoming increasingly blurred, leading to significant changes in the way the banking industry operates. The Banking Act of 1935 also made several changes to the structure and responsibilities of the Federal Reserve System. It reorganized the Federal Reserve Board into the Federal Reserve System we know today and gave the System the authority to change reserve requirements for member banks. These changes expanded the Federal Reserve's ability to manage the country's money supply and exercise monetary control, functions that remain central to its mission today.

But even as the regulatory landscape has evolved, the lessons learned from the banking reform of the Great Depression continue to resonate. The experience underlined the critical role that a stable banking system plays in the broader economy, and the importance of having a robust regulatory framework in place to maintain that stability. As such, the legacy of these reforms continues to shape the principles of banking regulation and financial oversight in America. Slowly, the bitter lessons of the Depression started to give way to a newfound stability. The economy gradually started to recover and, as the nation entered the 1940s, it was clear that the United States was entering a new era. In this forthcoming age, a different challenge would present itself - the upheaval of World War II.

4.5 Legacy

The legacy of the Great Depression has shaped the political, social, and economic landscape of the United States in profound ways. On the economic front, the Great Depression prompted a profound shift in the relationship between the government and the economy, in particular in the realm of financial regulation. This period of history was transformative, not just in the sense of immediate survival and recovery, but also in shaping the foundational principles that continue to guide financial policy and economic thinking.

One of the most visible legacies of the Great Depression is the creation of a robust system of financial regulation. The introduction of significant banking reforms, the establishment of the Securities and Exchange Commission (SEC), and the expansion of the Federal Reserve's role all were momentous changes that have endured to this day. The banking reforms led to the creation of a safer, more stable banking system that helped to avoid a similar financial collapse for several decades. The creation of the SEC was another crucial outcome of this era. By regulating the stock market and ensuring transparency in financial dealings, the SEC was instrumental in restoring public confidence in the financial markets, which had been shattered by the 1929 crash and the ensuing depression. By making the markets safer for investors, the SEC played a crucial role in encouraging the capital formation that has powered American companies and driven economic growth over the past eight decades.

On the macroeconomic front, the Great Depression significantly influenced the field of economic thought. The severity and length of the depression led to questioning of classical economic theories, which assumed that economies were self-correcting and that market forces would eventually restore equilibrium. The prolonged suffering and massive unemployment during the Great Depression challenged these assumptions, and led to the rise of

Keynesian economics, named after British economist John Maynard Keynes. Keynes argued that during severe downturns, the private sector may not be able to recover on its own, and that government intervention was necessary to stimulate demand and restore full employment. These ideas were influential in shaping the New Deal programs, and Keynesian economics has remained a major school of thought in economics, influencing policy makers in times of economic crisis, including the recent Great Recession of 2008.

The Great Depression led to a greater societal awareness of income inequality and the role of government in ensuring a basic standard of living. The hardship of the era exposed the stark disparities between the wealthy and the poor, leading to calls for reform. This led to the expansion of social safety nets, including the establishment of Social Security, unemployment insurance, and later, the introduction of minimum wage laws. These programs, born out of the crucible of the Great Depression, have become integral to American society, providing a measure of security to millions of Americans. The Great Depression also left a psychological legacy. Those who lived through it were marked by the experience, becoming more frugal and cautious about investing and borrowing. Even as the economy recovered and prospered, the memory of bank runs, lost savings, and unemployment lines remained fresh, influencing attitudes towards saving, investing, and debt for generations.

As the years passed and the memories of the Great Depression faded, so too did some of the caution it had instilled. Over time, a series of financial deregulations rolled back some of the safeguards put in place after the Depression. This culminated in the late 20th and early 21st centuries with a series of financial crises, most notably the 2008 financial crisis, that bore some eerie resemblances to the collapse that preceded the Great Depression. These later events serve as a reminder of the enduring lessons from the Depression about the dangers of financial instability and the importance of regulation to keep these risks in check. As we've explored the legacy of the Great Depression, we've seen that the economic impacts extended far beyond the decade of the 1930s. The changes that were implemented in response to the crisis have had long-lasting implications for the American financial system, societal structure, and global economic interactions. These changes continue to shape American financial practices and policies to this day, underscoring the transformative power of such a monumental event.

The Great Depression also influenced a redefinition of societal roles, in particular, the role of government. The vast social programs implemented as part of Roosevelt's New Deal reflected a new perspective, where government assumed the role of guardian against economic hardship. The public's expectation of government, hence, shifted significantly, with increased demand for regulations and social safety nets that would prevent a recurrence of such a disaster. This shift is an essential part of understanding the legacy of the Depression.

From an economic standpoint, the Depression also sparked critical analysis and evolution of economic theory. The shortcomings of the classical economic models in the face of the Depression led to the rise of Keynesian economics. Championed by British economist John Maynard Keynes, this theory advocated for increased government expenditures and lower taxes to stimulate demand and pull the global economy out of the depression. The prevalence of Keynesian economics in today's economic policy discussions testifies to the lasting impact of this paradigm shift. The influence of the Great Depression extended beyond politics and economics into the cultural sphere. The hardships and struggles that people endured during this time had a profound influence on the literature, music, and visual arts of the era, creating a cultural legacy that remains a significant part of American history.

The chapter on the Great Depression provides a valuable backdrop to understanding the long-term changes that took place in the American financial system. By examining the root causes of the Depression, the economic and societal impact, and the subsequent government response, we gain a nuanced understanding of this transformative era. By examining the significant banking reforms that took place and the lasting legacy of the Depression, we can appreciate the significant shifts in the financial system.

The Great Depression serves as a stark reminder of the deep interconnections within the global economy, the potential for economic theories to evolve in response to unprecedented challenges, and the enduring ability of a society to transform tragedy into lessons for future prosperity. As we explore the subsequent chapters, we will see how these lessons from the Depression era echo through the annals of American finance, shaping responses to future economic crises and influencing the evolution of financial systems in the decades to come.

5 Post War Prosperity

As the echoes of the Great Depression began to fade, a new era dawned on the United States, an era of rapid economic expansion, dynamic social change, and unprecedented prosperity. The end of World War II marked the beginning of a period that historians have come to call the Post-War Prosperity or the Golden Age of Capitalism. The economic landscape of the United States underwent a massive transformation during this period, and it profoundly shaped the trajectory of American finance.

The end of the war saw the country at a critical juncture. On one hand, there were grave concerns about the possibility of falling back into depression with the cessation of wartime production. On the other hand, there was a sense of hope and optimism, fueled by the technological advancements made during the war and the potential of a booming consumer market waiting to be tapped. As it turned out, the fears of a post-war depression proved unfounded. What unfolded instead was a period of extraordinary economic growth, largely due to the pent-up consumer demand that had accumulated during the war years, massive investments in infrastructure, and the strengthening of the manufacturing sector. An essential part of this era's narrative is the demographic shift that occurred during the period - the Baby Boom. The end of the war saw a surge in birth rates as millions of soldiers returned home and started families. This demographic phenomenon significantly affected the economy and the financial landscape in multiple ways. The population boom drove demand for goods and services, housing, education, and healthcare, leading to an unprecedented expansion in various sectors of the economy.

Simultaneously, the United States was witnessing a socio-cultural shift marked by the rise of suburbanization. The mushrooming of suburbs around the cities was not merely a shift in the housing pattern but an entire lifestyle shift that had significant financial implications. The move to the suburbs brought about changes in consumption patterns and gave rise to a culture of homeownership and consumer credit that transformed the American financial sector. The consumer boom that accompanied suburbanization would profoundly influence the development of the American economy and finance.

Then, there was the rise of consumerism, a significant social and economic development of the post-war era. The proliferation of mass-produced goods, the expansion of credit, and aggressive marketing strategies led to a consumer culture that reinforced the economic boom. The impacts of this rise in consumerism were far-reaching, influencing everything from business practices and advertising to personal finance and the national economy.

Amidst this robust growth and prosperity, new challenges also emerged. The economy of the United States, like any other, was not immune to cyclical fluctuations and the pressures of a changing world order. The latter part of the post-war era saw the emergence of inflation as a significant economic challenge. This led to a new set of policy considerations and economic debates, marking a shift in the financial landscape.

The post-war prosperity era was transformative and pivotal, providing a vibrant backdrop against which the story of American finance continued to evolve.

The exploration of this period is critical as it not only illuminates the past but also helps us understand the financial world we inhabit today.

5.1 Economic Growth

The economic growth experienced by the United States in the post-war years was nothing short of extraordinary. From 1945 to 1960, the nation's gross national product (GNP) nearly doubled, leading economists to refer to this period as the "economic miracle." This was a time of unprecedented economic expansion that redefined the contours of the American economy.

During the war years, the U.S. economy had been heavily geared towards supporting the war effort, with industries churning out tanks, ships, aircraft, and munitions. With the end of the war, these same industries now had to transition to peacetime production. This transition was not easy and was fraught with concerns about potential unemployment and economic stagnation.

These fears were largely unfounded. The economy not only avoided falling into a depression but entered a period of rapid growth that reshaped the American financial landscape. A variety of factors contributed to this economic boom. A major driving force was the pent-up consumer demand that had accumulated during the war years. Rationing and war production had severely limited the availability of consumer goods. With the war's end and the lifting of rationing, Americans were eager to spend their savings on goods and services that had been scarce during the war years. This unleashed a consumer spending boom that fueled the economy.

Significant technological advancements made during the war found their way into the civilian economy, further fueling economic growth. Industries that had been integral to the war effort, such as aviation, electronics, and synthetic materials, began to find new commercial applications. This spurred innovation and created new industries, generating jobs and driving economic growth. Government spending also played a crucial role in this economic boom. Massive investments in infrastructure, education, and research and development spurred economic activity. Programs like the GI Bill, which provided education and housing loans to returning veterans, injected money into the economy and led to increased demand for goods and services.

These factors combined to create a potent mix that resulted in a period of economic growth unlike anything the United States had experienced before. This growth was not confined to certain regions or sectors but was broad-based, with nearly all parts of the economy participating in the upswing. The manufacturing sector, in particular, experienced a period of extraordinary growth, with U.S. factories producing goods at an unprecedented rate. This industrial expansion played a crucial role in creating the modern American middle class, providing well-paying jobs to millions of workers. The rising incomes and increased job stability, emblematic of the post-war period, not only boosted economic growth but also led to an important demographic shift: the Baby Boom. Beginning in 1946, the United States experienced a marked increase in birth rates, which continued for almost two decades. This resulted in a significant expansion of the population, leading to both immediate and long-term effects on the economy and society.

This period of increased birth rates has been attributed to several factors. The return of soldiers from the war, combined with increased economic stability and optimism about the future, led to many couples starting or expanding their families. In addition, social norms of the time encouraged family formation, with marriage and parenthood considered an essential part of adult life. The Baby Boom had far-reaching implications for the economy. A larger population meant increased demand for goods and services, which in turn spurred further economic growth. Baby Boomers, as this generation came to be known, would grow up to be the largest group of consumers, workers, and investors the United States had ever seen.

The burgeoning population also increased the demand for housing, which led to a boom in the construction industry. The need for more homes to accommodate the growing families of the Baby Boomers would trigger significant shifts in American society, from changing patterns of housing and urban development to the evolution of the American financial system.

While the Baby Boom era was characterized by optimism and prosperity, it also posed challenges. The rapid population growth put pressure on public resources, including schools and healthcare services. Additionally, as this generation began to age, concerns arose about the ability of social security and other public pension systems to accommodate the growing number of retirees.

Despite these challenges, the Baby Boom was a defining period in American history, shaping the country's demographic, economic, and social landscape for decades to come.

5.2 Baby Boom

It is crucial to understand the scale of the Baby Boom to appreciate its profound effects. Over a period from the end of World War II in 1945 until the mid-1960s, approximately 76 million babies were born in the United States. This surge in births represented a 40% increase over the previous generation. This post-war euphoria, coupled with a thriving economy, resulted in an era of unprecedented growth and prosperity.

Baby Boomers, as those born during this period came to be known, represented a significant demographic shift. They constituted a generation that was larger and more influential than any before. Their sheer numbers allowed them to shape societal norms, values, and economic trends. As this group moved through their life stages—childhood, adolescence, adulthood, and now into retirement—their needs and desires influenced every sector of the economy, from housing and education to health care and retirement planning. The first significant economic impact of the Baby Boom was the rapid expansion of the consumer market. As millions of new babies were born, families required an array of products and services to care for them. Demand for baby food, clothing, toys, and a host of other products soared. Industries expanded to meet this demand, creating jobs and stimulating further economic growth.

As Baby Boomers grew, their needs evolved, and the economy shifted to accommodate them. The demand for larger family homes drove a boom in housing construction, particularly in the suburbs, altering the landscape of American cities. The education system expanded dramatically to educate this new generation, leading to the construction of new schools and universities and the creation of countless teaching jobs.

One of the crucial economic consequences of the Baby Boom was the creation of a highly influential consumer class. As this large generation grew older, their purchasing power grew with them. As teenagers, they drove demand for popular music, fashion, and other forms of entertainment. As young adults, they bought cars, homes, and the myriad appliances and furnishings needed to fill those homes. With this generational shift, consumer goods industries boomed, from automakers and homebuilders to manufacturers of refrigerators, televisions, and a whole new category of consumer electronics.

Their purchasing power was further amplified by cultural shifts. In contrast to their parents, who had lived through the Great Depression and World War II, Baby Boomers were more inclined to spend rather than save. They were confident in the ongoing prosperity of their era and felt secure in their economic futures. This readiness to consume helped fuel economic expansion, and provided a fertile environment for new financial products and services.

In response to the burgeoning market, companies started developing new financial products and services to cater to the unique needs of the Baby Boomers. Credit cards, for instance, became increasingly common. The concept of buying now and paying later appealed to the optimistic outlook of the Boomers. The availability of easy credit, in turn, boosted consumer spending, contributing to economic growth. The Baby Boom also had significant implications for the job market. With so many people entering their working years at the same time, the labor market expanded dramatically. This increase in workers supported economic growth, as more people earning wages meant more people spending money, fueling demand for goods and services.

But this wasn't the only impact of the Baby Boom on the labor market. As this generation entered the workforce, they brought with them new ideas and attitudes. They were better educated than previous generations and had high expectations for their careers. This resulted in a shift in the types of jobs that were in demand, with a greater emphasis on professional and technical roles, and less on manual labor. The Baby Boomers weren't just shaping the economy with their purchasing power; they were also transforming the very nature of work itself.

On the cusp of adulthood, the Baby Boomers entered a rapidly changing society. America in the mid-20th century was in the throes of what can only be described as a mass migration. But this wasn't the sort of migration that crossed oceans or continents. This was a migration from the cities to the suburbs. As these young people began establishing their own households, many of them did so in the burgeoning suburbs that were quickly transforming the American landscape. This shift towards suburbanization would have profound implications for the American economy. Throughout the 1950s and 1960s, new houses were being built at a staggering rate to accommodate the growing demand. These homes, with their manicured lawns and white picket fences, were often bought on credit, driving further growth in the financial sector. As these suburban communities sprang up, so too did the need for infrastructure to support them. Roads and highways were built, leading to a surge in automobile sales. Shopping malls, schools, and hospitals were also erected to cater to these burgeoning communities. This boom in construction not only contributed to economic growth, but also created numerous jobs, adding further fuel to the fire of the post-war economy.

Suburbanization also fostered a certain kind of consumer behavior. Suburban homes were often larger than their urban counterparts, leading to increased demand for furniture, appliances, and other household goods. Cars became a necessity rather than a luxury in these suburban communities, further driving the demand for automobiles.

This exodus to the suburbs wasn't merely a matter of demographics or economics. It was a cultural phenomenon, tied to deeply held American ideals of individualism and upward mobility. The suburban home was seen as a symbol of middle-class success. To own a home in the suburbs was to achieve the American Dream. This deeply ingrained cultural aspiration added a potent fuel to the economic engine driving the post-war boom.

While the suburbs may have embodied the American Dream for many, they also highlighted the stark divisions within American society. In many ways, the suburbs were emblematic of the social and economic disparities that marked this era of apparent prosperity. These implications of suburbanization, along with its economic impacts, are part of the larger narrative of post-war American finance.

5.3 Suburbanization

The growth of suburbs in the United States, starting in the mid-20th century, marked a substantial shift in the living patterns of many Americans. While the cities had always been the epicenter of economic activity, the decades following the Second World War witnessed an increasing number of people moving to the outskirts of cities, seeking a different lifestyle. Suburbanization, the term used to describe this phenomenon, would go on to have profound impacts on the American economy and the development of the financial sector. The roots of suburbanization can be traced back to several factors, one of the most prominent being the return of soldiers after World War II. As soldiers returned home, there was a pressing need for housing. Coupled with this was the newly acquired economic stability and growth, which meant that a larger number of people could afford homes. The GI Bill, signed into law in 1944, also played a pivotal role. It provided a range of benefits for returning World War II veterans, including low-cost mortgages, loans to start a business or farm, and tuition and living expenses to attend university or vocational education. These factors created a ripe environment for the construction of large-scale housing projects on the outskirts of cities.

One of the most famous of these projects was Levittown, a suburb of New York City. Created by the real estate developer William Levitt, Levittown was a planned community with thousands of identical homes. Levitt utilized assembly-line methods to construct these houses rapidly and affordably, offering many Americans their first opportunity to own a home. This innovative approach to housing marked a significant shift in the American real estate market, transforming housing from a luxury good to a widely accessible commodity. This democratization of home ownership had a significant impact on American finance, with the real estate and mortgage industries becoming key drivers of economic growth.

Yet, Levittown and other suburban developments were not just about housing. They embodied a particular vision of the American Dream—a dream of individual home ownership, economic prosperity, and a comfortable life away from the hustle and bustle of the city. This vision was powerfully appealing to many Americans in the post-war period, driving demand for suburban homes and spurring further economic growth. The growth of the suburbs didn't just transform housing; it reshaped the entire landscape of American consumption. As families moved away from city centers into newly formed suburban communities, the need for new services and infrastructure became apparent. This presented an opportunity for banks and financial institutions, which played a key role in financing the expansion of infrastructure such as roads, schools, and utilities, further fueling economic growth.

At the same time, the suburbs were a powerful engine for consumer spending. Newly suburban families needed cars to commute to work, furniture and appliances to fill their homes, and a multitude of other goods and services. The consumer culture that had begun to emerge during the Roaring Twenties exploded during the post-war period, with suburbanization playing a crucial role in its expansion. The advent of the shopping mall is a classic example of this trend. As families moved to the suburbs, traditional downtown shopping districts became less accessible. Retailers responded by building large shopping centers in suburban areas, offering a variety of stores in one convenient location. The first of these, the Southdale Center in Edina, Minnesota, opened in 1956 and quickly became a model for similar developments across the country. This shift in retail not only changed where Americans shopped, but also how they shopped, contributing to the rise of credit card usage and consumer debt, another significant development in the evolution of American finance.

But it wasn't all rosy. The growth of the suburbs also had a darker side, particularly in terms of social equity. During the early years of suburbanization, many suburbs were exclusively white, with minorities often denied housing due to discriminatory practices like redlining, a systemic denial of various services by federal government agencies, local governments, and the private sector to residents of specific neighborhoods or communities. These practices deepened economic and racial disparities in the United States, and their effects are still felt today.

The vast movement of people and resources to the suburbs also left many urban areas impoverished and neglected, creating a cycle of disinvestment and decline that would take decades to reverse. These challenges, while outside the direct scope of finance, would have significant implications for the evolution of American financial systems and policy in the years to come. As the suburbs grew, so did the appetites of the consumers living in them. The post-war economic boom had created a new, increasingly affluent middle class, with more disposable income than any previous generation. But it was the combination of this newfound wealth with the invention and proliferation of new consumer goods and the expansion of consumer credit that truly spurred the rise of consumerism that would come to define the latter half of the twentieth century.

Even as the government was encouraging suburbanization through policies like the GI Bill, private industry was finding new ways to attract and accommodate this swelling tide of consumers. Advertising underwent a revolution of its own, with Madison Avenue firms employing new techniques and technologies to entice and persuade potential buyers. Televisions, once a luxury item, became commonplace in American households, providing a new medium for advertisers to reach into the homes of potential consumers. The finance sector was not untouched by these developments. As consumers bought more, they also borrowed more. The rise of consumer credit is one of the defining features of this era. In 1950, Diners Club introduced the first universal credit card, offering customers the convenience of "buy now, pay later" across a wide range of businesses. Other companies soon followed suit, and by the 1960s, credit cards like Visa and Mastercard had become a fixture of American financial life.

Banks and other lending institutions saw the potential for profit in this new consumer culture and began offering personal loans, automobile financing, and other forms of credit to middle-class consumers, dramatically expanding the availability of consumer credit. By the 1970s, consumer spending accounted for more than 60% of the U.S. GDP, a trend that has continued into the 21st century. Meanwhile, the rise of consumerism was also reshaping the retail landscape. Department stores and shopping malls became the temples of the new consumer culture, replacing the traditional downtown shopping districts and accommodating the tastes and demands of a new suburban clientele.

As we look back at this period, we see that the rise of consumerism and suburbanization were intimately linked, each driving and reinforcing the other. Together, they played a crucial role in shaping the American economy, society, and financial landscape in the post-war era, setting the stage for the next phase in the evolution of American finance.

5.4 Rise of Consumerism

The suburbanization boom and the rise in disposable income, as previously discussed, paved the way for the rise of consumerism, an essential aspect of the Post War Prosperity era. But what did this surge in consumerism really mean, and how did it shape the economic and financial landscape of America?

The essence of consumerism lies in the promotion of the consumer's interests; it denotes the theory that an increasing consumption of goods is economically desirable. This theory came alive during the Post War Prosperity era, fueled by an explosion of new products, effective advertising, and the availability of credit. Following World War II, Americans saw a vast array of new products flooding the market. These were not only items that enhanced comfort and convenience in the home, such as washing machines, refrigerators, and television sets, but also goods that fed into the aspirational lifestyles being peddled by advertisers. Cars, for instance, became more than just means of transportation; they were status symbols, tangible evidence of one's place in the suburban middle class.

Behind this cascade of products was an industry that had undergone rapid expansion and innovation during the war years. Factories that had been producing military goods were retooled to cater to the civilian market, leading to a rise in production capacity. At the same time, technological advancements made during the war were applied to consumer goods, resulting in better quality products. The rapid expansion of television played a crucial role in fueling consumerism. In 1946, only 6,000 homes in America had television sets. By 1955, that number had jumped to over 30 million. Television not only changed how Americans spent their leisure time, but also how they shopped. The advent of TV advertising meant that companies could now showcase their products directly in the homes of consumers, making products more desirable through visual appeal and emotional connection.

Advertising in this era was all about creating a desire for products, associating them with an idealized version of life that consumers aspired to. It was about selling a lifestyle as much as selling a product. Companies became incredibly skilled at creating a sense of need for their products, often capitalizing on the insecurities and aspirations of the public. This was a drastic departure from the pre-war years, when advertising was more focused on the functional aspects of products.

The boom in consumerism also heralded a significant change in the financial landscape of the country. As demand for goods increased, so did the need for ways to finance these purchases. Consumer credit became a vital component of the economy, leading to significant changes in the banking and finance sectors. Credit cards, personal loans, and installment plans proliferated, giving consumers the ability to purchase goods on credit and pay back over time. The spread of consumer credit had profound effects on both the economy and the individual consumer. From an economic perspective, the rise of consumer credit contributed to increased demand for goods and services, stimulating economic growth. It also had a transformative effect on the retail industry. The concept of "buy now, pay later" allowed businesses to sell more expensive items, boosting profits and encouraging the development of new products and services. In many ways, this era can be considered the birth of the modern retail industry. Credit also had a profound effect on individual consumers. On the one hand, it allowed them to purchase goods and services that they would otherwise not have been able to afford. On the other hand, it also created a culture of debt. As the pressure to conform to the consumerist lifestyle grew, so did the level of indebtedness among Americans. Many found themselves living beyond their means, borrowing money to keep up with the consumerist lifestyle being advertised to them.

In addition to the rise of consumer credit, another key factor driving the surge in consumerism was the proliferation of large department stores and shopping malls. These retail behemoths became not just places to shop, but also centers of social activity. They offered a wide variety of goods under one roof, from clothing and furniture to appliances and electronics, making shopping a convenient and enjoyable experience. The shopping mall, in particular, became a symbol of post-war consumer culture. These enclosed, climate-controlled shopping centers provided a safe, clean, and convenient space for suburbanites to spend their leisure time and disposable income. They also played a crucial role in shaping the suburban landscape. Many suburbs were built around a central mall, reinforcing the consumerist lifestyle that was becoming increasingly ingrained in American society.

The rise of consumerism also had a profound impact on American culture. The emphasis on consumption and material wealth had implications for values, attitudes, and social norms. The notion of "keeping up with the Joneses" took hold, as people sought to emulate the consumerist lifestyle portrayed in advertisements and television shows. This focus on material wealth and consumer goods was seen by some as a sign of prosperity and success, but it was also criticized for promoting a shallow and materialistic culture.

Overall, the rise of consumerism was a defining feature of the Post War Prosperity era. It fueled economic growth and shaped American society in profound ways, some of which are still evident today. The consumer culture that emerged during this period laid the groundwork for the consumer society that we live in today, with all its benefits and challenges. Amid the wave of prosperity and consumerism, another economic phenomenon started to gain ground: inflation. This increase in the general price level of goods and services over time was not an unfamiliar concept, but it began to take a new significance in the post-war years. It's important to understand that inflation isn't necessarily a bad thing in moderation; in fact, a certain level of inflation can even be beneficial to an economy. It encourages spending and investment, as people prefer to use their money rather than hold onto it and lose purchasing power over time.

Unchecked or excessive inflation can have detrimental effects on an economy, diminishing the purchasing power of money, eroding savings, and creating uncertainty.

The post-war era was marked by several periods of inflation, often tied to economic growth, the rise of consumerism, and various policy decisions. As consumption rose, so did demand for goods and services. If this demand outpaced supply, prices would naturally rise. This was especially apparent in periods of strong economic growth, when high demand for goods and services put upward pressure on prices. The extensive use of credit also contributed to inflation. Credit expanded the money supply; when more money was available, demand increased, pushing prices up. Furthermore, businesses, observing that consumers were willing to take on debt to purchase their goods, may have felt more confident in raising prices, further fueling inflation.

Government policy also played a role in post-war inflation. Fiscal policies, such as government spending on social programs, infrastructure, and defense, injected money into the economy, which could fuel inflation if not carefully managed. Monetary policy, including decisions about interest rates and the money supply, also had implications for inflation.

This setting of rising prices posed new challenges and opportunities for consumers, businesses, and policymakers. For consumers, inflation meant that the money in their pockets had less purchasing power. It made it more expensive to live and forced consumers to grapple with the economic reality of rising prices. For businesses, inflation could lead to higher costs, but it could also allow them to raise prices and potentially increase profits. For policymakers, managing inflation became a key concern, influencing decisions on interest rates, money supply, and other aspects of economic policy. As we continue to explore the landscape of the post-war era, we'll see how the experiences of this time period—particularly the interaction of booming economic growth, the rise of consumerism, and the reality of inflation—played a pivotal role in shaping modern economic policy and public sentiment about the role of government in managing the economy.

5.5 Inflation

About Inflation, it's important to note that it was not a singular, static phenomenon. Rather, inflation ebbed and flowed in response to a variety of factors, including global economic conditions, shifts in supply and demand, and changes in monetary and fiscal policy. In the years following World War II, the United States experienced several significant inflationary periods. One of the first of these periods came immediately after the war. As we've discussed, the war had led to increased industrial production, technological advancements, and, subsequently, a boom in economic growth. The conversion of the wartime economy back to a peacetime one was a complex process, and it led to a brief but substantial period of inflation.

This initial post-war inflation was primarily demand-pull inflation, which occurs when demand for goods and services outpaces supply. As the soldiers returned home and transitioned back into civilian life, they and their families had pent-up demand for goods and services that had been scarce during the war years. This surge in demand, coupled with a supply that was still adjusting from producing military goods to consumer goods, resulted in a rapid rise in prices.

In the early 1950s, another wave of inflation hit as the United States entered the Korean War. This conflict triggered another shift towards war production and led to increased government spending, both of which contributed to rising prices. Again, this was largely a case of demand-pull inflation, with heightened demand for resources for the war effort putting pressure on the prices of goods and services. Interestingly, this period also saw the early stages of cost-push inflation, a type of inflation driven by rising costs of inputs like raw materials and labor. In this case, several factors contributed. One was the high demand for commodities needed for the war effort, which pushed up their prices. Another was the rising power of labor unions, which often secured wage increases for their members, increasing labor costs for businesses.

By the mid to late 1950s, inflation had again become a prominent issue. This was a time of rapid economic growth and prosperity, with rising wages, low unemployment, and increased consumer spending. Once again, the increased demand for goods and services put upward pressure on prices. This period also saw the continued rise of credit and consumer debt, which further fueled demand and inflation. The growth of consumer credit during this period was remarkable, with more and more Americans buying homes, cars, appliances, and other goods on credit. This easy access to credit not only facilitated the rise of the consumer society but also contributed to the inflationary pressure. Another interesting factor during this period that needs attention is the role of monetary policy in contributing to inflation. The Federal Reserve, the central bank of the United States, has the power to influence inflation through its control over the money supply. Essentially, when the Fed increases the money supply faster than the economy's ability to produce goods and services, it can create inflation.

In the 1960s, the United States was grappling with the cost of the Vietnam War and increased social spending under President Lyndon B. Johnson's Great Society programs. The Fed, under the leadership of Chairman William McChesney Martin, faced pressure from the Johnson administration to keep interest rates low to finance the government's spending. This policy, known as "guns and butter," led to an increase in the money supply, which contributed to rising inflation.

On a global scale, the post-war international monetary system, known as the Bretton Woods system, also played a role in the U.S inflation. Under Bretton Woods, the U.S. dollar was the world's reserve currency, linked to gold, and other currencies were linked to the dollar. In the 1960s, growing U.S. balance of payments deficits led to an oversupply of dollars in global markets, which contributed to inflation both domestically and internationally.

In the 1970s, the inflationary pressures were further exacerbated by several key events. Firstly, the 1973 oil crisis, when the members of the Organization of Arab Petroleum Exporting Countries (OAPEC) proclaimed an oil embargo, led to a sharp increase in energy prices. This increase in energy prices was a significant shock to the U.S. economy, leading to stagflation, a situation characterized by high inflation and high unemployment. The oil shock led to cost-push inflation, as the higher energy costs were passed on to consumers in the form of higher prices for goods and services.

In addition, the decision by President Richard Nixon in 1971 to end the U.S. dollar's convertibility into gold — effectively ending the Bretton Woods system — had profound implications for inflation. With the dollar no longer tied to gold, the Federal Reserve had more leeway to increase the money supply. This, combined with the oil shock and other factors, led to a period of high inflation in the 1970s and early 1980s. The period of post-war prosperity was indeed a complex one. It was marked by unprecedented economic growth, but also by periods of significant inflation. The inflation was driven by a multitude of factors, ranging from shifts in demand and supply, changes in monetary and fiscal policy, to global economic conditions and crises. The impact of this inflation was felt not only in the form of higher prices, but also in the economic decisions and policies that were adopted to manage it.

6 From Manufacturing to Service: Industrial to Postindustrial

It is against this backdrop that we must now turn our attention to a significant shift that has sculpted the structure of the American economy — the transition from an industrial to a postindustrial economy. This shift is characterized by a decrease in manufacturing and an increase in service-based industries, a change often called deindustrialization.

Inflation, along with various other factors, contributed to the restructuring of the American economy. This economic transformation unfolded in the latter half of the twentieth century, and has only accelerated in the twenty-first century. It fundamentally changed the face of the American workforce, the structure of the economy, and the nature of economic challenges and future trends.

The structural change in the economy significantly reshaped the nature of work and employment in the United States. The declining share of manufacturing jobs and the burgeoning growth of service sector jobs had profound implications for the labor force. There are myriad factors to consider here, such as changes in job security, income, skill requirements, and the socioeconomic implications of these shifts. Then, we will analyze how this transition impacted the broader economy. What does it mean for an economy to shift its emphasis from making things to providing services? How does this transition influence economic growth, trade, and the distribution of wealth? These are the questions that we will grapple with in our exploration.

The challenges that arose in this era of economic restructuring were multifaceted. These ranged from the dislocation of workers in declining industries, to the need for upskilling and reskilling the workforce, to managing the social and economic disparities exacerbated by these shifts. We will examine these complexities and their impact on both the individual and societal level.

Lastly, we will look towards the horizon of future trends. The movement from an industrial to a postindustrial economy is an ongoing process, and understanding where we might be heading is crucial. New technologies, changing demographics, and evolving consumer preferences will all play a role in shaping the postindustrial economy of the future.

6.1 Impact on Workforce

The transition from manufacturing to service, from an industrial to a postindustrial economy, marked a pivotal shift in the structure of the American workforce. As manufacturing jobs began to decline and service sector jobs increased, the effects were far-reaching, impacting job security, income levels, skill requirements, and various other dimensions of work. During the heyday of the industrial economy, manufacturing jobs were the backbone of the American workforce. These jobs often provided stable, long-term employment and were accessible to individuals with varying levels of education. The industrial economy was marked by the production of tangible goods — automobiles, appliances, furniture, clothing, and so on. Workers were typically involved in the direct production of these goods, and the skills required were often specific to the manufacturing process.

With the transition to a postindustrial economy, the manufacturing sector began to shrink. Factors such as automation, outsourcing, and globalization contributed to this decline. As manufacturing jobs were automated or moved overseas, many workers found themselves displaced. This displacement was not evenly distributed, and certain regions, often referred to as the "Rust Belt," were particularly hard-hit. In these areas, the loss of manufacturing jobs led to widespread unemployment and economic hardship.

On the other hand, the rise of the service sector opened up a whole new set of employment opportunities. Jobs in fields such as healthcare, education, retail, finance, and information technology began to increase. Unlike manufacturing jobs, many service sector jobs involve the provision of intangible services rather than the production of tangible goods. As a result, the nature of work in the service sector can be quite different from work in the manufacturing sector. In the service sector, interpersonal and problem-solving skills are often highly valued. For instance, a customer service representative needs to be able to communicate effectively and resolve issues, a healthcare worker needs to provide care and empathy, and a financial advisor needs to provide sound investment advice. As such, the skill requirements for service sector jobs can be quite different from those for manufacturing jobs.

The stability and security of service sector jobs can vary widely. Some service sector jobs, particularly those in fields like healthcare and education, can provide stable, long-term employment.

Other service sector jobs, such as those in retail or hospitality, may be more precarious, with less job security and lower wages.

Thus, the transition from an industrial to a postindustrial economy has led to a major restructuring of the American workforce. The decline of manufacturing and the rise of the service sector has had profound implications for workers, reshaping the landscape of employment opportunities, job security, income levels, and skill requirements.

Understanding these impacts is essential for shaping policies and strategies that can help to support workers and promote a thriving, inclusive economy. Alongside these shifts, changes in the workplace and labor market dynamics further compounded the impact on the workforce. As manufacturing jobs dwindled and service sector jobs grew, the trend towards casual, part-time, and temporary employment arrangements also gained momentum. This was partly due to the nature of service sector jobs, where customer demand can fluctuate, and workforce needs can vary accordingly. This trend has led to an increasing number of 'contingent' workers – those not in a permanent, full-time position.

Contingent work can offer some benefits such as flexibility, but it can also lead to job insecurity and lack of access to benefits like health insurance, paid leave, and retirement plans. This represents a departure from the traditional model of a stable, full-time job with benefits that was more common in the manufacturing sector. Further, the impact on the workforce was also reflected in the wage trends. Manufacturing jobs traditionally offered decent wages and helped build the American middle class in the 20th century.

The service sector is characterized by a wide wage disparity. On one end, there are high-paying jobs in fields like information technology and finance. On the other end, there are many low-wage jobs in areas like retail, food service, and personal care. Consequently, the transition to a service economy has been associated with growing income inequality.

In addition to these changes, the shift from manufacturing to service also altered the geographical distribution of jobs. Manufacturing jobs were often located in specific industrial regions, whereas service sector jobs tend to be more widely dispersed. Nevertheless, some types of service jobs, particularly high-paying ones, are often concentrated in metropolitan areas. This has led to growing economic disparities between urban and rural areas. Another dimension of the impact on the workforce relates to educational requirements. Many manufacturing jobs required specific vocational skills, but not necessarily a high level of formal education. In contrast, many service sector jobs require higher levels of education. For instance, jobs in fields like healthcare, finance, and IT often require a college degree or even advanced degrees. This shift has implications for educational policy and workforce development.

While some workers have been able to adapt to these changes, others have faced challenges. Workers who were displaced from manufacturing jobs, particularly older workers and those without a high level of education, have often struggled to find new jobs in the service sector. For these individuals, the transition to a service economy has been a difficult one, marked by job loss, retraining, and adaptation to new types of work.

The impact of the transition from manufacturing to service on the workforce is a complex and multifaceted issue. The changing nature of work, evolving labor market dynamics, shifting wage trends, and geographical and educational factors all play a role. Understanding these impacts is crucial for developing strategies to support workers and foster a prosperous, equitable economy in the postindustrial era. The impact on the workforce is just one aspect of the transition to a service economy. This transformation has also had profound implications for the broader economy, which we will explore in the next section.

6.2 Impact on Economy

The move from a manufacturing to a service-based economy has also had significant consequences on the broader economy. For instance, service industries often have different supply chains, capital requirements, and regulatory environments than manufacturing industries, which can influence macroeconomic variables like investment, productivity, and trade. In the arena of investment, for instance, manufacturing industries are often capital-intensive, requiring significant investments in physical assets such as machinery, equipment, and buildings. In contrast, service industries are typically more labor-intensive and may require less physical capital investment.

They often require significant investments in human capital, including education and training, as well as intangible assets like software and intellectual property. This shift can affect overall levels of business investment and influence economic growth.

Productivity growth rates also tend to differ between the manufacturing and service sectors. Historically, the manufacturing sector has seen relatively high productivity growth, thanks to technological advancements and economies of scale. On the other hand, productivity growth in the service sector has often been slower, although there are significant variations within the sector. For example, productivity growth in information technology services has been rapid, while it has been slower in areas like healthcare and education. Changes in the composition of the economy can thus influence overall productivity growth, which is a key driver of economic growth and living standards. In the realm of international trade, the rise of the service economy has contributed to changes in the composition of exports and imports. While the U.S. has a trade deficit in manufactured goods, it has a trade surplus in services. As the service sector has grown, service exports have become increasingly important. At the same time, the offshoring of service jobs has also become more common, due to advances in information and communication technology. This has led to new opportunities but also new challenges, such as how to support workers whose jobs are offshored.

The transition to a service economy has also influenced labor market dynamics. As previously discussed, service industries often have different employment structures than manufacturing industries, with more part-time, temporary, and contingent employment. These changes can affect labor market stability and workers' income and benefits. Further, wage disparities within the service sector can contribute to income inequality, which can influence consumer spending and economic stability. Additionally, service industries often have different tax and regulatory environments than manufacturing industries. For instance, sales taxes often apply differently to goods and services, and regulations may vary by industry. These differences can affect businesses' costs and incentives and can influence the distribution of economic activity across sectors.

In summary, the shift from manufacturing to a service-based economy has broad impacts on the economy, affecting investment, productivity, trade, labor markets, and government policy. These impacts are complex and interact with each other in numerous ways, which can present both opportunities and challenges for economic policymakers. While the shift to a service economy brings many benefits, such as new types of jobs and opportunities for economic growth, it also poses challenges, such as wage inequality and job insecurity for certain segments of the workforce. These challenges must be managed carefully to ensure that the transition to a postindustrial economy benefits all members of society. One notable aspect of the postindustrial economy's impact on the economic landscape is the change in the nature of goods and services. As a manufacturing-based economy, the United States once concentrated on producing tangible goods, such as cars, appliances, and clothing.

With the shift towards a service-based economy, the nation's production focus has largely pivoted towards intangible goods, often associated with knowledge and information. These include various professional services, such as consulting, education, healthcare, software development, and financial services.

The dominance of services in the U.S. economy represents a significant shift in the country's economic output. According to the U.S. Bureau of Economic Analysis, the service sector accounted for over 76% of the U.S. GDP in 2020, a figure that has been steadily increasing over the past few decades. This means that three-quarters of the economic value generated within the country comes from services, a stark contrast to the manufacturing-driven economy of the past. As a result, the role of services in the U.S. economy is fundamental and is expected to continue growing in the future.

A closer look at specific sectors within the service economy illustrates this trend. For instance, healthcare, one of the largest and fastest-growing sectors, has experienced significant growth due to several factors, including demographic shifts like the aging population and advances in medical technology. Similarly, the technology sector, particularly software and information services, has seen a rapid expansion with the rise of digital technologies and the internet.

Alongside these significant shifts, the transition from manufacturing to services has also brought about new challenges and complexities. For one, the rise of the service economy has resulted in increased income inequality. This is primarily because service-sector jobs span a wide spectrum of income levels, ranging from high-paying professional and technical roles to low-wage jobs in sectors such as retail and hospitality. This wage disparity is contributing to a widening income gap, a pressing concern for policymakers.

The evolution towards a service-based economy also raises questions about the sustainability of economic growth. In particular, the service sector's lower productivity growth, compared to manufacturing, is an area of concern. While certain segments of the service sector, such as technology, exhibit high productivity growth, others, such as healthcare and education, lag behind. Achieving consistent productivity growth across the service sector is thus a key challenge for maintaining overall economic growth in a service-dominated economy. In summary, the impact of the transition from manufacturing to services on the economy is profound, influencing the nature of goods and services produced, the composition of the GDP, wage levels, and productivity growth. As the United States continues to travel its path as a service-based economy, understanding these impacts will be crucial for shaping policies that promote economic prosperity and address emerging challenges.

6.3 Challenges

One of the fundamental challenges accompanying the transition from a manufacturing to a service-based economy is the change in employment patterns. The job market's structure has undergone a significant transformation. With the decline of manufacturing jobs, many workers have had to transition into service sector roles, often requiring different skills and training. In the manufacturing sector, jobs were traditionally full-time positions with benefits and the potential for upward mobility. Manufacturing jobs often required technical skills but not necessarily advanced education. This allowed a significant portion of the population to find stable, well-paying jobs without needing a college degree.

In contrast, the service sector is marked by a broader range of job types, including part-time, gig, and contract work. These jobs often have less job security and fewer benefits than traditional full-time positions. Additionally, many well-paying service jobs require a higher level of education or specialized training, creating barriers for workers from the manufacturing sector seeking to transition into service roles.

This structural shift in the job market presents significant challenges for workers and policymakers. Upskilling and reskilling programs are essential to equip workers with the skills needed in the service sector. Implementing these programs on a large scale is a significant task. This is particularly crucial given the rising importance of digital and technological skills in the service sector. Additionally, the growth of the gig economy, a significant part of the service sector, presents its own set of challenges. While it offers flexibility, it also introduces issues related to job security, income stability, and access to benefits. Policymakers must balance the need for labor market flexibility with protections for gig workers.

Another challenge is addressing the income inequality exacerbated by the shift to a service economy. As noted, service sector jobs span a wide income spectrum, contributing to growing wage disparities. Addressing this inequality requires thoughtful policy interventions, such as wage supports, progressive tax systems, and access to quality education and training. While we've already identified some significant challenges associated with the transition from an industrial to a postindustrial economy, such as changes in employment patterns, the requirement for upskilling, and the growth of income and regional disparities, there are more subtleties to this issue that warrant further exploration.

One crucial challenge lies in the environmental impact. The service sector, while often touted as less polluting than heavy industry, still carries considerable environmental burdens. For instance, the burgeoning IT industry has an energy consumption that is rising at an alarming rate. Data centers worldwide consume about 200 terawatt hours (TWh) per year, nearly 1% of global electricity demand, and the figure is growing. Despite efforts to use renewable energy, many data centers still rely on fossil fuels. The rapid pace of technological change that fuels the service sector also produces vast amounts of e-waste. According to the Global E-Waste Monitor, in 2019, the world generated 53.6 million metric tonnes (Mt) of e-waste, an average of 7.3 kg per capita. Only 17.4% of this was officially documented as properly collected and recycled. This trend suggests that the service industry, while less visibly polluting, still has environmental issues to address.

Next, there's the challenge of automation. As AI and machine learning become increasingly capable, more jobs, including those in the service sector, are threatened by automation. Research from McKinsey suggests that in the United States alone, 73 million jobs could be automated by 2030. While some believe this may create new jobs, others warn it could lead to widespread unemployment or underemployment, particularly for lower-skilled workers. This threat of automation puts additional pressure on the workforce to constantly upgrade their skills to stay relevant. It also puts pressure on education systems to evolve and keep up with the changing demands of the job market. This can be particularly challenging for developing countries that still struggle with basic education challenges.

The shift towards a postindustrial economy also comes with sociopolitical challenges. The rise of the gig economy has resulted in a new class of workers who operate outside the traditional employment relationship. This makes it more challenging to enforce labor rights and protections. While some gig workers appreciate the flexibility of their roles, others face instability and lack access to benefits and protections afforded to traditional employees. This issue requires significant policy attention to ensure fair treatment for all workers. Furthermore, the shift away from manufacturing can lead to social unrest. For instance, in areas where manufacturing was once the primary source of employment, its decline can leave communities economically depressed and socially destabilized. There's a need for policies that can facilitate a smooth transition and prevent the entrenchment of economic hardship and social problems in these areas.

These challenges are indeed formidable, but by no means insurmountable. They call for concerted effort, innovative thinking, and cooperation between different sectors of society – including governments, businesses, educational institutions, and individuals. There is another layer of complexity added to these challenges in the form of international trade and globalization. As countries increasingly become intertwined economically, the shift to a service-based economy doesn't only affect a single nation but has ripple effects across the globe. For instance, the offshoring of service jobs from developed to developing countries can lead to job losses in one country while boosting employment in another. This offshoring also raises questions about labor standards and working conditions in countries where these jobs are outsourced.

The rise of digital platforms is also a significant trend, especially in the service sector. These platforms facilitate transactions between users, whether they're individuals or businesses. Examples include online marketplaces like Amazon, ride-sharing apps like Uber, and accommodation platforms like Airbnb. While these platforms offer new opportunities for business and convenience for consumers, they also raise new regulatory challenges. As we shift further into the service economy, the question of inequality becomes increasingly pertinent. Many of the highest paying jobs in a service economy require high levels of education and skills. Simultaneously, many service jobs, especially those that can't be automated, are relatively low paid, such as jobs in retail or food service. This dichotomy can exacerbate income inequality within societies.

It is not all doom and gloom. Challenges also present opportunities. For instance, the demand for green services, such as renewable energy and energy efficiency, is growing. Service sector companies that can meet this demand will likely find ample business opportunities. The impact of technology also has a silver lining. While automation threatens some jobs, it can also create new ones. For example, the rise of data analytics, cloud computing, artificial intelligence, and other advanced technologies are spawning entirely new industries requiring new skills and expertise. As economies mature, there is a tendency for them to become more diversified and resilient. A diverse service economy, featuring a mix of industries such as finance, health, education, tourism, and technology, can be less vulnerable to sector-specific shocks than an economy heavily reliant on manufacturing or commodity exports.

The future of the postindustrial economy will be shaped by many factors, some of which we are only beginning to understand.

6.4 Future Trends

To venture a glimpse into the future of a postindustrial economy, one needs to understand the primary driving forces of change. These drivers are technological innovation, globalization, environmental sustainability, demographic change, and shifts in social values and behaviors. Each of these drivers will have an immense impact on future trends in the service industry. The first of these drivers, technological innovation, is already reshaping the service sector. The advent of digital technologies like big data, machine learning, artificial intelligence (AI), cloud computing, and blockchain, among others, is revolutionizing services. These technologies allow for new ways of delivering services, new business models, and the creation of entirely new services.

In the financial sector, for example, the rise of FinTech and blockchain technology is transforming how we transact and manage money. It is expected that these technologies will continue to disrupt the sector, leading to more automated, efficient, and customer-centric financial services. AI is another transformative technology expected to bring significant changes. It's likely that we'll see more service jobs, especially those involving routine tasks, become automated.

AI can also create new jobs and services. For instance, the demand for AI specialists is growing. Also, AI could enable more personalized and efficient services, such as personalized healthcare or personalized learning.

In the field of healthcare, telemedicine, AI, and personalized medicine are expected to become the norm. These changes could make healthcare more accessible and affordable, potentially improving health outcomes. Yet, technology is not the only driving force of change in the postindustrial economy. Globalization is another significant factor. With the world becoming more interconnected, service businesses need to operate on a global scale. This trend will likely continue, leading to more cross-border service delivery. Globalization will also intensify competition among service providers, pushing them to continually innovate and improve their offerings.

Another impact of globalization is the offshoring and outsourcing of services. As businesses seek to cut costs and access global talent, more service jobs are likely to be outsourced to countries with lower labor costs.

This trend could also lead to job losses in high-cost countries, contributing to economic inequality. Environmental sustainability is another critical driver of future trends. As the impacts of climate change become increasingly evident, there is growing pressure on businesses to become more sustainable. This trend is likely to reshape the service industry. For instance, we might see more demand for services that help businesses reduce their environmental footprint, such as energy efficiency consulting or sustainable supply chain management. There could also be increased demand for green services from consumers, such as renewable energy or sustainable tourism.

The demographic change, especially the aging population in many developed countries, will also shape the future of the service economy. An older population could lead to higher demand for health and social care services, as well as services that cater to the needs and preferences of older adults. Lastly, shifts in social values and behaviors will also influence future trends. For instance, consumers are increasingly seeking experiences over products, which could boost demand for experiential services like travel, dining, and entertainment. Also, consumers are becoming more socially conscious, seeking services from businesses that align with their values, whether that's sustainability, fair trade, or diversity and inclusion.

As these drivers interact, they will shape the trends that define the future of the service economy. In the next sections, we will explore these trends in more depth, examining their potential impacts on the workforce, the economy, and society at large. Moving forward, a pivotal future trend in a postindustrial economy lies in the realm of workforce development. There will be a continued shift towards jobs requiring higher skills and qualifications. The demand for workers with advanced technical skills, such as those related to digital technologies and data analysis, will increase. There will also be an increased need for 'soft' skills, such as critical thinking, creativity, and emotional intelligence. These skills will be crucial as tasks involving complex decision-making and human interaction are less likely to be automated.

This shift towards higher-skilled jobs means that education and training systems will need to adapt. Lifelong learning will become even more critical. Workers will need to continually upgrade their skills and learn new ones to stay relevant in the fast-changing job market. Thus, we may see a surge in demand for services that provide continuous learning opportunities, such as online learning platforms and professional development courses. At the same time, this trend could exacerbate economic inequality. Those with the means and access to acquire new skills may thrive, while those without may struggle. Addressing this potential divide will be one of the significant challenges in the postindustrial era.

Another future trend relates to the organization of work. We're already seeing a shift towards more flexible and remote work arrangements, driven by digital technologies. This trend is likely to continue, leading to changes in where, when, and how work is done. We might see more people working from home or co-working spaces, more flexible work schedules, and more project-based or gig work. This shift could provide more work-life balance and reduce commuting time and costs.

It could also blur the lines between work and personal life and lead to increased job insecurity. Furthermore, the importance of services in a postindustrial economy will make issues related to service quality and customer satisfaction even more critical. Businesses will need to focus on improving their service quality and building strong relationships with their customers. They might use technologies like AI and big data to gain insights into their customers' needs and preferences and provide personalized services.

They will also need to address concerns related to privacy and security, as these technologies involve collecting and handling large amounts of personal data.

The rise of the sharing economy is another trend we might see. This trend involves people sharing access to goods and services through digital platforms. Examples include ride-sharing services like Uber and accommodation-sharing services like Airbnb. This trend could lead to new service jobs and more efficient use of resources.

It also raises issues related to regulation, worker rights, and safety. Finally, sustainability will be a crucial consideration in the future service economy. Businesses will need to find ways to deliver their services in a way that minimizes their environmental impact. This trend could lead to innovations in service delivery and new 'green' service jobs.

It also poses a challenge as many current service practices are not sustainable.

In summary, the future trends in the service economy are shaped by various driving forces and have implications on multiple fronts.

7 Silicon Valley's Rise: Birth of Silicon Valley

As we take stock of these future trends, one stands out as being particularly transformative, and that is the proliferation of technology and its effects on all aspects of our lives. At the center of this technological revolution is an area known as Silicon Valley. Silicon Valley is more than a physical location—it's an ethos, an idea. It represents innovation, entrepreneurship, and the bold ambition to use technology to change the world. As we gaze into the future of the service economy, understanding the history and influence of Silicon Valley becomes more relevant.

In the mid-twentieth century, when industrial manufacturing still dominated the economic landscape, few could have predicted that a relatively quiet region in Northern California, known for its fruit orchards, would become the epicenter of a technological revolution that would forever change our economy and our society. The story of Silicon Valley is a testament to the power of innovation, entrepreneurship, and the transformation from industrial to postindustrial. Silicon Valley's emergence didn't happen in a vacuum. It was, and still is, a unique confluence of elements—entrepreneurial spirit, access to capital, presence of world-class universities, influx of skilled immigrants, and government support—that made this region a hotbed for tech innovation. It illustrates how geography, culture, and policy can combine to create an environment that nurtures innovation and economic growth.

This area has been the birthplace of many technological advancements and tech giants that have significantly influenced the course of the global economy. Companies like Apple, Google, Facebook, and many others started here and have gone on to redefine how we work, live, and communicate. These companies didn't just revolutionize technology—they also reshaped the economic landscape. They played a key role in the shift from the industrial to the postindustrial economy by driving the growth of high-tech services and creating new types of jobs. They also popularized new ways of working, such as flexible work hours, flat organizational structures, and a focus on innovation and creativity.

The tech industry's rise in Silicon Valley has had significant impacts beyond the region. It has inspired other cities around the world to cultivate their own tech hubs, leading to the globalization of the tech industry. It has also spurred discussions on various societal issues, such as income inequality, data privacy, and the role of technology in our lives. As we venture further into the postindustrial era, understanding the birth and rise of Silicon Valley is crucial. It offers insights into the factors that drive technological innovation and economic transformation, and it provides lessons on how to deal with the challenges and opportunities presented by the digital age. Let us then turn our attention to the birth of Silicon Valley and its meteoric rise as a technology and innovation hub.

7.1 Tech Startups

Tech startups are an integral part of Silicon Valley's identity and its economic prowess. They represent the spirit of innovation, risk-taking, and disruption that the region is known for. But what exactly are tech startups, and how have they come to play such a critical role in Silicon Valley and the broader global economy?

Tech startups are new businesses founded on technology or innovative ideas, with the aim of disrupting existing markets or creating entirely new ones. They are distinguished from traditional small businesses by their growth-oriented mindset. While small businesses often aim to provide a steady income for their owners and a few employees, tech startups typically aspire to rapid growth, significant market influence, and potentially enormous financial returns. Their ultimate goal is often to go public through an Initial Public Offering (IPO) or to be acquired by a larger company. Silicon Valley has been a breeding ground for tech startups since the mid-20th century. This explosion of startup activity can be traced back to a few pivotal moments in history. One of these was the founding of Stanford Industrial Park (now known as Stanford Research Park) in 1951, which marked a deliberate attempt by Stanford University to promote high-tech economic development in the region. This move attracted a number of high-tech companies to the area, including some early computer and semiconductor firms.

Stanford's investment in this research park also highlights the important role that research universities have played in Silicon Valley's startup culture. Universities like Stanford and UC Berkeley have been a source of cutting-edge research, technological innovation, and highly educated talent - all crucial ingredients for tech startups. Another major factor has been the availability of venture capital. Venture capitalists invest in startups in exchange for equity, or shares in the company. This type of funding is particularly suited to tech startups, which often require substantial up-front investment but also offer the potential for large returns. The venture capital model has enabled many Silicon Valley startups to take risks, innovate, and grow rapidly.

These factors - a supportive university environment, the availability of venture capital, and a culture of innovation and risk-taking - set the stage for the boom in tech startups that Silicon Valley would become famous for. These entrepreneurial ventures have not only shaped the business landscape of the region, but they have also had profound impacts on society and how we live our daily lives. Companies like Google, Apple, Facebook, and countless others began as small-scale projects and are now titanic forces in their respective industries.

The first generations of tech startups in Silicon Valley were heavily concentrated in hardware and semiconductors, with companies such as Fairchild Semiconductor and Intel leading the way. They developed the technologies that would lay the foundation for the personal computing revolution of the 1980s and 1990s. This wave of innovation was characterized by garage-based ventures, epitomized by the story of Steve Jobs and Steve Wozniak building the first Apple computer in Jobs's garage. This pattern of innovation continued into the 1990s, with the emergence of the internet opening up new vistas for tech startups. Companies such as Netscape, Yahoo, and later Google and Facebook, transformed the way we access information, communicate, and conduct business. This era saw a shift towards software and services, and the rapid growth of these companies underscored the potential for tech startups to reach global audiences and achieve enormous scale.

The period of the late 2000s and beyond has been characterized by the emergence of the "app economy," with smartphones and mobile devices becoming ubiquitous. Tech startups have been at the forefront of this transformation, creating applications and services that leverage the power of these devices. Companies like Uber and Airbnb are prime examples of how startups have used technology to disrupt traditional industries. Throughout each of these periods, the common thread has been the entrepreneurial spirit and the willingness to take risks. But it's not just about individual entrepreneurs. It's also about the ecosystem that supports them. In Silicon Valley, this includes not just venture capitalists willing to provide funding, but also a labor market rich with talented engineers and technologists, and a culture that accepts failure as a natural part of the innovation process.

All these elements combine to create an environment where tech startups can thrive and where innovation is constantly pushed forward. This culture of innovation and the supporting ecosystem are key reasons why Silicon Valley has remained the global center for tech startups. While the Silicon Valley tech startup story often focuses on the 'big hits' – those companies that quickly ascended to enormous valuations and continue to shape our lives – the road of each startup is a complex one, rife with challenges and lessons learned.

At the heart of many tech startups is the ethos of innovation and disruption. They set out with the mission to create new products or services that challenge the status quo, often using technology as the catalyst for change. A company like Uber, for example, leveraged mobile technology to disrupt the traditional taxi industry. Netflix, on the other hand, revolutionized the way we consume entertainment by introducing on-demand streaming, a shift from the conventional DVD rental model. These startups didn't just improve existing services – they redefined their entire industries. Alongside the drive for innovation is an intense focus on growth. Many tech startups operate on the principle of "blitzscaling" – a term coined by entrepreneur and lecturer Reid Hoffman to describe the rapid scaling of a company even in the face of uncertainty. This approach prioritizes speed over efficiency in the face of market uncertainty. It's a high-stakes strategy that can lead to extraordinary growth (as seen with companies like Amazon and Facebook) but can also result in equally spectacular failures if not managed effectively.

Another noteworthy aspect of tech startups is their lean and agile structure. Many follow the Lean Startup methodology, a principle popularized by entrepreneur Eric Ries, which emphasizes rapid iteration, customer feedback, and a "fail fast" approach. By staying lean and being open to pivoting, these companies can adapt quickly to market changes and efficiently validate their business ideas.

These high-growth, high-risk environments come with their own challenges. Funding, for one, is often a critical issue. While venture capital is abundant in Silicon Valley, securing it requires startups to demonstrate their potential for high returns, often leading to intense competition and pressure to continuously innovate. Silicon Valley's tech startups, in their quest for disruption and growth, have created an exciting but challenging environment.

While the spirit of innovation and the daring to challenge established norms is central to the success of tech startups, this indomitable spirit has to be bolstered by a resource that is fundamental to any business: capital. Funding serves as the lifeblood that sustains a startup's operations, fuels its growth, and allows it to weather the uncertainties and setbacks that inevitably arise along the way. In Silicon Valley, the epicenter of the world's tech industry, venture capital has played a pivotal role in enabling these startups to blossom and bring their disruptive ideas to life. Venture capital (VC) is a form of private equity financing that is provided by VC firms or funds to startups, early-stage, and emerging companies that have been deemed to have high growth potential or which have demonstrated high growth. These VC firms, represented by venture capitalists, are willing to take on the considerable risk associated with investing in relatively nascent and unproven companies, with the expectation of potentially outsized returns should these startups succeed and either go public or get acquired by a larger company.

Silicon Valley's narrative would be incomplete without acknowledging the instrumental role played by venture capitalists. Companies that now straddle the tech landscape as giants, such as Apple, Google, Facebook, and many others, were once fledgling startups that were propelled on their growth trajectories through the backing of venture capitalists. These financiers not only inject capital into the startups but also provide strategic guidance, mentoring, and access to their network of contacts, which can be invaluable to young, growing companies.

The relationship between venture capitalists and startups isn't without its own complexities and challenges. The quest for funding can become a high-stakes game, with startups vying for attention and resources in a fiercely competitive arena. There are also questions about control and decision-making, as venture capitalists often secure equity in the companies they invest in and can wield significant influence over the strategic direction of these companies.

7.2 Venture Capital

Venture capital in Silicon Valley, like its entrepreneurial spirit, is not a recent phenomenon. The roots of venture capital can be traced back to the mid-20th century, with the establishment of the first venture capital firms such as American Research and Development Corporation (ARDC) and J.H. Whitney & Company.

It was only in the late 1960s and 70s, concurrent with the emergence of Silicon Valley, that venture capital truly came into its own.

It was during this period that key venture capital firms like Kleiner Perkins, Sequoia Capital, and Accel Partners were established. These firms would go on to fund some of the most transformative companies of our time. Kleiner Perkins, for instance, backed companies like Amazon, Google, and AOL. Sequoia Capital, on the other hand, funded Apple, Cisco, and YouTube, among many others. The role of these venture capital firms extended beyond just providing funds. They also served as valuable mentors and advisors to the startups they funded, leveraging their industry knowledge and experience to guide these companies through their growth phases. This assistance often proved crucial in helping these young companies travel the often tumultuous road from a nascent startup to a successful, sustainable business. The venture capitalists would take on considerable risk with their investments, given that they were often dealing with unproven businesses in emerging industries.

The potential for outsized returns from a successful exit, either through an initial public offering (IPO) or a strategic acquisition, made this a risk worth taking. The successes of companies like Apple, Google, and Facebook, all of which delivered exceptional returns for their early-stage investors, underscore this point.

But this risk-reward dynamic also brought its own set of challenges. The high-stakes nature of venture capital investing meant that for every successful investment, there were many more that failed to deliver. This inherent risk led to a hypercompetitive environment for startups seeking funding, as venture capitalists became increasingly selective, backing only those companies that they believed had the potential to deliver the desired returns. The intense competition for funding also resulted in an increased emphasis on rapid growth and profitability, sometimes at the expense of other considerations.

Venture capital, in many ways, sowed the seeds for the next phase of Silicon Valley's evolution, a phase characterized by the rise of the internet. The mid-1990s marked the beginning of the internet revolution. The dot-com bubble, as it was known, saw an extraordinary influx of investments into startups focused on internet-based services and products. These were the years when many of today's technology giants, including Google, Amazon, and eBay, were born. The proliferation of the internet led to new business models and value propositions. Companies like eBay offered an online marketplace, connecting buyers and sellers worldwide. Google revolutionized the way we access information, making the vast expanse of the internet searchable and, in the process, creating a highly profitable online advertising model. Amazon, starting as an online bookseller, quickly expanded to other product categories, ultimately aspiring to be the world's most customer-centric company.

Venture capital firms were quick to recognize the potential of these internet startups. They were willing to provide the necessary funding despite the lack of immediate profitability, banking on the future potential of these companies. The venture capital model, with its emphasis on long-term returns, was perfectly suited to this new wave of startups. Venture capital funding enabled these startups to scale rapidly, taking advantage of the network effects inherent in the internet economy. Venture capitalists were not just passive investors in these startups. They played an active role in shaping the strategic direction of these companies, often serving on their boards and providing valuable guidance and mentorship to the founding teams. Through their investments, venture capitalists also helped validate the market potential of these startups, attracting further investments and helping these companies grow.

The internet revolution was not without its challenges. The rapid influx of investments led to a speculative bubble, with stock prices of dot-com companies reaching unsustainable levels. When the bubble burst in the early 2000s, many dot-com companies went out of business, leading to significant losses for investors. Yet, despite this setback, the internet revolution fundamentally transformed the landscape of Silicon Valley and set the stage for its next phase of evolution.

Today, the internet is an integral part of our lives, influencing how we communicate, shop, work, learn, and entertain ourselves. It has disrupted traditional industries and created new ones. And much of this change can be traced back to the startups that emerged from Silicon Valley during the internet revolution. As we look to the future, it is clear that the internet, and the technologies it has spawned, will continue to shape our world in ways we can only begin to imagine.

7.3 Internet Revolution

The Internet Revolution was indeed a transformative period not just for Silicon Valley, but for the entire world. The emergence of the World Wide Web in the 1990s made the internet widely accessible to the public, sparking a flurry of activity in Silicon Valley as startups raced to take advantage of this new platform.

One of the key drivers behind the internet revolution was the development of new technologies and protocols that allowed for the sharing of information over the internet. This included Hypertext Transfer Protocol (HTTP), which is the foundation of any data exchange on the web, and HTML (HyperText Markup Language), which allowed people to create and design their own websites. Together, these technologies transformed the internet from a niche tool used primarily by academics and scientists into a global platform for communication, information sharing, and commerce. As these new technologies emerged, a generation of entrepreneurs saw the potential to create value. Yahoo!, founded in 1994 by Jerry Yang and David Filo, became one of the first popular web portals, offering a directory of other websites. In 1995, eBay, founded by Pierre Omidyar, began as an online marketplace for the sale of goods and services for individuals. Amazon, founded by Jeff Bezos the same year, started as an online bookstore before evolving into a platform selling virtually everything.

This era also saw the birth of Google. Founded by Larry Page and Sergey Brin in 1998, Google's mission was to "organize the world's information and make it universally accessible and useful." Its PageRank algorithm revolutionized internet search by ranking webpages based on their relevance and importance, thereby delivering more accurate search results.

These companies, and many others, pioneered new ways of doing business online, creating innovative business models that leveraged the connectivity and scale of the internet. They built platforms that could reach millions of people around the world, offering services that were not constrained by physical boundaries. This led to unprecedented growth rates, with these companies quickly becoming major players in the global economy. The dawn of the Internet Revolution was not merely an ascendance of technology; it was a cultural shift. As more and more people got connected to the internet, it began to change how we live, work, and communicate. The office started to extend into the home, friendships could be maintained over long distances, and global communities formed around shared interests.

Simultaneously, the rise of social media redefined our notion of connectivity and digital identity. Sites like MySpace and Facebook in the early 2000s offered people a new way to connect with friends, share experiences, and present themselves online. These platforms provided a sense of community and belonging that was independent of physical location, contributing to the global cultural shift towards a more digital society.

In the realm of commerce, the internet provided a platform for new and disruptive business models. Traditional industries, like travel and retail, were transformed by online businesses like Expedia and Amazon. These companies leveraged the global reach and 24/7 availability of the internet to offer more choice, better prices, and greater convenience than traditional brick-and-mortar businesses. Furthermore, the ability to collect and analyze data on consumer behavior allowed these companies to personalize their offerings, improving customer satisfaction and loyalty. The widespread availability of information on the internet also democratized knowledge, changing the dynamics of industries like news and education. The proliferation of blogs, forums, and open-source software made information and tools readily available, allowing anyone with an internet connection to learn and create.

In Silicon Valley, this was a period of extreme optimism and exuberance. Entrepreneurs, armed with new technologies and a vision of a digital future, flocked to the area to start their own internet companies. The atmosphere was characterized by a strong belief in the transformative power of technology, and the idea that with enough ingenuity and ambition, anyone could create the next big thing.. By the late 1990s and early 2000s, the Internet Revolution was in full swing. It became clear that the widespread adoption of internet technology had far-reaching implications not just for the tech industry, but for the entire economy.

The internet enabled businesses to operate at an unprecedented scale. Companies like Amazon and eBay, which started as small operations, were able to reach a global audience and rapidly expand their customer base. This dramatic increase in reach, coupled with the ability to automate many aspects of the business, resulted in tremendous growth and profitability for these pioneering internet companies. But the economic impact of the Internet Revolution was not confined to the tech industry. Traditional businesses also benefited from the advent of the internet, which provided them with new ways to reach customers, streamline operations, and reduce costs. Businesses across sectors began to establish an online presence, setting up websites and later social media accounts to engage with customers and market their products.

At the same time, the internet also created new challenges for businesses and the economy as a whole. The democratization of information and the ease of online transactions led to increased competition in many industries.

The shift towards digital business models necessitated a rethinking of regulatory and legal frameworks to address issues such as online privacy, intellectual property rights, and e-commerce taxation. The job market also underwent significant changes. The demand for tech-savvy professionals skyrocketed, leading to a shortage of skilled workers in fields such as software development, data analysis, and digital marketing. On the flip side, certain jobs became obsolete with the automation of many routine tasks.

As we tread into the realm of the impact of Silicon Valley's rise on the broader economy, we find that the tale is one of both opportunity and disruption. A tale that sees traditional industries transformed, job markets reinvented, and the birth of entirely new economic sectors. The dynamism of Silicon Valley did not just change the face of technology but also played a pivotal role in shaping the modern economy.

7.4 Impact on Economy

The influence of Silicon Valley's tech revolution on the global economy cannot be overstated. With its symbiosis of innovation, investment, and industry, the region has changed the way we live, work, and communicate, creating significant economic implications along the way.

The rise of Silicon Valley has had a powerful effect on job creation and the labor market. A wave of new occupations, stemming from the growth of tech companies and the digital transformation of traditional industries, has dramatically shifted the landscape of employment. From data analysts to software engineers, UX designers to cybersecurity specialists, these roles, primarily concentrated within the tech sector, have become critical pillars of the modern economy. A substantial component of Silicon Valley's impact lies in its ability to catalyze the creation of new industries and subsectors. This has been seen in the rise of e-commerce, social media, digital advertising, cloud computing, and more recently, sectors such as artificial intelligence, robotics, and blockchain technology. Each of these industries represents a significant portion of the modern economy and continues to grow exponentially. These new sectors generate enormous amounts of revenue. Giants like Google, Facebook, and Apple have market capitalizations that rival the GDP of many countries. The taxes they pay, although a subject of ongoing debate, contribute significantly to public finances, and the wealth they create for investors fuels economic activity in other sectors.

Silicon Valley's technological advancements have also triggered a surge in productivity across all sectors of the economy. The digitization of business processes, the automation of routine tasks, the optimization of supply chains, and the more efficient communication systems are just a few examples. This increased productivity, although occasionally disruptive, has the potential to stimulate economic growth by allowing businesses to produce more with the same resources. Reflecting on the rise of Silicon Valley, it's clear that the region's transformation into a global hub for technology and innovation has profoundly influenced the economy at multiple levels. From the initial growth of tech startups fueled by a daring spirit and disruptive ideas, to the emergence of a robust venture capital landscape willing to back high-risk, high-reward enterprises, Silicon Valley has been the engine driving major economic shifts.

The rise of the Internet, arguably the region's most significant contribution, has not only revolutionized communication and commerce but has fundamentally changed the way we live and work, creating entirely new industries and employment opportunities. The Internet's transformative power extends to the education sector, the health sector, entertainment, finance, and even government, redefining the rules of engagement and creating new spaces for economic activity. Additionally, Silicon Valley's impact on the economy has been manifested in the physical expansion of companies, the creation of new service sectors, escalating real estate prices, and significant investments in research and development. Its influence, for better or worse, has been far-reaching, disrupting traditional sectors, reshaping the investment landscape, and increasing wealth generation while also amplifying issues of affordability and inequality.

This backdrop of rapid technological development and expansion sets the stage for the next chapter of our exploration: the Dot-Com Bubble and Bust. As we move forward, it's important to remember the lessons of Silicon Valley's rise. The audacity to innovate, the ambition to scale, and the willingness to take risks led to unprecedented economic growth. Yet, these same elements, when mixed with over-exuberance and a lack of financial caution, can precipitate a precipitous fall, as seen in the Dot-Com Bubble.

Understanding the balance between these dynamics can provide critical insights into the nature of economic booms and busts in the tech sector.

8 Dot Com Bubble and Burst

The late 1990s and early 2000s marked an era of extraordinary growth and subsequent collapse in the tech sector, most notably characterized by the Dot-Com Bubble and subsequent bust. This period, while filled with excitement and optimism about the potential of the internet and new technologies, also laid bare the stark realities of how speculative frenzy can lead to unsustainable economic conditions. As we entered the era of the Dot-Com, the promise of the internet appeared limitless. The rapid success of early internet businesses sparked a speculative mania, leading investors and venture capitalists to pour money into any company with a ".com" in its name. The stock market soared to new heights as the notion of traditional business metrics was cast aside in the quest for market share and the prospect of future profits. This period of "irrational exuberance," as it was later famously coined, saw valuations detached from underlying business fundamentals.

The lofty expectations soon collided with reality. Many internet startups, despite their high-flying stock prices, were not generating profits. The investor sentiment quickly shifted, leading to a catastrophic crash in the market known as the Dot-Com Bust. The collapse was swift and severe, wiping out fortunes and leading to a significant contraction in the tech industry. In the aftermath of the bust, tech companies were forced to reckon with the new economic environment. For some, this meant restructuring their business models or tightening their belts. For others, it led to bankruptcy and dissolution. The impact of the Dot-Com Bust on tech companies was substantial and long-lasting.

The Dot-Com Bubble and Bust provides us with important lessons about the delicate interplay between innovation, speculation, and financial prudence. The lessons learned during this period still resonate today, particularly as we discover new technological revolutions. The balance between the optimism of technological advancement and the realism of financial sustainability is a theme that will continue to permeate through our examination of economic history.

8.1 Irrational Exuberance

In the late 1990s, the rapid growth and potential of the Internet sparked an investment frenzy, leading to a phenomenon famously referred to as "Irrational Exuberance." This term, coined by the then-Federal Reserve chairman Alan Greenspan during a speech in 1996, perfectly encapsulates the atmosphere of the Dot-Com era. The euphoria led many investors to overlook traditional business fundamentals in favor of the promise of future profits from revolutionary technological advancements.

Irrational exuberance manifested itself in numerous ways. First and foremost, it was evident in the skyrocketing prices of tech stocks, particularly those of internet-related companies. The NASDAQ Composite, a stock index heavily laden with tech stocks, rose from just under 1,000 points in 1995 to over 5,000 points by March 2000. It wasn't just established tech companies driving this surge; new startups with little more than a business plan and a .com in their name saw their share prices rocket on the day of their initial public offering (IPO). Valuations of these companies were driven not by traditional measures like earnings or assets, but rather by metrics such as click-through rates or the number of website visitors.

Furthermore, venture capital played a significant role in fueling the irrational exuberance of this period. The promise of lucrative returns led venture capitalists to pour billions of dollars into internet startups. These investments allowed the startups to focus on growing their user base and market share, often at the expense of short-term profitability. The prevailing wisdom was that once a company established itself as a dominant player in the internet space, profits would inevitably follow.

The market's obsession with growth over profitability led to some questionable business practices. Many internet companies engaged in aggressive marketing campaigns and extravagant spending to promote their brand and attract users, with little regard for the bottom line. The prevailing attitude seemed to be that traditional business models and metrics didn't apply to internet companies. This disregard for fundamentals created an economic environment rife with speculation and unsustainable business practices. Ultimately, the bubble created by this irrational exuberance would burst, leading to one of the most significant market corrections in history. The scope of the irrational exuberance during the Dot-Com era was not limited to just investors and venture capitalists. It was a societal phenomenon that impacted a wide range of stakeholders, including the media, business schools, and even everyday consumers. The media played a significant role in stoking the fire of the tech boom. Stories of overnight millionaires and the limitless potential of the Internet dominated news coverage, creating a pervasive sense of optimism and reinforcing the perception that the rules of the economy had fundamentally changed.

A change in mindset was also visible within academia. Business schools started tailoring their curriculums to cater to the booming technology sector, emphasizing entrepreneurship and e-business strategies. There was a proliferation of courses on subjects like venture capital and digital marketing, reflecting the market's fascination with internet startups. Some students even dropped out to start their own online ventures, lured by the promise of immense wealth and the allure of being part of the digital revolution.

Everyday consumers, seduced by the allure of the digital age and the promise of easy wealth, also jumped on the bandwagon. People who had never invested in stocks before started buying tech shares, often without understanding the companies' business models or the risks involved. In some instances, people even quit their jobs to become full-time day traders, further adding to the speculative environment.

As we would soon discover, this era of irrational exuberance was not sustainable. The financial markets were operating on hype and speculation rather than grounded economic principles. Although the Internet did indeed represent a paradigm shift in the way business was conducted, the market's expectations far exceeded the reality of what these new tech companies could deliver. The gap between perception and reality would eventually lead to the devastating Dot-Com Bust, as we will discuss in the next section.

8.2 Dot Com Bust

The Dot-Com Bust, a dramatic and sudden collapse of the stock market centered around internet-based companies, began in early 2000 and marked the end of a speculative bubble that had been building since the mid-1990s. The term 'Dot-Com' referred to the domain name dot-com (.com) used by most businesses operating on the internet. The unprecedented growth of these companies, propelled by a widespread belief that the internet would revolutionize businesses and consumer habits, fueled the bull market of the late 1990s.

The Dot-Com Bust was essentially the bursting of this bubble, driven by the same factors that had caused its inflation: speculation, overvaluation, and the novelty of internet businesses. As 1999 rolled into 2000, investors, blinded by the dazzling growth figures of internet startups, poured money into these companies with little regard for traditional business metrics like profitability or revenue. The flood of capital led to skyrocketing valuations, with the NASDAQ Composite Index, which includes many technology companies, peaking at over 5,000 points in March 2000.

This period of rapid growth was short-lived. Just as swiftly as it had inflated, the bubble began to burst. The catalyst was a shift in investor sentiment, triggered by several high-profile Dot-Coms reporting disappointing earnings. These revelations started to raise doubts about the inflated valuations of internet companies. Investors began to question the sustainability of businesses that, despite their impressive user base and market reach, were not generating profits.

As skepticism mounted, the stock market took a nosedive. Many companies that had seen their stock prices skyrocket during the boom experienced a brutal correction. Internet companies' stocks began to fall, leading to a massive sell-off in the market. The NASDAQ Composite, which had been the epicenter of the

Dot-Com Boom, saw its value halved within a year of its peak. The bust resulted in many internet startups going bankrupt, leading to significant financial losses for investors. The speed and magnitude of the Dot-Com Bust were as remarkable as the frenzy that preceded it.

It is essential to understand the factors that fueled the Dot-Com Bust, the impact it had on the tech companies, and the lessons that were learned from it. In the aftermath of the Dot-Com Bust, a lot of the focus was centered around the phenomenon of 'burn rate.' This was a measure of how quickly these internet companies were spending their venture capital funds, with little to no return on investment. Many of these dot-coms were losing money on every transaction they made, but they hoped to make it up in volume. This was the infamous "get big fast" strategy, which encouraged companies to grow their customer base as quickly as possible, even if it meant massive losses in the short term.

When the investors' sentiment changed and they began to value profitability over growth, many dot-coms were left with no viable path to becoming profitable.

One infamous example of this was the online grocer Webvan. Founded in the late '90s, Webvan raised over $800 million in venture capital and had an impressive IPO. The company aimed to revolutionize the grocery industry by delivering products directly to customers' homes.

The business model proved to be deeply flawed. The logistics of delivering groceries, especially perishable items, were complicated and expensive. Coupled with a customer base that wasn't ready to fully transition to online grocery shopping, the company was unable to become profitable. Despite raising such a vast sum of money, Webvan filed for bankruptcy in 2001, less than two years after its IPO. Similarly, Pets.com became a symbol of the Dot-Com Bust. The company sold pet supplies to online shoppers and was best known for its sock puppet mascot, which even appeared in a Super

Bowl commercial. Pets.com had impressive growth in sales, but it also had high costs. The company spent massively on marketing and infrastructure while also selling its products at a discount. This dual pressure on its finances proved to be unsustainable. Despite a highly publicized IPO in February 2000, Pets.com folded by November of the same year, becoming one of the quickest dot-com failures.

These examples underline the fact that, during the Dot-Com Boom, basic business principles were often ignored in favor of rapid growth. The subsequent bust served as a stark reminder of the dangers of this approach.

As the dot-com bubble burst, the NASDAQ Composite lost 78% of its value as it fell from 5046.86 to 1114.11. Billions of dollars of wealth were effectively wiped out overnight, leading to a significant economic downturn. The speed and severity of the collapse took many by surprise, as investors had been riding high on the promises of the 'new economy.'

The ramifications of the dot-com bust were not confined to the technology sector or the stock market alone. As a result of the bust, there was a contraction in consumer spending and business investment. This, in turn, led to job losses and increased unemployment, particularly in the technology sector, further contributing to an economic slowdown. In addition, the bust had profound effects on the telecommunications sector. Telecom companies had invested heavily in building infrastructure such as fiber optic cables, in anticipation of high demand from internet service providers and dot-coms.

The demand did not materialize at the scale they had expected, leading to an oversupply. This was known as the 'telecoms crash,' which was a significant component of the wider dot-com bust.

Another casualty of the bust was the advertising industry. Many dot-coms had spent massively on advertising in an attempt to gain market share.

When these dot-coms went out of business, they left large unpaid bills and reduced future advertising expenditure, causing a contraction in the advertising industry.

The fallout from the bust also led to a crisis in confidence among investors. They became wary of the hype surrounding technology companies and began to look more critically at profitability and traditional business models. As we transition from discussing the Bust itself, we should now turn our focus towards the effect that this period had on the companies operating in the tech industry, as the implications for them were profound and far-reaching.

8.3 Impact on Tech Companies

The dot-com bust had a profound impact on tech companies, both those that survived the crash and those that did not. Many startups that had achieved multi-billion dollar valuations in a matter of months found themselves insolvent almost overnight. The aura of invincibility that had surrounded these companies quickly faded as reality set in. The companies that survived were those that were able to quickly adapt to changing market conditions, pivot their business models, or had sufficiently diversified income streams to weather the storm.

Among the many companies that faltered during the dot-com bust were highly publicized cases like Pets.com, Webvan, and eToys.com. Despite having high-profile marketing campaigns and impressive sales growth, they were fundamentally unprofitable businesses. When investor sentiment shifted and capital dried up, they were unable to continue their operations. Their rapid rise and fall served as a cautionary tale for future tech startups.

Not all tech companies succumbed to the dot-com bust. Some, like Amazon and eBay, managed to deal with the difficult conditions and emerged stronger on the other side. Their experiences during this period were formative and influenced their future strategies. Amazon, for instance, became more disciplined about its growth strategy, focused on long-term profitability, and diversified into areas like cloud computing with Amazon Web Services. eBay leveraged its already profitable model and expanded globally. While these companies were able to survive and ultimately thrive following the bust, they were exceptions rather than the rule. Many other tech companies either went out of business, were acquired for a fraction of their peak valuations, or limped along as shell of their former selves.

In the aftermath of the dot-com bust, the technology sector underwent a period of consolidation. Companies were forced to cut costs, streamline their operations, and refocus on their core businesses. This often involved layoffs, office closures, and the discontinuation of non-core product lines. The days of lavish employee perks, expensive marketing campaigns, and unprofitable growth strategies were largely over. A new era of fiscal discipline and shareholder accountability had begun. In the wake of the dot-com crash, a significant number of tech companies were left struggling. In many cases, those that had invested heavily in their online presences without a clear path to profitability were the hardest hit. The result was often a dramatic restructuring of their business models, if not outright failure. In many ways, the dot-com crash served as a reality check for the tech industry, forcing companies to reconsider the viability of their business strategies.

The primary focus for surviving tech companies post-bust was on building sustainable business models. Many transitioned from a "growth at all costs" mentality to a more balanced approach that considered both growth and profitability. This often involved cost-cutting measures, layoffs, and a reassessment of their product or service offerings. With the decline of advertising revenues that many internet companies relied on, a focus shifted to identifying alternative revenue streams. In the wake of the crash, many tech companies also refocused their efforts on meeting real customer needs rather than trying to create markets where none existed. This was a shift away from the mindset of the boom years, where companies often sought to "disrupt" established industries without a clear understanding of these industries or the problems they were attempting to solve. The bust brought home the importance of understanding customer needs and developing products and services that addressed them effectively.

Additionally, the crash resulted in significant layoffs across the tech sector. While this had a devastating short-term impact on those who lost their jobs, it also resulted in a dispersal of talent. Many of those who were laid off during the bust would go on to found or join new companies, taking with them the lessons they'd learned during the boom and bust. This led to a new wave of tech startups in the mid-2000s that were more prudent, focused, and resilient, contributing to the tech industry's eventual recovery.

Surviving tech companies also had to contend with a dramatic loss of public and investor trust. The bust exposed the flimsiness of many tech companies' claims about their business prospects. In response, companies began to emphasize transparency and accountability to regain that trust. This shift manifested in more rigorous financial reporting, better corporate governance, and more cautious projections of future performance.

Finally, the dot-com bust led to a reassessment of the role of venture capital in the tech industry. During the boom years, easy access to venture capital had allowed many tech companies to grow rapidly without needing to demonstrate profitability.

When the bust came, many of these companies were left vulnerable. In the aftermath, both venture capitalists and tech companies became more discerning, with a greater emphasis on due diligence and fiscal responsibility. This more cautious approach to investment and growth has remained a feature of the tech industry to this day.

8.4 Lessons Learned

The dot-com bust served as a significant turning point in the technology industry, prompting reflection and learning that would shape the sector's future. One of the critical lessons drawn was the importance of sustainable and realistic business models. The bust underscored the fact that high growth rates and potential alone aren't sufficient for long-term survival. Startups needed to demonstrate a clear path to profitability, emphasizing the development of stable revenue streams, efficient cost structures, and viable products and services that met real customer needs.

The bust highlighted the importance of fiscal discipline. During the dot-com boom, it was common for companies to spend extravagantly in the pursuit of growth, often with little consideration for profitability. But the bust showed that this type of spending was not only unsustainable but could also lead to catastrophic consequences when market conditions changed. Consequently, tech companies and investors became much more conservative in their spending and investment decisions. This emphasis on fiscal discipline has remained a defining feature of the technology industry since the bust. The dot-com bust also served as a stark reminder of the inherent riskiness of the tech sector. Many investors who had poured money into dot-com startups in the expectation of massive returns found themselves facing significant losses instead. This led to a greater appreciation of risk management in investment decisions, with investors becoming more diligent in assessing the potential downsides of their investments.

Furthermore, the bust highlighted the importance of adaptability. The rapid change in market conditions that accompanied the bust caught many tech companies off guard, leading to their downfall. Those companies that survived were typically those that were able to adapt quickly to the changing environment, whether by shifting their business models, cutting costs, or finding new revenue sources. This lesson has since been taken to heart by tech companies, which today place a high premium on adaptability and agility. The importance of regulatory oversight was another crucial lesson from the dot-com bust. The boom years had been characterized by a relatively lax regulatory environment, which allowed many of the excesses of the period to occur. The bust led to a recognition of the need for stronger regulatory oversight to prevent such excesses and to protect investors and the broader economy from the fallout of a potential bust. As a result, regulations surrounding financial reporting, corporate governance, and other aspects of corporate behavior have been strengthened. Finally, the dot-com bust taught the tech industry the value of resilience. Despite the devastation that the bust wrought, the industry was able to rebound and go on to even greater heights. This resilience was driven by a combination of factors, including the continued belief in the transformative potential of technology, the adaptability of tech companies, and the lessons learned from the bust. It served as a powerful reminder that while the tech sector is prone to cycles of boom and bust, its long-term trajectory is one of growth and advancement.

Indeed, the lessons from the dot-com bust have continued to resonate in the tech industry. They have informed the ways in which startups are built and funded, how risks are managed, and how companies respond to changing market conditions. As such, while the bust was undoubtedly a painful period for the tech industry, it was also a formative one that has significantly influenced its subsequent development. Building on the lessons learned from the dot-com bubble and bust, tech companies started paying greater attention to the durability and scalability of their business models. They were also more conscious of regulatory compliances and took proactive steps to ensure transparency and adherence to business ethics. This period marked a significant transition in the tech industry, focusing more on the long-term sustainability of businesses than rapid, often uncontrolled, expansion.

The fallout of the dot-com bubble also changed the financial market landscape. The internet, which was initially seen as a medium to disseminate information quickly, also became a medium for executing financial transactions. Investors became more comfortable making investment decisions based on information they found online, and online trading platforms became more mainstream. This transition was one of the many ways the dot-com bubble contributed to the technological transformation of the financial industry. A comprehensive review of this era would be incomplete without acknowledging the resilience of the tech industry. Despite the tumultuous period, many companies emerged stronger, innovated, and eventually became industry giants. The likes of Amazon, Google, and eBay got through the crisis, made necessary adjustments, and today, they are among the most influential players in the global tech industry. In retrospect, the dot-com bust offered valuable lessons that reshaped the tech industry's approach to innovation, investment, and business growth.

Transitioning into the new era of the 21st century, the significant shift in the financial markets brought about by technological advancement became evident.

9 Technology's Impact on Finance Electronic Trading

In the backdrop of the resilient tech industry, a quiet revolution was happening in the finance sector, laying the groundwork for the modern age of electronic trading. It's been a transformative experience, evolving from the open outcry pit trading systems of the past, with brokers screaming buy and sell orders across the trading floor, to a world where the vast majority of trading is done electronically. The transition brought significant changes to the way markets operate, offering unprecedented speed, precision, and transparency.

At the heart of this transformation was technology, leveraging computing power and internet connectivity to bring about fundamental changes in the way financial transactions were conducted. While the advent of electronic trading offered an efficient and accessible platform for trading securities, the impact of technology on the finance industry extended beyond trading floors. Mobile devices and the internet allowed consumers to interact with their banks and manage their finances without having to step into a physical bank branch. As a result, services that were once confined to bank branches or personal computers could be availed right from the palm of your hand, anywhere and at any time. This transformation wasn't just limited to traditional banking activities but extended to various other financial services.

Meanwhile, the financial markets also witnessed a paradigm shift. With high-speed computers and advanced mathematical models, trading turned from a human-driven activity into one that is largely automated. The rise of algorithmic trading has not only changed the speed and nature of trading but also redefined the skills required to be a successful trader.

The intersection of technology and finance also witnessed the emergence of financial applications that have democratized access to financial services. Today, buying shares, managing investments, tracking expenses, or even applying for a loan can all be done through a smartphone app. Looking into the future, the fusion of finance and technology holds promises and challenges that will likely continue to transform the landscape of the finance industry.

9.1 Mobile Banking

Mobile banking represents a significant leap in the way people manage their finances, ushering in an era of unprecedented convenience and access. It has turned the ubiquitous smartphone into a portable bank, allowing users to transact, invest, and manage their money anytime and anywhere. This has drastically changed the consumer-banking relationship and led to a shift in how banks operate and deliver their services. The genesis of mobile banking can be traced back to the early 2000s, with the advent of online banking. While online banking required a desktop or a laptop with internet access, mobile banking took it a step further by making banking services accessible right from the customer's pocket. SMS banking, where customers could check their balance or receive transaction alerts via text messages, was one of the first forms of mobile banking.

It was with the advent of smartphones and mobile apps that mobile banking truly came into its own.

Mobile banking apps are now capable of performing a wide array of functions. From basic tasks such as checking account balance and transaction history to making payments, transferring funds, depositing checks via mobile check deposit feature, applying for loans, investing in stocks or mutual funds - the list is nearly endless. These services have significantly reduced the need for physical bank visits, saving customers' time and adding an element of speed and convenience to banking operations. In fact, the flexibility and ease of mobile banking have made it a preferred choice for many, significantly influencing the way consumers interact with their banks. owever, the rise of mobile banking is not without its challenges. Security is paramount in the world of banking and finance, and the digital platform presents a new set of threats. Cyberattacks, phishing scams, and data breaches have become increasingly common, requiring banks and financial institutions to continually enhance their security measures. Nevertheless, the potential of mobile banking continues to grow, and it has set a new standard in financial services, establishing itself as an integral part of the modern banking landscape.

In addition to the rise of mobile banking in the traditional banking sector, the impact of technology on finance has also led to the emergence of mobile-only banks, often referred to as "neobanks." Neobanks are digital-only banks with no physical branches, offering services exclusively through a mobile app and a website. They have further pushed the boundaries of what's possible in mobile banking, offering streamlined services and innovative features that cater to the digital-native generation. The rise of mobile banking has not just transformed the customer experience but also prompted banks to rethink their business models and operational strategies. The shift to mobile has led to a reduction in the need for physical branches, prompting banks to optimize their branch networks and focus more on enhancing their digital offerings. Simultaneously, it has opened up new avenues for customer engagement and personalized services, providing banks with valuable insights into customer behavior and preferences. As a result, banks are now more customer-centric, leveraging technology to deliver personalized and efficient services that align with the digital age.

The impact of mobile banking extends beyond banks and consumers. It has socio-economic implications, contributing to financial inclusion. In many parts of the world, particularly in developing countries, access to traditional banking services is limited. Mobile banking has bridged this gap, providing an accessible and affordable platform for banking services, thus playing a crucial role in promoting financial inclusion. It has empowered individuals and businesses with financial tools and services, paving the way for economic growth and reducing income inequality. As we look ahead, the future of mobile banking seems promising. With advancements in technology, we can expect to see more innovative features and services that will make banking even more convenient and personalized. From biometric authentication and voice-enabled services to AI-powered financial advisors, the possibilities are boundless. As banks and financial institutions continue to embrace digital transformation, mobile banking is set to play a pivotal role in shaping the future of the banking industry.

The rise of mobile banking is just one aspect of how technology has revolutionized the finance sector. It's also a testament to the dynamic nature of technology and its ability to disrupt and reshape industries.

The success stories of various banks and financial institutions adopting mobile banking are testament to this transformative power. One of the best examples of the transformative power of mobile banking is M-Pesa, a mobile phone-based money transfer, financing, and microfinancing service launched in Kenya in 2007 by Vodafone and Safaricom, Kenya's largest mobile network operator. The platform initially aimed to create a simple method for repaying microloans.

It quickly expanded to offer a wide range of services, including money transfers, bill payments, and even salary disbursements. Today, M-Pesa is not only one of the most popular payment methods in Kenya but also has a significant presence in several other countries, including Tanzania, Afghanistan, South Africa, India, and parts of Eastern Europe.

M-Pesa's success story is unique because it effectively leveraged mobile technology to fill a significant gap in the market. Before M-Pesa's launch, many Kenyans didn't have access to traditional banking services due to the country's large rural population and a lack of banking infrastructure in these areas. M-Pesa provided an accessible and affordable platform for these individuals, transforming the country's financial landscape. By leveraging the ubiquity of mobile phones, M-Pesa was able to provide financial services to those who were previously unbanked or underbanked. The platform has since become a crucial tool for financial inclusion, helping to reduce poverty levels and stimulate economic growth in regions where it operates.

Another interesting example of mobile banking transformation is seen in the rise of neobanks, like Revolut and N26, that offer a purely digital banking experience. These banks provide all of their services through a mobile app, completely eliminating the need for physical branches. Users can open an account, make transfers, apply for loans, and even access investment services right from their smartphones. Revolut, for instance, has amassed millions of customers globally by offering competitive currency exchange rates, seamless international money transfers, and a range of other financial services. It uses data-driven insights to offer personalized financial advice to its users, showing how mobile banking is not just about transactional services but also about helping users manage their finances more effectively.

These examples illustrate how mobile banking has disrupted the traditional banking model and laid the groundwork for a new era in financial services. They underscore how financial institutions, both large and small, can leverage mobile technology to reach out to underserved markets, meet changing customer expectations, and compete effectively in an increasingly digital world. Mobile banking has undeniably been a significant development in the world of finance, reshaping the way people conduct financial transactions and interact with their banks. Yet, this is just the tip of the iceberg when it comes to the transformation brought about by technological advancements in the finance industry. This transformation extends far beyond the individual consumer and impacts the global financial markets at large. One example of such a paradigm shift is the rise of algorithmic trading.

As we transition from the world of mobile banking to the sphere of financial markets, we enter a realm where speed, precision, and the ability to process vast quantities of data are of paramount importance. Here, technology has ushered in a new era characterized by automation and efficiency - the era of algorithmic trading. Algorithmic trading, or algo trading, refers to the use of advanced mathematical models and formulas to make high-speed trading decisions. It involves the use of complex algorithms to analyze market data and execute trades at speeds and frequencies that are beyond human capabilities.

Algo trading has several advantages. It can process and analyze large volumes of market data in real time, enabling traders to make rapid decisions based on the latest market trends. It reduces the risk of human error in trading and enables more systematic trading. For instance, it eliminates the emotional and psychological factors that often affect human traders. It also allows for backtesting, i.e., testing trading strategies using historical data, which can help in refining them before their application in the live market.

This shift towards algorithmic trading also comes with its own set of challenges. The increased use of algorithms can lead to increased market volatility, as seen in instances of 'flash crashes' where markets plunge rapidly due to aggressive algorithmic trading. While algo trading reduces human error in decision-making, it introduces the risk of technological failures or glitches, which can also lead to significant market disruptions.

9.2 Algorithmic Trading

The advent of algorithmic trading has completely revolutionized the operations of global financial markets, transforming the ways trades are executed, and the strategies that traders employ. Algorithms in trading are used to automate complex and quantitative trading strategies that involve buying and selling financial instruments in various markets. At the most basic level, an algorithm might be programmed to place a buy order for a particular stock when its price falls below a certain threshold, or to sell when the price reaches a specified level.

In practice, trading algorithms can be far more complex, taking into account multiple factors such as volume, timing, price levels, and a multitude of other market parameters.

Algorithmic trading holds several advantages over traditional trading. One of the key benefits is speed. Algorithms can scan dozens of public and private markets simultaneously, analyze large amounts of data, and execute trades based on the analyzed data all within fractions of a second. Such speed provides a significant edge in a world where market conditions can change in the blink of an eye.

Algorithmic trading can be more cost-efficient. By rapidly executing trades, it ensures that traders get the best possible price at any given time. This efficiency, in turn, reduces the costs associated with trading, such as the bid-ask spread. Additionally, by automating the trading process, algorithmic trading reduces the need for traders to constantly monitor the markets and manually place trades, thus freeing up valuable time and resources. The accuracy and precision offered by algorithmic trading are another advantage. It eliminates the risk of human errors in placing trades. Furthermore, by using algorithms, traders can execute complex strategies that would be virtually impossible for humans to manage manually, allowing for more sophisticated and potentially profitable trading strategies.

9.3 Financial Apps

With the rise of algorithmic trading and technology's pervasive integration into the world of finance, we find a new landscape emerging that provides a democratization of access to financial tools and resources. This landscape is replete with a plethora of financial applications that put the power of financial management and investment in the palm of your hand.

The development of financial applications has gone hand in hand with the broader digital transformation of finance. Today, numerous apps are available that cater to a wide variety of financial needs, from personal finance management to investing in stocks and other securities. Take the realm of personal finance management, for example. Applications like Mint and YNAB (You Need A Budget) have transformed the way individuals manage their personal finances. These apps allow users to track their income, expenses, and savings, all in real time and from their smartphones. Such capabilities were previously unheard of for the everyday individual without extensive financial knowledge or access to expensive financial management tools.

In the investing space, applications such as Robinhood and Etoro have not only simplified the process of investing in stocks and other securities, but they have also significantly reduced the cost of entry. These platforms have done away with traditional trading fees, making it possible for anyone with a smartphone and a few spare dollars to become an investor. What's more, many of these applications are leveraging the power of AI and machine learning to provide personalized advice and insights to their users. For example, apps like Acorns and Stash don't just facilitate investing; they also provide investment recommendations based on the user's financial goals and risk tolerance. This kind of tailored advice was once the preserve of wealthy individuals who could afford a personal financial advisor. Today, thanks to these financial apps, such advice is available to the masses.

In short, financial apps are transforming the landscape of personal finance and investment. They're putting power back in the hands of individuals, making financial management and investing more accessible than ever before. It's an exciting time in the world of finance, with technology continually reshaping what's possible. As we move forward, we stand at the precipice of the next chapter in this transformation: the future of finance, and the role that technology will play in shaping that future. Financial apps aren't limited to budgeting and investing, either. There's also a wide array of applications aimed at addressing more specific financial needs. For instance, several apps help users manage their student loans or automate savings for specific goals. Others provide platforms for peer-to-peer payments, eliminating the need for cash or checks when splitting a dinner bill or paying a friend back.

One of the significant benefits that these apps have brought to the table is financial literacy. Many of these applications come with educational resources that help users understand complex financial concepts. As such, they've become instrumental in increasing financial awareness and knowledge, especially among younger generations. In this way, financial apps are playing a crucial role in closing the financial literacy gap. Apps like Credit Karma and NerdWallet, for example, provide insights into credit scores and help users understand the factors that influence their creditworthiness. These tools make what was once a mysterious and often confusing topic much more accessible and understandable. The democratization of this knowledge can have a significant impact on individuals' financial health, helping them make informed decisions about borrowing and debt management.

The convenience and user-friendliness of these apps cannot be overstated. With sleek interfaces, intuitive controls, and user-centered design, these apps make financial management less of a chore and more of a seamless part of daily life. They're designed to integrate smoothly into users' daily routines, facilitating financial management without the need for extensive time or effort. In conclusion, financial apps represent a significant stride in the digitization of finance. They're providing users with unprecedented access to financial tools, fostering financial literacy, and making financial management more seamless and accessible than ever before. As they continue to evolve and innovate, one can only imagine the possibilities for the future of finance.

9.4 Future of Finance

As we gaze into the crystal ball of the future of finance, a few key trends and potential developments stand out. Firstly, it's undeniable that artificial intelligence (AI) and machine learning will continue to have a profound impact on financial services. With the ability to analyze vast amounts of data at lightning speed, these technologies are expected to revolutionize everything from risk assessment to personalized financial advice.

Today, AI is already being used to improve fraud detection and enhance customer service through chatbots and virtual assistants. But in the future, its role could become even more central. Imagine personalized AI financial advisors that can monitor all aspects of a user's financial life, offer timely advice, and even make transactions on their behalf. Given the pace of AI development, such a scenario is not far-fetched. Secondly, we should expect further growth and diversification in the field of financial applications. As we've seen, mobile banking and financial apps have already changed the way we interact with our money.

This could be just the tip of the iceberg. Future financial apps could provide even more services, from comprehensive financial planning and management to highly specialized offerings tailored to individual user's needs.

Blockchain technology, the underlying tech behind cryptocurrencies like Bitcoin, could also become a more significant player. Its potential extends beyond just digital currencies. Blockchain's ability to provide secure, decentralized records could transform various financial processes. For example, it could be used to create more efficient and transparent systems for settling transactions or verifying identities. While blockchain technology is still in its relative infancy, its potential impact on the financial sector is enormous.

Finally, another key trend is the continuing shift towards a more customer-centric approach. As competition in the financial sector heats up, service providers are increasingly focusing on improving the user experience. This means making services more convenient, intuitive, and tailored to individual needs. We've already seen this with the rise of mobile banking and financial apps, and it's likely that this trend will only intensify in the future. All these developments point towards a future of finance that's increasingly digital, personalized, and user-focused. But underlying many of these trends is a broader shift that's changing the face of the financial sector. This is the rise of FinTech, a term that encompasses a range of technologies and innovations aimed at transforming financial services. As we move forward, the influence of FinTech will become more and more apparent, redefining what's possible in the realm of finance.

The exploration of the future of finance would not be complete without discussing the implications of big data. Big data refers to the vast quantities of information generated by our digital activities, and its role in finance is becoming increasingly significant. Financial institutions have begun harnessing big data for various purposes, from predictive analytics to customer segmentation and targeted marketing. In the realm of investment, for instance, big data allows for more informed decisions. Quantitative analysts, or "quants," are increasingly relying on big data to create complex financial models and analyze market trends. With the ability to process and interpret vast amounts of data in real-time, financial institutions can identify profitable opportunities more quickly, manage risks more effectively, and respond more agilely to market changes.

Furthermore, there's a growing interest in the field of "social trading." This involves leveraging social media data to gain insights into market trends and investor behavior. Social trading platforms are already allowing individual traders to share their strategies and performance data with others, creating a more collaborative and transparent investment environment.

Yet, big data also brings challenges, especially regarding data privacy and security. As financial institutions collect and store more personal information, they become attractive targets for cybercriminals. Thus, a significant part of the future of finance will involve developing more advanced security measures to protect sensitive data and maintain customer trust. Another potential game-changer for the future of finance is the concept of "open banking." Open banking is a system where banks open up their APIs (Application Programming Interfaces) to third-party developers. This allows these third parties to build new financial products and services, from payment apps to budgeting tools. Open banking has the potential to foster greater competition and innovation in the financial sector, leading to more choices and better services for consumers.

While it's impossible to predict the future with absolute certainty, one thing is clear: technology will continue to drive transformation in the financial sector. As we have seen, this transformation is multi-faceted, affecting all areas of finance from mobile banking to investment and beyond. Yet, all these trends have one thing in common: they are all underpinned by the rise of FinTech – the convergence of finance and technology. This key shift is setting the stage for a future of finance that is more connected, more efficient, and more customer-centric than ever before.

10 The Birth of Fintech

The whirlwind of innovation that has characterized the technology sector in recent decades has not left the financial industry untouched. This evolution, characterized by the seamless merger of financial services with technology, has given birth to a dynamic and rapidly evolving sector: FinTech. The amalgamation of these two industries heralds a revolution that's shaking the traditional financial institutions to their core and changing the way we interact with money. In a broad sense, FinTech represents a new wave of companies that leverage advanced technologies to provide financial services in innovative ways. They are driven by a desire to disrupt the conventional norms, offering services that are typically more efficient, convenient, and cost-effective than those offered by traditional financial institutions. They embody the philosophy that financial services, like any other consumer service, should evolve with the needs and demands of its users, adapting to the digital landscape we live in today.

Banks, once viewed as towering monoliths, have often been slow to adapt to the digital revolution. This has created a vacuum, one that has been rapidly filled by innovative FinTech companies. These firms have identified and exploited gaps in the banking sector, providing services that traditional financial institutions often overlook or ignore. Whether it's peer-to-peer lending, mobile payments, robo-advising, or cryptocurrency trading, the scope of their operations is vast and ever-expanding. While the rise of FinTech companies promises a more inclusive and democratized financial ecosystem, it is not without its challenges. One of the most significant issues lies in the realm of regulation. The financial sector is among the most heavily regulated in the world, given the potential for fraud, economic instability, and the need to protect consumers. FinTech companies operate in a unique space, often treading the thin line between being a financial service provider and a technology firm. This ambiguity presents regulatory hurdles that these firms must consider as they grow and evolve.

Looking forward, the question isn't whether FinTech will continue to shape the landscape of the financial industry – that seems to be a foregone conclusion. Instead, the question revolves around how these changes will play out and what the future holds for both the disruptive newcomers and the traditional financial institutions they're challenging. From artificial intelligence and machine learning to blockchain and cryptocurrency, the tools driving this transformation promise a future of exciting possibilities and profound changes in the financial industry. In summary, FinTech is redefining the contours of the financial industry, promising a future that is more inclusive, efficient, and responsive to customer needs.

10.1 Fintech Companies

FinTech companies, the nucleus of this digital revolution in the financial world, are worth discussing in more detail to comprehend their role, their impact, and the unique offerings they bring to the market. Coming in all shapes and sizes, from startups to established corporations, these firms are radically redefining financial services and posing considerable challenges to traditional financial institutions.

The emergence of FinTech companies represents a shift in the paradigm of financial services delivery. Traditionally, the domain of financial services was reserved for large banks and financial institutions, with a high entry barrier.

The advent of digital technologies and the internet has significantly lowered these barriers, enabling new players to venture into this space. These newcomers, referred to as FinTech companies, are essentially technology-driven firms that focus on providing innovative financial services. They leverage technology to design and deliver financial services that are typically more convenient, efficient, and user-friendly than traditional financial offerings. They operate in a wide array of financial sectors, including payments, lending, insurance, wealth management, and more. For example, firms such as PayPal and Stripe have revolutionized the payments sector by facilitating easy and quick online transactions. On the other hand, companies like LendingClub and Prosper have created peer-to-peer lending platforms, bypassing traditional banks and providing alternative financing solutions for consumers. These companies do not follow the traditional business model of banks and financial institutions. Instead, they leverage digital technologies to create novel business models that are typically lean, agile, and customer-centric. This approach enables them to deliver services more efficiently and at a lower cost than traditional financial institutions, providing considerable value to their customers. In the backdrop of all these remarkable developments, it becomes evident that the rise of FinTech companies has initiated a major shift in the banking sector. Banks have traditionally been the gatekeepers of financial services, with a long-established infrastructure and way of conducting business.

the emergence of FinTech companies has sparked an incredible transformation in this area, prompting a comprehensive reassessment of how banking services can be provided and accessed.

One of the most significant changes brought about by FinTech companies is a drastic shift in customer expectations. Customers now expect financial services to be as easy, intuitive, and accessible as the other digital services they use every day, such as online shopping or social media. They demand 24/7 accessibility, rapid response, personalization, and seamless multi-channel experiences. Companies like Monzo and Revolut in the UK, or Chime and Varo Money in the US, have responded to these needs by offering fully digital banking services, featuring real-time notifications on spending, automated savings tools, and personalized insights into financial habits.

Furthermore, FinTech companies have also managed to serve market segments that have been traditionally underserved by banks. Whether it's providing microloans for small businesses, offering financial services to the unbanked and underbanked populations, or enabling cross-border payments for migrants, FinTech companies are filling gaps that were previously untapped by traditional financial institutions. Notable examples include Kiva, a platform that facilitates crowdfunding of microloans for entrepreneurs in developing countries, and TransferWise (now Wise), which offers transparent and low-cost international money transfers. Importantly, the competition posed by FinTech companies has spurred innovation within the traditional banking sector. It's prompted many banks to invest heavily in digital transformation, to partner with FinTech startups, or even to create their own FinTech solutions. A prime example is Goldman Sachs' digital banking offshoot, Marcus, which offers online savings accounts and personal loans, while JP Morgan has launched its own digital-only bank, Chase, to compete in the UK banking market.

This new dynamic has fostered a more vibrant and competitive financial ecosystem, one that is more responsive to the evolving needs of consumers and businesses alike. It's a world where finance and technology are deeply intertwined, creating unprecedented opportunities and challenges. It's also the world where the traditional boundaries of banking are being stretched, prompting us to reimagine what the future of banking might look like. As we move into this future, the impact of FinTech companies on banking continues to grow, reshaping not just how we bank, but our relationship with money itself.

10.2 Impact on Banking

In assessing the impact of FinTech on the traditional banking sector, it's crucial to grasp the ways in which it has been a disruptive force. From reshaping business models to altering customer expectations, the rise of FinTech has indeed led to substantial changes in how banking services are delivered. Initially, banks and other traditional financial institutions seemed to consider FinTech companies as their adversaries. These nimble startups, with their customer-centric, digitally-driven approaches, appeared to pose a direct threat to the banks' long-standing business models. FinTech companies leveraged technology to provide faster, more efficient, and often cheaper services, outperforming banks in various aspects. For example, FinTech firms made it possible for individuals and businesses to make payments, borrow money, and invest, all without stepping into a physical bank or going through time-consuming procedures.

An area in which FinTech companies have particularly excelled is the user experience. Banks, with their cumbersome legacy systems, have often struggled to provide a smooth, modern digital experience. On the other hand, FinTech companies, unencumbered by outdated technology and procedures, have been able to prioritize customer experience from the start. They've capitalized on mobile technology to offer intuitive, easy-to-use apps, featuring seamless sign-up processes, instant updates, and personal finance management tools. This focus on customer experience has led to a shift in consumer expectations, as people increasingly demand the same level of convenience and functionality from their banks as they get from their FinTech services.

The relationship between banks and FinTech companies has been far from purely adversarial. On one hand, FinTech companies have indeed presented a competitive threat, but on the other hand, they have also provided traditional banks with opportunities for transformation and innovation. The pressure exerted by FinTech companies has acted as a catalyst, pushing banks to digitize and modernize their services.

Beyond customer service, FinTech companies have also helped banks to streamline their internal processes and make them more cost-effective. For instance, FinTech solutions like Robotic Process Automation (RPA) and Artificial Intelligence (AI) have been utilized to automate routine tasks such as data entry, account reconciliation, and loan origination, thereby reducing operational costs and error rates. AI and Machine Learning algorithms have been used to enhance risk assessment and fraud detection capabilities, adding another layer of security to banking operations.

A classic example of how FinTech has transformed traditional banking is the adoption of mobile and online banking. A few decades ago, customers had to physically visit the bank for nearly every transaction or service they needed. Today, due to technological advancements spearheaded by FinTech companies, customers can perform a vast majority of banking tasks from their mobile phones or computers. They can check their account balances, transfer money, pay bills, apply for loans, and even deposit checks digitally without having to visit a physical bank branch. This change has not only increased convenience for customers but also reduced operational costs for banks. In addition, FinTech has also revolutionized the lending sector, traditionally dominated by banks. The rise of peer-to-peer (P2P) lending platforms has opened up a new avenue for individuals and small businesses to access capital. These platforms connect borrowers directly with investors, cutting out the middleman, i.e., the banks, and often providing faster, cheaper, and more flexible loan options. For instance, LendingClub, a prominent P2P lending platform, has issued billions of dollars in loans, helping individuals consolidate debt, finance home improvements, and more. This kind of innovation has posed a considerable challenge to traditional banks, compelling them to rethink their loan offerings and pricing structures to stay competitive.

FinTech companies have also introduced innovative products and services that were unheard of in the traditional banking sphere. Cryptocurrencies, for example, have emerged as a new asset class thanks to the rise of FinTech. Companies like Coinbase have made it easy for people to buy, sell, and store cryptocurrencies, contributing to their popularity. Such developments have led banks to explore new possibilities, with some even contemplating launching their digital currencies. Indeed, the impact of FinTech on banking has been profound. FinTech has pushed the boundaries of what is possible in the financial world, creating a myriad of opportunities and challenges for traditional banks. As technology continues to evolve, the symbiotic relationship between FinTech and banking will continue to shape the future of finance. The next era of financial services may well see even more profound changes, as banks and FinTech companies continue to learn from, compete with, and complement each other.

Apart from the positive impacts, FinTech has also triggered some serious concerns within traditional banking. For instance, the fast-paced, innovation-driven nature of FinTech often leaves banks struggling to keep up. As customers become more tech-savvy and demand more digital services, banks are under immense pressure to enhance their digital capabilities, an endeavor that often requires substantial time and investment. The fact that FinTech companies are usually much smaller and more agile than large banking institutions makes the competition even tougher for banks.

FinTech has also brought about a heightened level of competition in the financial sector, putting a squeeze on the profit margins of traditional banks. While competition is generally good for consumers, as it drives innovation and better service, it also means that banks are now forced to reinvent themselves to stay relevant. They need to find ways to differentiate their services, whether through superior customer service, better product offerings, or unique selling points that can't easily be replicated by FinTech firms.

Then there is the risk of disintermediation. With FinTech firms providing a range of financial services, customers are finding less need to rely on banks as their sole financial providers. This shift in consumer behavior has led to a decrease in customer loyalty and an increase in customer churn, which could potentially lead to a decline in banks' market share over time.

Finally, FinTech has also exposed banks to new forms of risks. Cybersecurity, for instance, is a critical concern for both banks and their customers. As financial transactions become increasingly digital, the risk of cyber attacks, data breaches, and online fraud also increases. Banks must therefore invest heavily in securing their systems and protecting customer data, adding another layer of complexity to their operations. Despite these challenges, it's important to note that many banks are embracing the changes brought about by FinTech and leveraging them to their advantage. Rather than viewing FinTech firms solely as competitors, some banks are collaborating with them to improve their offerings and better serve their customers.

While FinTech's impact on banking has been profound and multi-faceted, another significant aspect that deserves our attention is the regulatory challenges it presents. Given the disruptive nature of FinTech, it poses unique regulatory and legal challenges that need to be addressed to ensure a level playing field and protect the interests of all stakeholders involved.

10.3 Regulatory Challenges

FinTech has created numerous regulatory challenges as it changes the landscape of financial services. One of the most prominent challenges is how to regulate an industry that is constantly evolving and creating new products and services. Traditional regulatory frameworks are often ill-suited to handle the innovation and speed of FinTech. Existing laws and regulations were primarily designed for traditional financial institutions and may not adequately address the risks posed by FinTech companies.

One primary area of concern revolves around consumer protection. As FinTech firms increasingly provide services that were traditionally handled by banks and other financial institutions, ensuring that consumers are protected becomes more complicated. For instance, peer-to-peer lending platforms need to ensure that their users understand the risks associated with lending and borrowing on their platforms. Digital payment systems need to provide adequate protection against fraud and unauthorized transactions.

Another challenge is data privacy and security. FinTech firms handle a large amount of sensitive customer data, and breaches can have severe consequences. Ensuring that these companies follow best practices in data security is crucial. But the task is not straightforward, given that data privacy laws vary significantly across different jurisdictions, making compliance a complex task for FinTech companies operating globally. Additionally, the regulatory environment for FinTech is often fragmented, which can create uncertainty for these companies. Different regulators may have jurisdiction over different aspects of a FinTech company's operations, leading to potential overlaps or gaps in oversight. This lack of clarity can impede innovation and deter investment in the sector. Furthermore, the fragmented regulatory landscape can create challenges in ensuring consistent consumer protection across different FinTech services.

The above challenges underscore the need for a regulatory framework that is flexible enough to accommodate innovation, yet robust enough to protect consumers and maintain the integrity of the financial system. The regulatory approach should strive to balance the promotion of innovation with the need to manage risk and ensure financial stability. Regulatory sandboxes, for instance, are one way that regulators can facilitate the development of FinTech while maintaining oversight. These are controlled environments where FinTech firms can test their innovations under the supervision of regulators. This approach enables regulators to better understand emerging technologies and to develop appropriate regulatory responses. Lastly, the global nature of FinTech also raises important issues around international cooperation among regulators. Given that many FinTech firms operate across borders, there's a need for greater coordination among different jurisdictions to ensure consistent regulation. For example, a FinTech firm licensed in one country might provide services to customers in another country via the internet. This could potentially create regulatory arbitrage opportunities and expose consumers to risks if the regulatory standards in the home country are lower than those in the customer's country.

The challenges faced in regulating FinTech are significant, yet they also present opportunities for regulatory innovation and for better alignment of regulation with the realities of the digital age. As the FinTech industry continues to evolve, it will be important for regulators to keep pace and ensure that their approach to regulation supports both innovation and the protection of consumers and the integrity of the financial system. As FinTech companies increasingly make use of cutting-edge technologies such as artificial intelligence, machine learning, and blockchain, this creates new regulatory challenges. One of these is ensuring algorithmic accountability. AI and machine learning are increasingly used in FinTech applications such as credit scoring, fraud detection, and investment advisory services. While these technologies can greatly enhance the efficiency and effectiveness of financial services, they can also create risks. For instance, the algorithms might inadvertently discriminate against certain groups of consumers or make decisions that are difficult to explain and scrutinize. Therefore, regulators are faced with the challenge of ensuring that these technologies are used in a way that is fair, transparent, and accountable.

The use of blockchain technology and cryptocurrencies in FinTech is another area that poses significant regulatory challenges. On the one hand, these technologies have the potential to revolutionize areas such as cross-border payments and smart contracts. On the other hand, they also raise issues around consumer protection, money laundering, and financial stability. Regulating these technologies is a complex task that requires a deep understanding of their workings and potential impacts. Regulators need to strike a balance between enabling innovation and managing the associated risks. A further regulatory challenge arises from the platform nature of many FinTech businesses. Many FinTech companies operate platforms that bring together different types of users, such as lenders and borrowers, buyers and sellers, or senders and receivers of payments. These platforms can create network effects that lead to the concentration of market power in a few large platforms. This concentration of power can raise competition issues and potentially result in unfair practices. Regulators need to monitor these developments and ensure that competition is preserved in the FinTech sector.

Regulation technology, or RegTech, is an area that could potentially help address some of the regulatory challenges posed by FinTech. RegTech refers to the use of technology to enhance regulatory processes. This includes technologies for monitoring compliance, reporting regulatory data, and identifying regulatory breaches. By making regulatory processes more efficient and effective, RegTech can help regulators keep pace with the rapid evolution of the FinTech industry.

The adoption of RegTech also poses its own challenges, such as ensuring the security and privacy of regulatory data. The dynamic nature of the FinTech industry implies that regulatory challenges will continue to emerge as new technologies and business models are developed. Addressing these challenges will require regulators to be proactive and forward-looking. They will need to engage with industry stakeholders, understand emerging technologies, and be willing to adapt their regulatory approaches as needed. This will help ensure that regulation supports the healthy development of the FinTech industry while adequately protecting consumers and the financial system.

One cannot overlook the challenges presented by cybersecurity when discussing regulatory issues in the FinTech industry. Cyber threats are an ever-present concern in a world increasingly dominated by digital transactions and services. FinTech firms, with their innovative applications and platforms, can be attractive targets for cybercriminals. Protecting consumer data and maintaining the integrity of financial transactions is paramount, but achieving this requires sophisticated, constantly evolving defenses. Therefore, cybersecurity regulation is a significant challenge, as it requires a deep understanding of complex, technical matters and must be agile enough to adapt to the ever-evolving landscape of threats. Notably, despite the challenges faced by regulators, the value and transformative potential of FinTech cannot be overstated. It's reshaping the way consumers interact with their finances, making financial services more accessible, convenient, and efficient.

Nevertheless, ensuring that these services are secure, fair, and transparent remains an ongoing task for regulators worldwide.

The future of FinTech is a particularly exciting subject as it opens up endless possibilities. How regulators respond to these developments will play a significant role in shaping this future. As we move towards that, it becomes clear that the FinTech revolution is only just beginning. Innovation will continue at a rapid pace, with emerging technologies such as artificial intelligence, machine learning, and blockchain driving new developments.

Already, we can foresee several significant trends that will shape the future of FinTech. One such trend is the increasing integration of financial services into everyday life. This phenomenon, often referred to as "embedded finance," involves the incorporation of financial services into non-financial platforms. For example, social media platforms might offer payment or lending services, or online retailers might provide insurance products. This trend is likely to continue, with financial services becoming increasingly intertwined with other areas of our lives. The continued development of new technologies will also shape the future of FinTech. Advances in artificial intelligence and machine learning will drive the development of more sophisticated FinTech applications, from robo-advisors to fraud detection systems. Blockchain technology also holds significant potential for the future of FinTech. While it is perhaps best known for its role in cryptocurrencies, blockchain's potential uses in FinTech are vast, ranging from smart contracts to decentralized finance (DeFi).

Ultimately, the future of FinTech is a story yet to be written, and it's a story that will undoubtedly be shaped by both the triumphs and challenges.

10.4 Future of Fintech

The future of FinTech promises to be a fascinating one, not just for those who work in the field, but for everyone who uses financial services, which is virtually all of us. The rapid technological advancements, combined with an ever-growing demand for convenient, efficient, and secure financial services, will continue to push the boundaries of what is possible in the realm of FinTech.

Artificial Intelligence (AI) and machine learning are expected to have a significant impact on the future of FinTech. These technologies have already begun to revolutionize the way financial services are delivered and consumed, and this trend is likely to continue. Machine learning algorithms can analyze vast amounts of data, identify patterns, and make predictions with a level of accuracy that would be impossible for a human analyst. This has numerous applications in finance, such as predicting market trends, automating trading decisions, and detecting fraudulent activity. AI is also set to transform customer service in the financial sector. Chatbots, virtual assistants, and other AI-driven tools can provide customers with instant, personalized service, drastically improving the customer experience. By automating routine tasks, these tools can also help financial institutions streamline their operations and reduce costs.

The potential of blockchain technology is another aspect that is worth considering. Blockchain offers a secure, decentralized method for recording transactions, making it an ideal foundation for many FinTech solutions. Blockchain can provide increased transparency, reduced fraud, and lower costs, particularly in areas such as cross-border payments and contract enforcement. While blockchain is most famously associated with cryptocurrencies, its potential applications in the realm of FinTech are broad and varied. DeFi, or decentralized finance, is a particularly promising application of blockchain technology. DeFi platforms aim to recreate traditional financial systems, such as exchanges and lending platforms, in a decentralized, peer-to-peer manner. While DeFi is still a relatively new field, it has seen rapid growth and could potentially revolutionize the way we interact with financial services.

Biometric technology is also expected to play a significant role in the future of FinTech. While it's currently used for identity verification and access control, its potential extends much further. Biometric data, such as fingerprints, voice patterns, and facial recognition, can provide an additional layer of security for financial transactions, reducing the risk of fraud and identity theft. Additionally, as the technology becomes more sophisticated, we could see it integrated into various aspects of financial services, enabling a more personalized and seamless user experience.

Mobile technology will continue to be a major driving force in the FinTech landscape. We've already seen how smartphones have transformed banking, payments, and other financial services, making them more accessible and convenient than ever. As mobile technology continues to evolve, we can expect to see even more innovative FinTech solutions designed for the mobile platform. For example, the use of Near Field Communication (NFC) for contactless payments or the utilization of Augmented Reality (AR) in financial planning apps.

The rise of 5G technology is expected to further fuel this trend. With its ultra-fast speeds and low latency, 5G has the potential to enable real-time financial services that were previously unthinkable. It could also enable more robust and sophisticated mobile banking applications, allowing users to perform a wider range of financial activities from their smartphones. Data will also continue to play a central role in the future of FinTech. The ability to collect, analyze, and use data effectively is becoming increasingly crucial in the financial sector. Big Data analytics can provide valuable insights into customer behavior, market trends, and risk factors. This data-driven approach allows financial institutions to make more informed decisions, offer personalized services, and better manage risks.

Open banking is another trend that's expected to shape the future of FinTech. Under the open banking model, banks share customer data with third-party developers (with the customer's consent), who can then create innovative new financial apps and services. This model fosters competition and innovation in the financial sector, resulting in a wider range of choices for consumers. Artificial intelligence (AI) and machine learning (ML) are expected to have a transformative impact on the FinTech sector. They are capable of learning from and making predictions based on data, a characteristic that makes them ideal for applications within the financial services industry. As the capabilities of AI and ML advance, we are likely to see more financial institutions incorporate these technologies to enhance their decision-making processes, improve service delivery, and optimize operational efficiency. For instance, AI and ML can be used in credit scoring models to better predict borrower risk or in investment strategies to optimize portfolio performance.

The Internet of Things (IoT) is poised to disrupt the FinTech sector. The connectivity between devices can provide an unprecedented amount of data, offering valuable insights for financial service providers. This could facilitate the development of innovative financial products and services tailored to individual needs. Additionally, with IoT, possibilities like smart contracts on blockchain technology become more feasible, potentially automating many aspects of banking and finance.

Another important trend is the shift towards green and sustainable finance. As society becomes more conscious of environmental issues, there's growing pressure on the financial sector to support sustainability. FinTech could play a crucial role in this transition by providing platforms that facilitate investment in green projects or by developing tools that enable companies to assess and disclose their environmental impact. Cryptocurrencies and blockchain technology will also continue to evolve and influence the FinTech sector. Although these technologies are still in their early stages and face numerous regulatory and adoption challenges, they hold great promise. The ability to conduct secure, transparent transactions across a decentralized network has wide-ranging implications for financial services. Beyond cryptocurrencies, blockchain could revolutionize areas like cross-border payments, contract enforcement, and asset management.

While the future of FinTech is exciting, it's also shrouded in uncertainty. Regulatory developments, technological advancements, and changes in consumer behavior could all steer its path in unexpected directions. Nonetheless, the ongoing digital transformation in finance is likely to bring about profound changes in how we manage our money, invest, and engage with financial institutions. As we look towards the future of FinTech, it's important to note that this advancement does not exist in isolation. It is tightly intertwined with other sectors of the economy, influencing and being influenced by them.

One such sector, which has seen its own dramatic transformation, is the housing market. Just as technology has revolutionized finance, it has also had significant implications for housing. This interplay becomes particularly noticeable when we examine notable events like the housing bubble.

11 The Housing Bubble

As we continue our exploration of the intersections between technology and finance, we must not forget the significant events that shaped our economic landscape. Among the most critical in recent history was the housing bubble of the 2000s. This period, characterized by a rapid rise in real estate prices followed by a sharp and painful crash, left an indelible mark on our economy and society at large. The housing bubble was not merely a fluctuation in the property market but a complex phenomenon influenced by a confluence of factors. Advances in technology played a part, allowing for new types of financial products and services, such as complex mortgage-backed securities. These financial instruments contributed to an environment of easy credit, fueling speculative buying in the housing market.

The bubble's burst was as dramatic as its build-up. The ripple effects of the collapse extended far beyond the housing market, wreaking havoc on the global economy. This phase witnessed the subprime mortgage crisis, an event that resulted in a tidal wave of defaults and foreclosures. Many financial institutions faced severe difficulties, leading to widespread economic distress and precipitating the worst recession since the Great Depression. The government's response to the crisis was critical in steering the course of the economy's recovery. The actions taken in the immediate aftermath, as well as the long-term measures, fundamentally altered the financial landscape. These developments reshaped regulations, brought about shifts in the financial services industry, and left lasting impacts on households and businesses alike.

11.1 Causes

In dissecting the causes of the housing bubble, one must appreciate the complexity and interdependence of the numerous factors at play. A confluence of economic, financial, and policy elements combined to fuel a speculative frenzy that led to a dramatic rise in housing prices.

At the heart of the housing bubble were the dynamics of supply and demand. The demand for housing skyrocketed during the early 2000s due to a variety of reasons. First, demographic factors played a significant role as the baby boomer generation reached their peak home-buying years. Secondly, there was a surge of optimism regarding homeownership, partly driven by the perception that housing prices would continue to rise indefinitely. On the supply side, home construction could not keep pace with the rising demand, leading to a shortage in housing supply. This lack of supply further drove up the prices of homes, causing a speculative frenzy in the real estate market. Investors began buying homes, not for their intrinsic value as a place to live, but with the intention of selling them at a profit when prices rose further. This speculative buying exacerbated the demand-supply mismatch and contributed to the formation of the housing bubble.

Concurrently, financial innovations and lax lending standards also played a significant role in fueling the bubble. During this period, financial institutions began offering new kinds of mortgages, such as adjustable-rate mortgages and interest-only mortgages, which initially had low "teaser" interest rates that would reset to higher rates after a few years. These mortgages were bundled into mortgage-backed securities (MBS), which were then sold to investors worldwide. The influx of capital from investors, combined with the ease of obtaining credit, made mortgages readily available, even to borrowers with low creditworthiness, known as subprime borrowers. This ease of credit further stimulated demand for housing, pushing prices higher. The belief that housing prices would continue to rise made these risky lending practices appear less risky at the time.

Furthermore, there were significant policy factors that also contributed to the housing bubble. The Federal Reserve, the central bank of the United States, maintained low-interest rates during the early 2000s, making borrowing cheaper. This policy facilitated the expansion of credit and encouraged risk-taking by investors and homeowners. There was a significant lack of oversight and regulation of the financial institutions involved in mortgage lending and securitization. Regulatory authorities failed to keep pace with the rapid financial innovation occurring in the mortgage market, leading to a regulatory vacuum that allowed risky practices to proliferate unchecked.

Finally, the economic environment in the years leading up to the housing bubble also played a role. The economy was booming in the early 2000s, fueled by a technology-driven productivity boom. Unemployment was low, and wages were rising, making homeownership affordable for more people. This prosperity contributed to the optimism that was a hallmark of the housing bubble era.

These factors and more culminated in a perfect storm, leading to a rapid escalation in housing prices, thus forming the housing bubble. The causes were multi-faceted and interdependent, a mixture of economic, financial, policy, and societal elements. In the next section, we'll explore the impact that this bubble had on the broader economy.

11.2 Impact on Economy

When the housing bubble burst, it unleashed a chain of events that reverberated throughout the entire economy. This was due to the interconnected nature of the financial system and the central role of housing in the American economy. The bursting of the housing bubble not only led to a sharp decline in housing prices but also sparked a full-blown economic recession, the Great Recession, that lasted from December 2007 to June 2009.

Firstly, the collapse in housing prices led to a massive erosion of household wealth. For many households, their home is their most valuable asset, and the dramatic drop in home values resulted in a negative wealth effect. Homeowners felt poorer, and this influenced their spending behavior, leading to a contraction in consumer spending, which is a crucial component of the gross domestic product (GDP). This contraction in consumption had a ripple effect throughout the economy, leading to lower business revenues, job losses, and further reductions in spending in a vicious cycle. In addition, the decline in housing prices also left many homeowners with mortgages worth more than the value of their homes, a situation known as being "underwater" on their mortgage. This led to a surge in mortgage defaults and foreclosures, with serious consequences for both homeowners and financial institutions. Homeowners faced eviction and the loss of their homes, while financial institutions faced substantial losses on their mortgage-related investments.

For financial institutions, the burst of the housing bubble exposed the risks and losses tied to their extensive involvement in subprime mortgages and related securities. Many of these institutions found themselves saddled with so-called "toxic assets" — mortgage-backed securities whose value had plummeted due to high default rates on the underlying mortgages. This led to a crisis of confidence in the financial system. Banks became wary of lending to each other due to fears about exposure to these toxic assets, leading to a freezing of credit markets and a full-blown financial crisis. As the crisis unfolded, businesses found it increasingly difficult to access credit, leading to reductions in investment and further job losses. The contraction in business investment was another factor that contributed to the depth and length of the recession. This financial crisis wasn't confined to the United States, it quickly spread to other economies leading to a global financial crisis.

The bursting of the housing bubble also had significant fiscal implications. The decline in economic activity led to a decrease in tax revenues just as government expenditures were rising due to increased demand for safety net programs like unemployment insurance and food stamps. This resulted in large budget deficits and an increase in public debt. At the same time, the government was forced to bail out several major financial institutions to prevent a complete collapse of the financial system, which further increased public debt. The housing bubble and its burst have also had a lasting impact on the structure and behavior of the economy. Many of the jobs lost during the recession, particularly in the construction and manufacturing sectors, have not returned. This has led to a structural shift in the labor market, with a greater emphasis on jobs in the service sector. Furthermore, the experience of the housing bubble has led to changes in the behavior of consumers and businesses. Consumers are now more cautious about borrowing, and businesses are more wary of risk. This newfound prudence has shaped the slow and uneven nature of the economic recovery.

The impacts of the housing bubble on the economy also reflected deeply on various sectors. The banking sector, for instance, was fundamentally reshaped by the crisis. Many small to medium-sized banks, particularly those heavily invested in the housing market, faced insolvency and were either closed or merged with larger institutions. Larger banks, despite their initial troubles, emerged from the crisis even larger and more influential than before, leading to an increased concentration in the banking sector. The real estate sector also underwent significant changes. The bubble's burst led to an excess inventory of homes due to the combined effect of foreclosures and reduced demand. This glut of properties put downward pressure on prices and stalled new housing construction, leading to job losses in the construction sector. The crisis also changed the perception of homeownership. What was once seen as a safe investment and a path to wealth accumulation is now viewed with more caution. These changes led to a shift towards rental housing, and the percentage of Americans owning homes dropped from a peak of 69% in 2004 to 64% a decade later.

One of the broader, more insidious impacts of the housing bubble was on societal inequality. The effects of the crisis were unevenly distributed, with disadvantaged groups suffering the most. Lower-income homeowners, who were disproportionately the targets of subprime lending, were more likely to lose their homes. These groups also faced higher unemployment during the recession. The uneven impact of the crisis has exacerbated wealth and income disparities, adding to the societal challenges that the US continues to grapple with today.

Finally, the psychological impacts of the housing bubble and subsequent crash should not be overlooked. For millions of people, the crisis meant the loss of a home, savings, or job. This has led to a sense of financial insecurity that persists even years after the end of the recession. The public's trust in financial institutions and the government has also been eroded, with many feeling that the response to the crisis favored big banks over ordinary citizens. This sentiment has influenced public discourse and attitudes towards economic policy to this day.

In summary, the impact of the housing bubble on the economy was profound and far-reaching. Its effects extended beyond the financial losses during the crash and continue to shape economic and social realities. Its lessons on risk, regulation, and inequality are ones that will inform economic policy and public attitudes for many years to come.

The housing bubble had a ripple effect that extended to various aspects of the economy. Perhaps one of the most notable impacts was the effect on consumer spending. As home prices skyrocketed during the bubble, many homeowners felt wealthier and increased their spending, often using home equity loans to finance their purchases. This phenomenon, known as the wealth effect, contributed significantly to economic growth during the bubble years.

When home prices collapsed, so did the perceived wealth, leading to sharp reductions in consumer spending, which played a substantial role in the depth of the ensuing recession. The bubble's burst also drastically influenced the job market. In the run-up to the peak of the housing bubble, the construction industry saw a substantial increase in employment as the demand for new homes soared.

With the bubble's burst and the subsequent fall in housing demand, the construction sector faced a significant contraction. The number of jobs in this sector dropped sharply, leading to an increase in unemployment rates. The effect was not limited to construction jobs alone. Real estate brokers, mortgage lenders, and even jobs in related sectors like home furnishing and appliances faced losses.

As an example, consider the city of Las Vegas, which was one of the most severely affected areas during the housing crisis. During the bubble, the city experienced a construction boom with numerous new homes, casinos, and hotels being built.

As the bubble burst, construction halted, and the city faced one of the highest unemployment rates in the country. Even today, the city is still dealing with the aftermath, with many of these constructions left as incomplete "ghost buildings." The impact on the financial sector was, of course, enormous. The collapse of the housing market led to significant losses for banks and financial institutions holding mortgage-backed securities. This loss in assets put a significant strain on the banking sector, leading to liquidity crises for many institutions and causing some of them to fail entirely. Those banks that survived had to be more stringent in their lending, leading to a credit crunch. This scarcity of credit further deepened the recession as businesses could not borrow to invest and expand, and consumers could not borrow to spend.

In essence, the impact of the housing bubble on the economy was both immediate and prolonged. It caused considerable disruption in the economic activities during its burst, but its effects lingered for years in the form of slow economic recovery, high unemployment, and a lasting impact on consumer behavior.

11.3 Subprime Mortgage Crisis

With the collapse of the housing bubble, one particular area of the mortgage industry bore the brunt of the crisis: the subprime sector. Subprime mortgages are loans given to borrowers who are considered a higher credit risk, often due to a low credit score. These mortgages were a significant contributor to the housing bubble because they allowed individuals who typically would not have been able to qualify for a mortgage to purchase homes. Subprime mortgages often came with higher interest rates to compensate for the increased risk, but they also frequently included adjustable rates, which started with low "teaser" interest rates that would reset to much higher rates after a few years.

The issues of the housing bubble went beyond just high-risk lending. The securitization of these subprime mortgages—whereby they were bundled together and sold as mortgage-backed securities (MBS)—spread the risk to the broader financial system. The demand for these MBS was high because they offered attractive returns, and their risk was supposedly low, as they were backed by real estate, which was assumed to be continually rising in value. When housing prices started to fall, many homeowners found themselves in a precarious situation known as being "underwater"—owing more on their mortgages than what their homes were worth. As these homeowners started to default on their mortgages, the mortgage-backed securities tied to these loans also began to fail. The financial institutions, insurance companies, and even pension funds that held these securities found themselves facing significant losses.

To compound the issue, the bursting of the housing bubble coincided with the reset dates of many subprime mortgages. The initial low teaser rates expired, and the higher interest rates kicked in, leading to a sharp increase in mortgage payments for many homeowners. This increase, coupled with the fall in home prices, led to a surge in defaults and foreclosures.

The subprime mortgage crisis was thus not just a crisis in the housing market. Its roots were deeply intertwined with the practices of the financial sector. It represented a failure in understanding and managing financial risks, and its effects were felt not only by the homeowners and the housing industry but also by the wider financial system and the economy as a whole. The fallout from the crisis was severe and marked the beginning of the most significant economic downturn since the Great Depression. This dramatic period of financial and economic distress, known as the Great Recession, was a testament to the far-reaching consequences of the subprime mortgage crisis. Transitioning into the heart of the crisis, we begin to explore the intricacies of the subprime mortgage crisis, its development, and its profound and far-reaching effects on the economy and society.

The Subprime Mortgage Crisis, as a critical aspect of the housing bubble, was centered around the implosion of a large sector of the American housing market: the subprime mortgages. The increasing number of defaults and foreclosures on these high-risk loans sparked a chain reaction of financial calamities, culminating in a severe and far-reaching economic crisis.

As mentioned earlier, subprime mortgages were loans given to borrowers with lower credit ratings who, under typical underwriting standards, would not be eligible for traditional loans. These loans carried a higher risk of default and, consequently, higher interest rates. This was part of a broader trend towards offering more accessible credit to a wider range of individuals, an approach often referred to as democratizing credit.

The problems arose from the structure of these subprime loans. Most of them were adjustable-rate mortgages (ARMs), which offered an introductory low interest rate (the "teaser rate") for an initial period before resetting to a much higher rate. This meant that after the teaser rate period ended, borrowers faced substantial increases in their monthly payments. In the housing boom years, this wasn't seen as a problem as borrowers could refinance their mortgages with the rising equity in their homes. But when the housing bubble burst and property prices fell, refinancing became impossible for many homeowners, leading to widespread defaults and foreclosures. Simultaneously, there was another factor contributing to the subprime mortgage crisis: securitization. In securitization, financial institutions bundled these subprime mortgages into mortgage-backed securities (MBSs) and sold them to investors worldwide. These securities offered attractive returns and were highly rated by credit rating agencies, making them appealing to a broad range of investors. The demand for MBSs led to more demand for subprime mortgages to back these securities, further inflating the housing bubble.

But, when the wave of defaults and foreclosures hit, the mortgage-backed securities tied to these subprime loans began to collapse. The resulting losses were not confined to the US; they rippled through the global financial system, causing significant financial distress and contributing to the global financial crisis. This cataclysmic series of events underscored the interconnectedness of the global financial system and the domino effect a collapse in one sector can have on the wider economy. In this broader context, the subprime mortgage crisis was a stark demonstration of the risks inherent in financial innovation and lax regulatory oversight. It highlighted the dangers of overreliance on complex financial instruments, the limitations of credit rating agencies, and the consequences of irresponsible lending practices. The ramifications of the subprime mortgage crisis were far-reaching, affecting not only the banking sector but also the real economy, with severe impacts on employment, income, and wealth.

To better comprehend the depth of the Subprime Mortgage Crisis, consider the case of a hypothetical homeowner, let's call him John. In the early 2000s, John, like many Americans, was captivated by the promise of home ownership. Despite his low credit score and limited income, John was granted a subprime mortgage loan with an adjustable rate for a home he could only afford at the teaser rate. He was assured by his lender that he could refinance his mortgage when the rate reset. John, elated at the prospect of owning a home, readily agreed.

For a while, all seemed well. The housing market was booming, and John's home was appreciating in value. But the scenario changed abruptly when the bubble burst. Housing prices fell dramatically, and John found himself owing more on his mortgage than his house was worth. Around the same time, his mortgage rate reset to a much higher level, and his monthly payments skyrocketed. John tried to refinance, but with his home's reduced equity and his precarious financial situation, he was not eligible for a new loan. Unable to meet his mortgage payments, John defaulted on his loan, and his home went into foreclosure. John's story was not unique; it was shared by millions of Americans. As more and more subprime borrowers defaulted on their loans, the effects were felt not just in the housing market but also in the broader financial sector. The mortgage-backed securities tied to these subprime loans, which were held by banks and investors worldwide, began to lose their value rapidly. Financial institutions that had heavily invested in these securities suffered substantial losses, leading to a crisis of confidence in the banking system.

Consider another example, this time from the banking sector's perspective. A large investment bank, let's call it XYZ Corp, had heavily invested in mortgage-backed securities. When homeowners like John began to default on their subprime mortgages, the securities that XYZ Corp held started to plummet in value. Soon, the bank's losses were mounting, and it faced severe liquidity issues. Eventually, XYZ Corp collapsed, sparking panic in the financial markets. Investors began to question the health of other banks, leading to a full-blown banking crisis. This example underscores the multiplier effect of the subprime mortgage crisis. What started as an issue within the housing sector quickly spread to the broader financial system and then spilled over into the real economy. The rapid and extensive spread of this crisis was partly due to the interconnectedness of the financial system, with the default of subprime mortgages triggering a chain reaction of financial distress.

This crisis also shed light on the flaws in the financial system. The role of financial institutions in promoting subprime lending, the lack of adequate risk assessment, the complacency of credit rating agencies, and the regulatory failures all came under scrutiny. The harsh lessons from this crisis provided important insights into the functioning of the financial system and led to a renewed focus on financial stability and regulatory reforms.

The reverberations of the subprime mortgage crisis extended far beyond the individuals and institutions directly implicated. As the crisis deepened, a range of economic and social consequences became apparent. One of the most immediate impacts was on employment. As financial institutions faced mounting losses, they began to lay off workers in large numbers. Meanwhile, as credit markets tightened, businesses found it harder to access the funds they needed to maintain or expand their operations, which further increased job losses.

The unemployment rate, which had been relatively low before the crisis, began to rise sharply, peaking at around 10 percent in the United States. This increase in unemployment had significant knock-on effects. With less income, people reduced their consumption, which resulted in lower business revenues and further job cuts, creating a vicious cycle. The stress of job losses and reduced income also had a significant impact on people's mental health, contributing to a rise in mental health issues. The crisis had a significant effect on public finances. As tax revenues fell due to lower incomes and corporate profits, government spending rose as it tried to mitigate the crisis's impact through various means, such as unemployment benefits, stimulus packages, and bank bailouts. This led to a sharp increase in public debt, posing additional challenges for governments in the years following the crisis.

On the international front, the crisis highlighted the global financial system's interconnectedness. The decline in U.S. housing prices and the rise in mortgage defaults didn't just affect U.S. banks and homeowners. Financial institutions worldwide had invested heavily in mortgage-backed securities, and as these securities plummeted in value, banks outside the U.S. also found themselves facing significant losses. This led to a global financial crisis, with countries around the world grappling with similar issues of banking instability, rising unemployment, and slowing growth. Additionally, the crisis led to a shift in economic thinking and policy. The belief in self-regulating markets that had prevailed in the pre-crisis years was seriously questioned as the crisis highlighted the financial sector's vulnerability to systemic risks. This prompted calls for stronger regulation and oversight of the financial industry to prevent a recurrence of such a crisis. Indeed, in the years following the crisis, significant regulatory reforms were undertaken in many countries to increase the resilience of their financial systems.

The crisis also revealed significant gaps in economic models and highlighted the need for better tools to understand the financial system's complexities. It spurred new research in fields like behavioral economics to understand the irrational behaviors that had contributed to the housing bubble and subsequent bust. It also motivated the development of macroprudential policy frameworks to manage systemic risks in the financial sector. These developments have had a lasting impact on how we understand and manage economic and financial systems. In sum, the subprime mortgage crisis was a watershed moment in global finance. It brought to light the weaknesses of the existing financial system, prompted significant regulatory changes, and reshaped economic thinking. Its legacy continues to influence financial and economic policy-making to this day.

11.4 Government Response

Following the subprime mortgage crisis, governments worldwide were forced into a delicate balancing act. On one hand, they needed to stem the crisis's immediate effects, such as rising unemployment, falling housing prices, and deteriorating consumer and investor confidence. On the other hand, they had to address the underlying structural issues that had contributed to the crisis, including lax regulatory oversight and risky lending practices. The initial response was largely focused on stabilizing the financial sector. As the credit market froze and numerous financial institutions faced the threat of bankruptcy, governments stepped in to shore up the banking system. This was done through various measures, such as injecting capital into troubled banks, providing guarantees on bank deposits and debt, and even nationalizing some banks. In the U.S., the Troubled Asset Relief Program (TARP) was established, which purchased distressed assets, notably mortgage-backed securities, and equity from financial institutions to strengthen the financial sector. While these measures were effective in preventing a complete meltdown of the financial system, they also raised a number of concerns. For one, there was widespread public dissatisfaction with the notion of using taxpayer money to bail out financial institutions that were largely seen as the main culprits of the crisis. This also raised moral hazard issues, as it could potentially incentivize reckless behavior by financial institutions in the future, knowing that they would be bailed out if things go wrong.

To mitigate these concerns and prevent a repeat of such a crisis, governments implemented a raft of regulatory reforms aimed at improving the financial system's stability. These included measures to increase transparency, enhance risk management, limit risky lending practices, and increase the resilience of financial institutions. In the

U.S., the Dodd-Frank Wall Street Reform and Consumer Protection Act was enacted, bringing significant changes to financial regulation.

While stabilizing the financial sector was crucial, it was only one part of the response. The crisis had resulted in a severe economic contraction, and there was a need to stimulate economic activity and mitigate the social impact of the crisis. To this end, governments implemented a range of fiscal and monetary policy measures. Central banks around the world lowered interest rates, in some cases to near zero, and implemented quantitative easing measures to stimulate lending and investment. Meanwhile, governments increased spending and implemented tax cuts to boost demand and create jobs.

These responses played a crucial role in mitigating the crisis's impacts, and lessons from these interventions continue to inform policy responses to financial and economic crises.

The crisis also had lasting effects, and the recovery process was long and difficult. This aspect of the crisis – the aftermath and the efforts to rebuild in its wake – is another critical facet of understanding the housing bubble and its effects on the global economy. The global response to the financial crisis was marked by significant coordination between nations, a testament to the interconnectedness of the world economy. While the crisis started in the United States, the shockwaves were felt across the globe, revealing just how closely tied the world's economies had become. To stem the tide of the crisis, countries adopted comprehensive measures on a scale unseen since the Great Depression.

The International Monetary Fund (IMF) and the World Bank played critical roles in coordinating global efforts to mitigate the crisis's effects. These institutions provided financial assistance to countries facing balance-of-payment problems due to the crisis, helped design policy responses, and promoted cooperation among countries. In several instances, the IMF extended financial packages to countries experiencing significant capital outflows, helping them stabilize their economies. Another notable aspect of the government response was the shift in monetary policy paradigm. Prior to the crisis, central banks primarily relied on interest rates as their primary tool to manage the economy. With interest rates near zero, they had to resort to unconventional policy tools. These included forward guidance, in which central banks communicate their future policy intentions, and quantitative easing (QE), a policy of buying large-scale assets to inject money into the economy. The aim was to reduce longer-term interest rates, encourage borrowing and spending, and bolster investor confidence.

Quantitative easing, in particular, became a cornerstone of the crisis response, with the U.S. Federal Reserve, the European Central Bank, and the Bank of England launching large-scale QE programs. While these measures were initially seen as temporary, they remained in place for many years after the crisis, and their withdrawal has been a complex and delicate task for central banks. These unconventional monetary policies have had significant implications for the global economy and continue to shape the economic and financial landscape.

While these immediate responses were critical, governments also recognized the need for long-term structural reforms. The crisis exposed various weaknesses in the financial system, and there was a broad consensus on the need to address them. This led to a comprehensive overhaul of financial regulation, aimed at making financial systems more resilient and less prone to crises. The reforms included higher capital requirements for banks, stricter oversight of the shadow banking system, and measures to improve transparency and risk management in financial markets.

These regulatory reforms also sparked debates. Some argued that the stricter rules could stifle innovation and growth in the financial sector. Others contended that the reforms didn't go far enough and that more drastic measures were needed, such as separating commercial banking from investment banking. These discussions reflect the complexity of regulating a constantly evolving financial system and balancing the need for stability against the benefits of innovation and growth. Ultimately, the government response to the financial crisis was a complex, multifaceted process that involved both immediate crisis management and long-term structural reforms. These actions have had profound implications for the global economy, shaping the economic and financial landscape in the years following the crisis. The crisis and the subsequent response have offered invaluable lessons for managing financial crises, underscoring the importance of effective regulation, sound macroeconomic policies, and international cooperation in maintaining global financial stability.

The enactment of these financial regulatory reforms and economic recovery measures laid the groundwork for what would become the new normal in the financial landscape. As the dust settled and economies started to regain stability, the aftermath of the crisis became apparent. The measures taken had not only contained the crisis but had also profoundly transformed the global economic and financial systems. One notable shift in the post-crisis period was the increased role of central banks in economic policy. The crisis had pushed central banks into uncharted territories, prompting them to take on a broader range of responsibilities and use new tools to manage their economies. In the wake of the crisis, central banks continued to play an active role, implementing measures such as low-interest rates and quantitative easing to stimulate economic growth and maintain stability. This expanded role of central banks has been a key feature of the post-crisis economic landscape.

The crisis also had far-reaching implications for financial institutions and markets. Banks faced stricter regulatory requirements, which affected their operations and profitability.

These new regulations pushed banks to reevaluate their business models and strategies. In some cases, this led to significant restructuring, as banks divested from risky activities and focused on their core business areas. The crisis also sparked a wave of consolidation in the banking industry, with weaker banks being absorbed by stronger ones. These changes led to a more resilient but also more concentrated banking sector. Furthermore, the crisis triggered a significant shift in investor behavior. The sharp losses incurred during the crisis led investors to become more risk-averse, favoring safer assets over riskier ones. This change in investor sentiment affected capital flows and had implications for financial markets worldwide. It also spurred the growth of new investment strategies, such as those based on environmental, social, and governance (ESG) factors, as investors sought to align their investments with their values and manage risk more effectively.

It also had significant social and political ramifications. The severe economic downturn, high unemployment, and austerity measures implemented in many countries led to widespread social discontent. This social unrest manifested in various forms, from protests and strikes to changes in political leadership and policy orientations. The crisis also highlighted issues of inequality and the need for more inclusive growth, which became key themes in policy debates and political discourse. The crisis underscored the need for international cooperation in managing global economic and financial issues. The global nature of the crisis highlighted the interconnectedness of the world's economies and the importance of coordinated action to maintain global financial stability. This recognition led to enhanced cooperation among countries and international institutions, which played a crucial role in managing the crisis and shaping the post-crisis economic landscape.

The aftermath of the crisis, therefore, is not just about economic recovery but also about a fundamental reshaping of the global economic and financial systems. The crisis has brought to the forefront the complexities and challenges of managing a globalized economy, highlighting the need for sound policy, effective regulation, and international cooperation. The lessons learned from the crisis continue to inform policy debates and shape the trajectory of the global economy, even as the world grapples with new challenges and uncertainties.

11.5 Aftermath

The post-crisis period marked a profound and complex transformation in the global economic landscape. Countries, societies, and individuals alike had to find their way through a drastically altered economic environment, replete with both unprecedented challenges and new opportunities.

Banks and financial institutions, having experienced a period of turbulence, sought to fortify their operations against future upheavals. This period was characterized by a renewed focus on building more robust risk management frameworks. Enhanced scrutiny from regulatory bodies and an increased public demand for financial transparency spurred institutions to overhaul their systems and processes, investing heavily in technology and data analytics to better manage and predict risks. The crisis served as a catalyst for innovation in the financial sector. Recognizing the need for more resilient and inclusive financial systems, many institutions began exploring new technologies and business models. In this environment, digital financial services and fintech companies flourished, offering new ways of delivering financial services that were often more accessible, efficient, and cost-effective than traditional banking models. This period also witnessed the rise of financial inclusion as a major policy goal, as governments and institutions sought to ensure that the benefits of financial services reached all sections of society.

The post-crisis period also ushered in a renewed focus on sustainable development. The crisis had laid bare the vulnerabilities of economies to shocks, prompting calls for more resilient and sustainable economic models. This perspective shift led to increased emphasis on green finance, responsible investment, and other strategies aimed at aligning economic activities with social and environmental goals. Investors increasingly turned to ESG

(Environmental, Social, Governance) criteria in their decision-making, leading to a substantial growth in sustainable finance.

It highlighted the importance of collaboration and collective action in addressing global challenges. The response to the crisis underscored the value of cooperation among nations, regulators, and market participants. In its aftermath, there was a concerted effort to build more robust mechanisms for international coordination in economic and financial matters. The creation of the Financial Stability Board, tasked with promoting global financial stability, was a testament to this effort. The aftermath of the crisis can thus be seen as a period of resilience, innovation, and transformation. The challenges brought on by the crisis necessitated a rethinking of many aspects of the global economy, prompting innovations and changes that have shaped the economic landscape of today. While the scars of the crisis remain, they also serve as reminders of the lessons learned and the strides made in building more resilient, inclusive, and sustainable economies.

The post-crisis world witnessed a renewed emphasis on consumer protection. The financial crisis exposed numerous unscrupulous practices that preyed on unsophisticated investors and individuals with limited financial literacy. The securitization of subprime mortgages and their sales to unsuspecting investors was a case in point. In the aftermath, regulatory bodies across the world were tasked with creating more transparent, accountable, and consumer-friendly financial markets. For instance, in the United States, this led to the creation of the Consumer Financial Protection Bureau, aimed at ensuring consumers get the information they need to make financial decisions that are best for them and their families.

The importance of financial education and literacy came to the forefront. There was a recognition that consumers need to be well informed to protect themselves in increasingly complex financial markets. Governments, NGOs, and financial institutions embarked on a range of initiatives to improve financial literacy. This encompassed everything from incorporating financial education in school curricula to launching awareness campaigns about different financial products and their risks.

Regulators also focused on improving transparency and fairness in financial markets. This was driven by the realization that the opacity of financial products and markets had been a contributing factor to the crisis. Efforts were made to ensure that financial products are understandable and that their risks are clearly disclosed. The role of credit rating agencies came under scrutiny, and reforms were implemented to ensure that their ratings provide an accurate assessment of risk.

Banks and other financial institutions underwent significant structural changes in the wake of the crisis. The objective was to build a financial system that is resilient to shocks and fit for the future. Capital and liquidity requirements were increased to ensure that banks have a stronger buffer to absorb losses. 'Too big to fail' became a focal point of regulatory efforts, with measures taken to ensure that the failure of a large bank does not result in systemic risk.

In summary, the aftermath of the financial crisis witnessed a fundamental rethinking of the principles that guide financial markets and institutions. The lessons learned from the crisis led to regulatory reforms aimed at creating a financial system that is resilient, transparent, fair, and consumer-friendly. The focus was on creating an environment where financial markets contribute to sustainable economic growth and prosperity.

12 Lehman Brothers and AIG

As we continue the history of financial markets, we come to a pivotal moment of crisis that left a profound impact on the global financial landscape. Two of the most significant events of the 2008 financial crisis revolve around the failure of Lehman Brothers and the near-collapse of AIG, both of which sent shockwaves through financial markets worldwide.

Lehman Brothers, once a respected and influential investment bank, succumbed to the weight of its risky investments and declared bankruptcy in September 2008. The fall of Lehman Brothers was monumental as it was the largest bankruptcy filing in U.S. history and marked the most significant casualty of the subprime mortgage crisis. The bank's fall highlighted the extent of the risk and malpractice that had come to characterize certain aspects of Wall Street behavior, triggering serious doubts about the stability and trustworthiness of the entire financial system.

AIG, on the other hand, was a different case. While not a bank, its activities in the financial sector through its financial products division had significant ramifications. The company had insured billions in mortgage-backed securities and other assets via complex financial instruments called credit default swaps. As the housing market plummeted and defaults rose, AIG found itself on the brink of failure. The company's potential collapse posed a systemic risk due to its interconnectedness with numerous financial institutions globally.

Together, the downfall of Lehman Brothers and the near-collapse of AIG unveiled the depth of the issues within the financial system and served as critical triggers for the severe economic recession that ensued. The fallout of these events led to widespread changes in the financial industry, from regulatory measures to shifts in corporate governance and risk management.

The ramifications of these events and the subsequent responses provide critical insights into the functioning of global financial markets and offer lessons for future financial stability.

12.1 Lehman Brothers' Fall

The fall of Lehman Brothers was an event of unprecedented scale and consequence. This 158-year-old investment banking firm, which had weathered everything from the Great Depression to two World Wars, suddenly found itself unable to withstand the damage done by a wave of mortgage defaults in the United States. The firm's fall didn't occur in a vacuum or overnight. It was the culmination of risky practices and decisions made over several years that finally caught up to the firm. In the years leading up to the crisis, Lehman Brothers was heavily involved in issuing and underwriting mortgage-backed securities (MBS). The firm bought mortgages from lenders, bundled them into securities, and sold those securities to investors. This process was initially lucrative and successful, as rising house prices ensured that mortgage defaults remained low.

The situation started to change as the housing market began to decline.

Lehman Brothers, along with many other financial institutions, had placed substantial bets on the continuous growth of the housing market. When the market started to collapse, the firm found itself exposed to large amounts of bad debt. The value of the mortgage-backed securities they held started to plummet, and Lehman Brothers was unable to sell these assets or find the funding needed to offset their declining value. As these assets became increasingly toxic, confidence in Lehman Brothers evaporated, causing other banks and investors to withdraw their support. By mid-2008, Lehman Brothers was facing a liquidity crisis. Efforts to secure funding, or a possible merger or acquisition, proved unsuccessful. The firm's stocks plunged as market confidence dwindled, and credit rating agencies downgraded the firm's debt, making it even more challenging to secure funding. In an increasingly precarious position, the firm started to sell off assets to raise liquidity, but the efforts were too little, too late. The firm declared bankruptcy on September 15, 2008, making it the most significant bankruptcy filing in U.S. history. The fall of such a major player in the financial industry sent shockwaves across the world, and the bankruptcy marked a pivotal point in the 2008 financial crisis. It was a stark reminder of the potential consequences of reckless risk-taking and lack of adequate oversight in the financial sector, further exacerbating the already tumultuous financial landscape. It led to a severe contraction in the global credit market, as banks became increasingly wary of lending to each other due to fears of counterparty risk. The collapse also ignited a severe loss of confidence in the financial system, prompting financial institutions and investors worldwide to reevaluate their risk exposure. The depth of Lehman Brothers' involvement in the mortgage-backed securities market was the catalyst for its precipitous fall. At its peak, the firm had approximately $111 billion in tangible assets, but it also held about $619 billion in liabilities, a substantial portion of which were tied to the deteriorating housing market. Such a massive gap between assets and liabilities laid bare the vulnerability of Lehman's financial structure. The bank was excessively leveraged, meaning it had borrowed extensively to finance its investments. While leverage can magnify profits in good times, it also amplifies losses when investments go sour, as was the case with Lehman Brothers.

Lehman's balance sheet woes were further compounded by its use of Repo 105 transactions, a type of short-term borrowing that allowed it to temporarily remove securities from its balance sheet. This practice created the illusion of a healthier financial state than was truly the case. The Repo 105 transactions essentially masked the level of risk Lehman was taking on and gave false reassurances to investors, credit rating agencies, and even its own employees about the firm's financial stability. It's demise was also exacerbated by failures in corporate governance and risk management. Despite warnings from some employees about the firm's risky strategies, Lehman's top executives continued to make large bets on the subprime mortgage market, seemingly oblivious to the escalating risks. Furthermore, the firm's risk management protocols were inadequate and largely ignored, as the lure of quick profits took precedence over cautious decision-making.

The downfall of Lehman Brothers was not just a failure of one firm. It was a symptom of a larger systemic problem within the financial sector – an over-reliance on risky financial products, lack of transparency, and insufficient regulatory oversight. The absence of a robust risk management framework and a culture that prized short-term gains over long-term stability led to decisions that were detrimental to the firm's health. Even when the risks became apparent, the firm was so deeply entangled in the web of toxic assets that it was impossible to extricate itself without significant losses.

A significant aspect of the Lehman Brothers' saga was its timing. Its bankruptcy came at a time when the global financial system was already under strain from the bursting of the housing bubble. Lehman's failure exacerbated this crisis, causing a domino effect that intensified the global financial downturn. The financial markets were paralyzed by fear and uncertainty in the wake of Lehman's bankruptcy, leading to a sharp contraction in lending and a steep decline in asset prices. As a result, the global economy slipped into what would become known as the Great Recession. In the end, Lehman Brothers' fall served as a stark reminder of the dangers of unchecked risk-taking and the fragility of financial systems.

In the months following Lehman Brothers' collapse, a palpable feeling of fear and uncertainty gripped Wall Street and global financial markets. The realisation that a firm as entrenched as Lehman could crumble so quickly sent shockwaves across the industry, leading many to question which institution might be next. The general mood was one of trepidation, as it was becoming increasingly clear that the financial crisis was far from over. The bankruptcy of Lehman Brothers exposed the interconnectedness of global financial institutions and the systemic risk that this could pose. Lehman was not an isolated entity; it was linked to numerous other financial institutions through a complex network of derivative contracts, debt obligations, and other financial ties. As such, its failure had far-reaching consequences, prompting other financial institutions to reassess their own vulnerabilities.

In this tumultuous environment, attention soon turned to the insurance giant, American International Group (AIG). AIG, like Lehman Brothers, had made significant investments in the subprime mortgage market.

AIG's exposure was not through mortgage-backed securities, but through a financial product known as credit default swaps (CDS). AIG had issued billions of dollars in these swaps, effectively insuring other companies' investments in mortgage-backed securities against default. As the housing market declined, these swaps resulted in massive liabilities for AIG, and the firm soon found itself on the brink of collapse.

Unlike Lehman Brothers, whose bankruptcy filing was swiftly followed by chaos in the financial markets, the U.S. government chose to intervene to prevent AIG's failure. The circumstances surrounding AIG's imminent downfall were different from those of Lehman, and the potential implications of AIG's failure were deemed too severe to allow. The next phase in the unfolding drama of the financial crisis had begun – the controversial bailout of American International Group.

12.2 AIG Bailout

The U.S. government, recognizing the potential disastrous domino effect AIG's failure could trigger in the global financial system, chose to intervene. It was feared that AIG's collapse could lead to a catastrophic chain reaction, with the potential to exacerbate the already fragile economic situation further. Given AIG's significant role as an insurer for numerous banks through credit default swaps, the failure of the company would have meant massive losses for these institutions. Such a scenario was seen as a systemic risk too large to ignore.

In September 2008, the Federal Reserve extended an $85 billion loan to AIG in exchange for a 79.9% equity stake in the company. The rationale behind this was to prevent the systemic risk posed by the insurer's collapse, protect policyholders, and contain the ripple effects of AIG's potential bankruptcy on the broader economy. This was the first time in its history that the Federal Reserve had bailed out an insurance company, illustrating the unprecedented nature of the crisis. This move was not without controversy. Critics argued that the bailout created a moral hazard by signaling to large financial institutions that the government would come to their rescue in times of distress, thereby encouraging reckless behavior. Others pointed out the inconsistency in the government's actions – Lehman Brothers was allowed to fail, while AIG was saved. Despite these criticisms, government officials maintained that the bailout was a necessary step to stabilize the financial system and protect the economy from further damage.

The AIG bailout marked a critical juncture in the financial crisis. It signaled the government's commitment to intervene in the market to avert further disaster.

The action taken was not just about saving one company; it was about preventing a systemic failure that could have further destabilized an already fragile global financial system. The complexities and ripple effects of such a decision go beyond the immediate need for financial stabilization. They highlight the intricacies of the interconnected global economy and raise questions about the role of government in managing financial crises.

The magnitude of AIG's bailout also highlighted the scale of the company's operations and their systemic significance. The insurer's extensive dealings in derivatives, in particular, credit default swaps, exposed the lack of transparency and regulation in the vast world of complex financial products. Many of these financial instruments were poorly understood, even by those trading them, and were only disclosed in the fine print of financial statements, if at all.

The bailout process itself was fraught with challenges. The initial $85 billion loan from the Federal Reserve turned out to be insufficient to stabilize the company, leading to further rounds of financial assistance. In the end, the total financial aid to AIG amounted to more than $180 billion, making it the largest bailout in U.S. history. The vast majority of these funds were used to pay off AIG's obligations on its massive portfolio of credit default swaps. These payouts, in turn, were directed to the banks that were counterparties to these swaps, effectively leading to a further indirect bailout of these institutions.

Through its support of AIG, the government was essentially stepping in to fulfil obligations that AIG could not, preventing a cascade of defaults that could have devastated the global banking system. On the one hand, this move was seen as necessary for the greater good of the economy. On the other hand, it raised serious concerns about the extent of risk and liability the government was willing to assume on behalf of private companies. The AIG bailout demonstrated the government's readiness to cross traditional boundaries to avert a total collapse of the financial system. Yet, it also underlined the dire need for greater regulation and oversight in the financial sector, particularly in the largely unregulated world of derivatives. The lessons learned from this crisis would later lead to significant reforms aimed at preventing such a scenario from recurring in the future.

The ramifications of AIG's near-collapse extended far beyond the company's direct stakeholders. The ripple effects of the crisis became apparent in the global financial markets, which saw drastic falls in value as confidence in the financial system plummeted. The Dow Jones Industrial Average and S&P 500 suffered significant losses in the days following the announcement of the AIG bailout, reflecting the widespread fear and uncertainty that had engulfed the markets. These effects were not confined to the US alone, with markets around the globe experiencing comparable turbulence. Investors fled from perceived risky assets, leading to a flight to safety which primarily benefitted traditionally safe assets such as government bonds and gold. As a result, yields on these securities fell to record lows. Conversely, the cost of borrowing for companies rose sharply, as reflected in the widening of credit spreads. These shifts in market dynamics highlighted the magnitude of the systemic risk that AIG had posed and the extent of the disruption caused by its near-collapse.

The AIG episode was a stark reminder of the interconnectedness of the global financial system. The fact that the troubles of a single, albeit massive, company could have such far-reaching consequences was a wake-up call for regulators, policymakers, and market participants alike. It underscored the inherent vulnerabilities within the system, and the need for more robust safeguards against the risks posed by too-big-to-fail institutions.

In the wake of AIG's bailout, the discourse around financial regulation and the responsibility of large financial institutions came under intense scrutiny. The financial markets, having been battered by the fallout of the AIG saga, were now poised to undergo significant transformations. Regulatory bodies and market participants alike braced for a new era, one which was hoped would bring increased transparency, stability, and resilience to the financial markets. The effects of the AIG saga had indeed left an indelible mark on the world's financial landscape, paving the way for a period of change and adaptation.

12.3 Impact on Financial Markets

As the dust began to settle following the AIG bailout and the fall of Lehman Brothers, the impact on the global financial markets was gradually becoming clearer. Banks and financial institutions worldwide had lost billions of dollars, causing a marked downturn in the financial industry and economy as a whole. Lending tightened dramatically as banks became increasingly wary of the potential risks involved. This credit crunch made it exceptionally difficult for businesses and individuals to secure loans, which in turn led to a slowdown in economic activity. As consumer spending declined, many companies faced lower sales and profits, leading to layoffs and further exacerbating the economic downturn.

The turmoil in the financial markets also had profound implications for global trade. With the tightening of credit, it became more difficult for businesses to finance their international trade operations. This led to a decrease in global trade volumes, contributing to the slowdown of economic growth worldwide. The World Trade Organization reported a 12% decline in the volume of world merchandise trade in 2009, the largest decline since World War II. Countries highly dependent on export-led growth, such as China and Germany, were significantly affected by this downturn in trade. Simultaneously, the fallout from the AIG bailout and Lehman Brothers' collapse caused a significant shift in investor sentiment. Confidence in the financial markets plunged, and investors began to question the safety of their investments. This led to a mass sell-off in the stock market, causing stock prices to plummet and wiping out trillions of dollars in wealth. The period from late 2008 to early 2009 was marked by extreme volatility in the stock market, as investors grappled with the uncertainties of the financial crisis.

On the flip side, safe-haven assets such as gold and government bonds experienced a surge in demand. Investors were looking for places to park their money that would provide some measure of security in the face of the financial turmoil. This led to a rise in the prices of these assets, demonstrating the flight to safety behavior that typically occurs during times of financial crisis.

This also meant that the yields on these assets fell, providing lower returns for investors. The bond market, in particular, saw an influx of capital, leading to historically low interest rates that persisted for several years following the crisis.

The financial crisis, precipitated by the fall of Lehman Brothers and the bailout of AIG, resulted in a massive disruption of financial markets. In addition to the stock market plunging and currency volatility, there were far-reaching impacts on commodities, bonds, and other financial instruments. Let's explore these impacts further. As the crisis took hold, demand for commodities plummeted. Prior to the crisis, commodities had been on a bull run, driven by strong demand from emerging economies such as China.

As the crisis set in and global economic activity slowed, demand for commodities fell sharply. Prices for a broad range of commodities from oil to copper took a hit. Countries and companies reliant on commodities exports, particularly in emerging markets, were significantly affected. The drop in commodity prices further exacerbated their economic difficulties.

In the bond markets, the crisis led to a sharp increase in risk premiums, especially for corporate and high-yield bonds. As investors became more risk-averse, they demanded a higher yield to hold these bonds, which pushed their prices down. Credit spreads—the difference in yield between corporate bonds and government bonds—widened dramatically. This made it more expensive for companies to raise capital by issuing bonds, adding to their financial distress. It also triggered an unprecedented level of volatility in financial markets. Financial instruments such as derivatives, which are used to manage risk, saw their values fluctuate wildly as market participants struggled to accurately price in the risks. The CBOE Volatility Index, or VIX, often referred to as the "fear gauge" of the market, spiked to record levels during this time. This high level of volatility made it challenging for market participants to deal with the financial markets, contributing to the sense of panic and confusion.

The market for securitized products, particularly mortgage-backed securities, also suffered a severe blow. These were at the heart of the financial crisis. As defaults on the underlying mortgages increased, the value of these securities fell dramatically. This led to substantial losses for the financial institutions holding them, further shaking confidence in the financial system.

In the aftermath of this widespread turmoil in financial markets, it became glaringly apparent that the regulatory framework at the time was inadequate to prevent such a crisis. The existing system had failed to keep pace with the growing complexity and interconnectedness of financial markets. It had not fully grasped the risks building up in the system, especially in the shadow banking sector, which includes activities such as securitization and money market funds. In the face of these massive market disruptions and their devastating impact on the economy, a major rethinking of financial regulation was clearly required.

In the face of such systemic failure, governments and regulators around the world were impelled to respond, leading to the most significant overhaul of financial regulation since the Great Depression. This regulatory response aimed to address the shortcomings revealed by the crisis and to build a more resilient financial system that could better withstand future shocks. While the specific measures taken varied across countries, they shared a common objective of strengthening the stability and integrity of the financial system.

12.4 Regulatory Response

The worldwide financial crisis prompted a sweeping reform of the regulatory landscape in an effort to prevent such an event from happening again. These changes aimed to address the many deficiencies in the regulatory framework that had been exposed by the crisis. Regulatory authorities took extensive steps to increase oversight, ensure transparency, and promote financial stability.

One of the most significant regulatory responses to the crisis was the passing of the Dodd-Frank Wall Street Reform and Consumer Protection Act in the United States in 2010. This comprehensive legislation included a number of key measures aimed at reducing systemic risk, enhancing transparency, and improving the accountability and governance of financial institutions. Key provisions of the Act included the Volcker Rule, which restricted banks from making certain types of speculative investments, and the creation of the Consumer Financial Protection Bureau, designed to protect consumers in their financial dealings. In addition to Dodd-Frank, the U.S. also introduced the Stress Test (Comprehensive Capital Analysis and Review), which required banks to demonstrate that they would be able to maintain adequate capital levels even under severe economic stress scenarios. This was a significant step towards ensuring the resilience of individual banks and the banking system as a whole.

Europe also saw significant regulatory changes following the crisis. The creation of the European Systemic Risk Board in 2010 was one of the most important steps taken to enhance the regulation of the European financial system. This body was tasked with identifying and monitoring potential threats to financial stability and taking corrective measures when necessary. In response to the weaknesses revealed in the bank capital adequacy rules known as Basel II, the Basel Committee on Banking Supervision developed a new set of guidelines, known as Basel III. These new standards, agreed upon in 2010, sought to enhance the resilience of banks by requiring them to hold more and better-quality capital and to maintain higher levels of liquidity.

These regulatory responses represented a profound shift in the approach to financial regulation, moving away from a narrow focus on the safety and soundness of individual institutions and towards a broader concern with the stability of the financial system as a whole. This new approach, known as macroprudential regulation, recognizes the interconnectedness of financial institutions and markets and the systemic risks that can arise from their collective behavior.

In this vein, regulatory authorities also took steps to improve the oversight and regulation of the shadow banking sector, which had played a key role in the buildup to the crisis. This sector, comprising activities such as securitization, derivatives trading, and money market funds, had largely escaped regulatory scrutiny prior to the crisis. New regulations aimed to increase transparency in this sector and limit its potential to generate systemic risk. In addition to these broad-based reforms, regulators also focused on specific areas of the financial system that had contributed to the crisis. These included efforts to strengthen the regulation and oversight of credit rating agencies, which had come under severe criticism for their role in the crisis. Further, regulators worked to enhance the transparency and oversight of the derivatives market, including the market for credit default swaps, which had been a key factor in the amplification of the crisis.

The regulatory response to the financial crisis was not just about putting new rules in place. It also involved a fundamental rethink of the regulatory philosophy and approach. It represented a shift from a reactive, rules-based approach to a more proactive, principles-based approach, which aimed to identify and mitigate potential risks before they could lead to a crisis. This shift required a significant change in the culture and mindset of regulatory authorities. It necessitated a more forward-looking, risk-focused approach, which considered not just the current state of the financial system but also potential future developments and risks. This new approach involved a more holistic view of the financial system, recognizing the interconnectedness of different parts of the system and the systemic risks that can arise from their collective behavior. An example that further illustrates the regulatory response is the case of the United States and the sweeping reforms enacted by the Dodd-Frank Wall Street Reform and Consumer Protection Act. Prior to the financial crisis, risk-taking by banks and other financial institutions was largely unchecked. This was partly due to the prevailing regulatory philosophy that markets were self-correcting and that financial institutions, especially large ones, were best placed to manage their own risks.

The financial crisis revealed the flaws in this laissez-faire approach.

In response, Dodd-Frank introduced a broad range of reforms aimed at enhancing regulatory oversight and curbing excessive risk-taking. A key aspect of Dodd-Frank was the Volcker Rule, named after former Federal Reserve Chair Paul Volcker. This rule sought to limit speculative trading by banks, a practice that had contributed significantly to the crisis. Under the Volcker Rule, banks were prohibited from engaging in proprietary trading, that is, trading for their own profit rather than on behalf of clients. They were also limited in their ability to own or invest in hedge funds and private equity funds. Dodd-Frank also led to the creation of the Financial Stability Oversight Council (FSOC), a regulatory body tasked with identifying and responding to risks to the financial system as a whole. FSOC was granted the power to designate certain financial institutions as systemically important, meaning that their failure could pose a risk to the entire financial system. These institutions would then be subject to heightened regulatory scrutiny and higher capital requirements.

Another example can be found in the regulatory response in the United Kingdom. The crisis highlighted the problems with the country's tripartite regulatory system, which split responsibilities between the Bank of England, the Financial Services Authority (FSA), and the Treasury. The system was criticised for its lack of clarity and for the gaps in oversight that it allowed. In response, the UK underwent a significant regulatory overhaul. The Financial Services Act 2012 abolished the FSA and replaced it with two new regulatory bodies: the Financial Conduct Authority (FCA) and the Prudential Regulation Authority (PRA). The FCA was tasked with protecting consumers, promoting competition, and ensuring the integrity of the UK's financial markets. The PRA, a part of the Bank of England, was responsible for the prudential regulation of banks, insurers, and large investment firms. This reform sought to create a more effective and accountable regulatory structure.

Similarly, on a global scale, the Basel Committee on Banking Supervision revised its guidelines for bank capital adequacy, stress testing, and market liquidity risk with the introduction of Basel III. This new standard was developed in response to the regulatory deficiencies exposed by the financial crisis. The primary aim of Basel III was to improve the banking sector's ability to absorb shocks from financial and economic stress, improve risk management and governance, and strengthen banks' transparency and disclosures.

While regulatory authorities around the world took steps to strengthen the resilience of the financial system, these efforts were not without challenges. There was a need to balance the goals of financial stability, economic growth, and innovation. Excessive regulation could stifle innovation and economic growth, but inadequate regulation could leave the financial system vulnerable to shocks. Striking the right balance was, and continues to be, a key challenge for regulators. Another major challenge for regulators was the need for international coordination. The financial system is global in nature, and financial crises do not respect national borders. Therefore, effective regulation requires international cooperation.

This can be difficult to achieve given the differing interests and priorities of different countries. The successful implementation of the Basel III standards, for instance, required extensive negotiation and compromise among the member countries of the Basel Committee.

As regulators worked to enhance the stability of the financial system, they also had to deal with the reality that the financial system was changing rapidly. New technologies, such as fintech and blockchain, were transforming the way financial services were delivered, creating new challenges and risks for regulators. Regulators had to ensure that their frameworks were flexible and adaptable enough to keep up with these changes.

Despite these challenges, the regulatory response to the financial crisis marked a significant shift in the approach to financial regulation. It recognised the importance of systemic risk, the interconnectedness of financial institutions and markets, and the need for proactive, risk-focused regulation. While the success of these reforms will only be fully understood in the context of future financial crises, they represent important steps towards a more stable and resilient financial system. Yet, it's worth noting that regulatory responses, while they aim to prevent a recurrence of such a crisis, have to be continuously evaluated and updated. The financial landscape doesn't remain static, and regulations need to keep pace with the evolution of financial markets, products, and innovations. The fallout of Lehman Brothers and AIG had demonstrated that the costs of complacency can be devastating. Thus, the pursuit of a stable, transparent, and resilient financial system remains an ongoing process, adjusting to the ever-changing dynamics of global finance.

This process is informed not only by a deeper understanding of the underlying factors that contributed to the crisis but also a broader appreciation of the role of regulation in fostering financial stability. The experience of the crisis served as a stark reminder of the potential consequences of excessive risk-taking and inadequate oversight. It underscored the importance of robust and effective regulation in maintaining confidence in the financial system and promoting sustainable economic growth. Yet, as we turn our gaze to the future, the inherent complexities and challenges that come with regulating an ever-evolving financial landscape remain. The crisis had far-reaching effects, and in the aftermath, the financial landscape has changed dramatically. The regulatory responses were one part of a broader narrative, yet, there was more to the story. The aftermath and the lessons learned from the fall of Lehman Brothers and AIG carried profound implications for the financial world and beyond, shaping the future course of the global economy.

12.5 Lessons Learned

One of the most significant lessons learned from the fall of Lehman Brothers and the bailout of AIG was the importance of risk management. Prior to the crisis, financial institutions had often taken excessive risks, fuelled by a desire for higher returns and a belief that the good times would continue indefinitely.

The crisis showed that this approach was unsustainable. Financial institutions that had overextended themselves were unable to absorb the shocks when the markets turned against them, leading to a cascading series of failures. Thus, one of the primary lessons of the crisis was the importance of prudent risk management. Financial institutions need to have robust systems in place to identify, measure, and manage their risks. They must also ensure that they have sufficient capital to absorb losses in the event of adverse market movements.

The crisis also underscored the role of regulators in overseeing the financial system and ensuring its stability. Prior to the crisis, regulatory oversight had often been lax, with regulators either unable or unwilling to rein in the excessive risk-taking of financial institutions.

The crisis highlighted the limitations of this approach. Regulators have a crucial role to play in ensuring the stability of the financial system. They need to have the tools and the authority to monitor the activities of financial institutions, intervene when necessary, and impose penalties for non-compliance. Furthermore, the crisis highlighted the interconnectedness of the financial system. The fall of Lehman Brothers and the troubles at AIG were not isolated events; rather, they were part of a broader systemic crisis. Financial institutions are intricately linked, both directly through their financial transactions and indirectly through their exposure to common risks. Therefore, the failure of one institution can quickly spread to others, leading to a systemic crisis. This interconnectedness underscores the importance of macroprudential regulation, which focuses on the stability of the financial system as a whole, rather than just individual institutions.

In addition, the crisis served as a wake-up call about the dangers of financial innovation that is not matched by equivalent advancements in risk management and regulation. Financial engineering had created complex products that were poorly understood by both investors and the institutions themselves. This lack of understanding, combined with inadequate risk management and regulatory oversight, created a "perfect storm" that led to the crisis. Therefore, one of the lessons of the crisis is the need for financial innovation to be accompanied by an understanding of the associated risks and appropriate risk management and regulatory frameworks.

Finally, the crisis demonstrated the vital importance of transparency and trust in the financial system. In the run-up to the crisis, many financial institutions had become increasingly opaque, with complex business models and financial products that were difficult for outsiders to understand. This lack of transparency eroded trust in the financial system, making it more vulnerable to shocks. When the crisis hit, the lack of trust exacerbated the panic, leading to a freeze in many financial markets. Therefore, enhancing transparency and rebuilding trust must be central goals for financial institutions and regulators alike.

13 Post Crisis Recovery

In the aftermath of the financial crisis, the world experienced a period of deep economic recession, with the collapse of major financial institutions and an unprecedented amount of government intervention. The crisis had profound and far-reaching impacts, affecting economies worldwide and reshaping the global financial landscape. Following the crisis, economic recovery was a gradual and at times, a challenging process. As economies around the world attempted to bounce back, they faced a difficult balancing act. On one hand, there was a need to stimulate economic growth and create jobs; on the other, there was a need to ensure financial stability and prevent a similar crisis from happening in the future.

Regulatory changes were a crucial part of this post-crisis environment. In the aftermath of the crisis, regulators worldwide embarked on a major overhaul of financial regulation. This effort was aimed at addressing the shortcomings in the regulatory framework that had been exposed by the crisis and ensuring that financial institutions were better prepared to withstand future shocks. The banking industry, too, faced its own set of challenges and transformations in the post-crisis world. The crisis and the subsequent regulatory changes had far-reaching implications for the banking industry, affecting its business models, its risk management practices, and its relationship with regulators and the public.

While the crisis was a painful experience, it also provided important lessons for policymakers, regulators, financial institutions, and society as a whole. Understanding these lessons and applying them to future practices is key to preventing a similar crisis in the future.

13.1 Economic Recovery

Delving deeper into the period of economic recovery following the financial crisis, it's crucial to understand the myriad of factors that played a role in restoring stability and fostering growth. Following the downturn, economies worldwide sought to recuperate from the damage inflicted and get back on track, a process characterized by varying degrees of success and numerous challenges.

A key driver of this recovery was the implementation of economic stimulus packages. Governments around the world enacted large-scale fiscal measures designed to reignite economic growth and halt the spiral of recession. The United States, for instance, launched the American Recovery and Reinvestment Act of 2009, a historic $787 billion stimulus package. The funds were channeled into various sectors of the economy, including infrastructure, education, health, and renewable energy. The intent was to stimulate spending, bolster job creation, and instill confidence in the economy's ability to rebound. Monetary policy also underwent significant shifts during this period. Central banks across the globe slashed interest rates to record lows and embarked on unconventional measures such as quantitative easing. The goal was to pump money into the economy, promote borrowing, and encourage investment. Quantitative easing, which involved the large-scale purchase of government bonds, served to lower long-term interest rates and ensure the free flow of credit.

These measures provided an essential lifeline for economies mired in recession, but recovery was by no means a swift or linear process. The severity of the financial crisis meant that many economies experienced what is often termed a 'U-shaped' recovery, with a prolonged period of low growth before a gradual upturn. In many cases, GDP growth rates remained below pre-crisis levels for several years, and unemployment rates were slow to fall.

Despite these challenges, the post-crisis period was also one of transformation and resilience. Economies began the arduous task of restructuring, diversifying, and strengthening their economic models. They sought to decrease dependency on certain volatile sectors and instead fostered growth in more sustainable industries. Innovation and technological progress became key drivers of growth during the recovery phase. The advent of the digital age opened up new opportunities for business and consumerism, significantly aiding the recovery process. During the economic recovery, countries also took strides towards enhancing financial inclusion. The financial crisis had underscored the importance of access to reliable financial services for all sections of society. Efforts were made to bridge the gap and ensure that the benefits of economic growth were shared more equitably, which in turn, further fueled economic recovery.

Despite the numerous hurdles, by the mid-2010s, most economies had managed to recover a significant portion of the ground lost during the recession.

The road to complete recovery was long and fraught with challenges. Indeed, the post-crisis recovery period served as a testament to the resilience of economies worldwide, even in the face of the most severe financial crisis since the Great Depression. Economic recovery in the aftermath of the financial crisis was a multi-faceted process that required both an immediate response to the crisis and a more long-term plan for economic stability. One element that served as a significant propeller of growth was the shift towards a more globalized economy. While globalization had been on the rise before the crisis, the post-crisis period saw an even more profound integration of economies worldwide. The proliferation of technology, an increased focus on international trade, and a deeper interconnection of financial markets all contributed to this trend.

The role of innovation was also substantial in stimulating recovery. Technological advancements, particularly in the realm of digital technology, served as a catalyst for economic growth. The digital revolution transformed numerous sectors, ranging from retail to finance, and opened up new avenues for investment and business development. It also spurred consumer spending, which is a significant contributor to GDP growth. Sustainability also became a significant focus during the recovery phase, as the crisis had underscored the pitfalls of unchecked and unsustainable economic practices. Consequently, the push for sustainable and responsible business practices gained momentum. Green investments increased, and more corporations began incorporating sustainability into their business models.

Nevertheless, the process of economic recovery was not without its setbacks. Even as economies clawed their way back to pre-crisis levels, the scars of the financial crisis were evident. For one, income inequality was exacerbated in many countries, causing social and political tensions. Additionally, despite the overall progress, many sectors, particularly those hardest hit by the crisis, struggled to regain their footing.

Despite the challenges, the post-crisis period demonstrated the capacity of economies to adapt, innovate, and recover in the face of adversity. It highlighted the resilience of the global economic system and the potential for transformation in the face of crisis.

As economies experienced the recovery process, it became apparent that a significant part of the solution would involve implementing systemic changes. The crisis had exposed numerous flaws in the existing regulatory framework, highlighting the need for robust and comprehensive regulation. This recognition paved the way for sweeping regulatory changes aimed at strengthening the financial system and preventing a recurrence of such a devastating crisis. In this context, the post-crisis recovery period witnessed a marked shift in the regulatory landscape, reflecting the lessons learned from the crisis.

13.2 Regulatory Changes

The period following the financial crisis witnessed sweeping regulatory changes in response to the weaknesses and gaps in the financial system that the crisis had starkly exposed. The urgency to revamp the financial system's regulation and oversight was keenly felt worldwide, given the broad consensus that lax regulatory oversight had played a significant role in facilitating the crisis.

One of the most profound changes to emerge during this period was the introduction of the Dodd-Frank Wall Street Reform and Consumer Protection Act in the United States in 2010. This piece of legislation was one of the most significant overhauls of financial regulation since the reforms following the Great Depression. The Dodd-Frank Act aimed to reduce various risks in the U.S. financial system by imposing stricter regulations on banks and other financial institutions. It introduced measures to prevent another occurrence of the too-big-to-fail problem by establishing protocols for the orderly liquidation of large failing financial institutions. Furthermore, it increased transparency in derivatives trading, established the Consumer Financial Protection Bureau to protect consumers, and put in place measures to restrict risky trading behaviors.

Simultaneously, across the Atlantic, the European Union also introduced a series of regulatory reforms to strengthen its financial system. These included changes to the capital requirements directive, the introduction of the European Systemic Risk Board for macro-prudential oversight, and a revision of the directive on deposit guarantee schemes. Notably, the concept of macroprudential regulation gained prominence during this period. Unlike micro prudential regulation, which focuses on the safety and soundness of individual financial institutions, macroprudential regulation concerns itself with the stability of the financial system as a whole.

It aims to mitigate systemic risks, i.e., risks that could cause the entire financial system to malfunction. This approach was largely a response to the realization during the financial crisis that systemic risks could emerge from the collective behavior of financial institutions and not merely from the failure of individual ones. In addition to these regulatory changes, the post-crisis period also saw increased scrutiny of the role of credit rating agencies. These agencies had come under heavy criticism during the financial crisis for their role in facilitating the subprime mortgage bubble by assigning overly optimistic ratings to mortgage-backed securities. Therefore, in the wake of the crisis, regulators across the world introduced measures to enhance the transparency and accountability of these agencies.

These sweeping changes weren't without controversy or criticism. The process of regulatory reform was fraught with complexities, involving a careful balancing act between preventing another financial crisis and not stifling economic growth. The reforms raised important questions about regulatory harmonization, especially in an increasingly interconnected global financial system. While the need for regulatory changes was broadly agreed upon, the specifics of what those changes should look like sparked intense debates among policymakers, economists, and industry participants.

The reformation did not solely focus on high-profile measures such as the Dodd-Frank Act or the EU's capital requirements directive. The changes were indeed much more wide-ranging, extending to numerous areas of financial regulation and supervision. In the U.S., the Volcker Rule, part of the Dodd-Frank Act, stood as one of the significant reforms. This rule prohibited banks from conducting certain investment activities with their own accounts and limited their ownership of and relationships with hedge funds and private equity funds. It aimed to restrict risky trading behaviors, considered a contributing factor to the crisis.

It has been contentious since its inception due to concerns about its impact on market liquidity and banks' ability to manage risk.

Another remarkable part of the Dodd-Frank Act was the creation of the Consumer Financial Protection Bureau (CFPB). The CFPB's formation was a response to the crisis-driven recognition that consumer protection had been fragmented and inconsistent across different types of financial products. The CFPB aimed to ensure that all consumers had access to markets for consumer financial products and services and that these markets were fair, transparent, and competitive.

The Basel III international regulatory framework for banks was another cornerstone of the post-crisis regulatory changes. Developed by the Basel Committee on Banking Supervision, Basel III sought to strengthen bank capital requirements and introduce new regulatory requirements on bank liquidity and bank leverage. It required banks to hold more high-quality capital to withstand periods of stress better and reduced the risk of spillover from the financial sector to the real economy.

Similarly, the Financial Stability Board (FSB) was established to coordinate the work of national financial authorities and international standard-setting bodies, developing and promoting the implementation of effective regulatory, supervisory, and other financial sector policies. It aimed to maintain global financial stability by strengthening the financial system and safeguarding against systemic risks. Despite these various regulations and oversight bodies, it is important to note that implementing these regulations did not come without challenges. The regulations have been subjected to much debate, both for their effectiveness and for the burdens they impose on the financial industry. Critics argue that these regulations may have unintended consequences, including inhibiting economic growth and innovation or encouraging risk-taking in unregulated parts of the financial system. The effects of these regulatory changes continue to evolve as the financial industry adjusts to the new regulatory landscape.

These regulatory changes were not uniform worldwide; differences across jurisdictions were pronounced. This discrepancy posed another challenge – ensuring global financial stability in a world of diverse financial systems. Given the global nature of the financial industry, divergent regulatory regimes could lead to regulatory arbitrage, where financial institutions move activities to jurisdictions with less regulation. Therefore, efforts have been made to harmonize regulations across jurisdictions to ensure that all financial centers have robust regulatory regimes.

In conclusion, the post-crisis regulatory changes brought about significant shifts in the way financial institutions and markets operate. While these changes have undoubtedly had a profound impact, the long-term implications of these regulatory reforms continue to be a topic of intense study and debate among policymakers, regulators, and financial industry professionals.

13.3 Impact on Banking

As we cast our eyes over the post-crisis landscape, it is unmistakable that the banking sector was one of the most profoundly affected areas of the economy. The financial crisis brought about significant change in banking, not just in terms of regulatory compliance but also in operational practices, customer relationships, and business models. One of the most immediate impacts was the restructuring of many banks, particularly in countries where the financial crisis hit hardest. A notable number of banks had to be nationalized or received state aid to survive. Others were bought by larger institutions, leading to a wave of consolidation in the banking sector. This consolidation was a direct result of the increased pressure to maintain profitability in the face of higher regulatory capital requirements, increased regulatory costs, and a low-interest-rate environment that compressed net interest margins.

Simultaneously, the increased capital requirements brought about by Basel III and other regulatory reforms made certain business activities less profitable for banks. Traditional banking activities such as lending were affected as higher capital charges made loans more expensive. As a result, banks began to rethink their business models, with some choosing to focus on core banking activities and retrench from riskier lines of business. Some banks shifted from a model of universal banking towards a more focused approach, specializing in certain areas where they could earn a reasonable return on capital.

The increased focus on risk management was another significant change in the banking industry. Prior to the crisis, risk management in many banks was inadequate, with insufficient attention paid to the systemic risks posed by complex financial products and high levels of leverage. The crisis highlighted these shortcomings, prompting banks to invest in more robust risk management systems. Banks today place a much higher emphasis on understanding their risk profile and maintaining adequate capital buffers to absorb potential losses. Furthermore, the crisis changed the way banks interacted with their customers. Trust in banks declined significantly during the crisis, as many customers felt let down by the financial industry. Banks had to work hard to regain this trust, with many focusing on improving their customer service and transparency. Some banks introduced more customer-friendly products, made efforts to simplify their fee structures, or focused on responsible lending practices to regain customer confidence.

The post-crisis period also witnessed the rise of digital banking and fintech companies. With the increased regulatory scrutiny and cost, and decreased trust in traditional banking, the stage was set for disruptive innovation. The emergence of new technologies provided an opportunity for fintech companies to challenge traditional banks, particularly in areas such as payments, lending, and wealth management. These companies, unburdened by legacy systems and high regulatory costs, were able to offer innovative, user-friendly services that attracted many customers. In response, many banks had to accelerate their digital transformation initiatives to keep up with these new competitors. The impact on the banking sector post-crisis is multifaceted, extending far beyond increased regulation. The changes have reshaped the sector, forcing banks to reassess and adjust their strategies. The industry is undoubtedly more resilient and better capitalized than before the crisis, but it is also grappling with new challenges such as increased competition from fintech companies, low-interest rates, and the ongoing need to restore trust with the public. The interplay of these factors continues to define the trajectory of the banking sector in the post-crisis era.

In this ongoing transformation of the banking sector, understanding the intricacies is crucial. When looking at the operational landscape of banking, one can observe a greater level of stringency in operational procedures, risk management, and compliance practices. Banks have had to dramatically enhance their operational resilience, risk monitoring, and stress testing capabilities to mitigate the risk of future crises. For instance, stress testing became a cornerstone of bank regulation in the aftermath of the crisis, helping institutions and regulators assess the potential impact of adverse economic scenarios on a bank's capital position. From an investment perspective, banks have been prompted to apply a more rigorous and discerning approach towards their portfolio management. Prior to the crisis, investment decisions were often overly reliant on credit rating agencies' assessments.

The crisis highlighted the limitations of this approach, with many highly-rated securities suffering significant losses. In response, banks have been incentivized to strengthen their own credit assessment capabilities and to diversify their investments to manage risk better.

Another key area that experienced significant change is the lending landscape. Before the crisis, credit was readily available, and lending standards were often lax. In the aftermath of the crisis, banks tightened their credit standards, scrutinizing borrowers more carefully and demanding higher levels of collateral. Consumer lending and mortgage lending, in particular, saw significant changes. Lenders implemented more stringent underwriting standards and verification processes to ensure borrowers could afford the loans they were taking on.

The increased regulation also had a profound impact on the profitability and efficiency of banks. Higher capital and liquidity requirements, as well as stricter oversight, have led to higher costs and reduced returns for many banking activities. To adapt to this new reality, banks had to reassess their business models and look for new avenues for growth. They explored opportunities in emerging markets, leveraged technology to improve efficiency, and developed new services to generate fee income.

Despite these challenges, many banks managed to craft the new landscape successfully, adjusting their operations to comply with new regulations, streamlining their businesses to improve efficiency, and embracing technology to meet changing customer expectations. The shift toward digital channels has been particularly noteworthy. Many traditional banks accelerated their digital transformation efforts, developing mobile apps, online platforms, and other digital services to compete with fintech startups. This digital transition was not without its challenges, but it also presented significant opportunities for banks to improve their customer service, operational efficiency, and competitiveness. Yet, the technological shift also amplified cybersecurity risks, forcing banks to significantly ramp up their investments in cybersecurity measures to protect their systems and customer data. In the era of digital banking, cyber threats have become one of the most significant challenges, adding another layer to the already complex regulatory and operational environment.

In essence, the impact of the financial crisis on banking can be seen as a catalyst for a more robust, risk-aware, customer-centric, and technologically adept banking system. The transformative effects are still being felt, continually reshaping the sector and challenging its participants to adapt. The post-crisis banking environment remains complex and challenging, but these challenges also present opportunities for banks to evolve and improve.

14 The Rise of Cryptocurrencies

As we continue our exploration of modern financial history, it is impossible to overlook the dramatic influence of one particularly disruptive innovation: the rise of cryptocurrencies. Cryptocurrencies, digital or virtual currencies that utilize cryptography for security, have carved out a unique niche within the financial sector, with their potential to radically alter the ways in which we conduct transactions and store value. The story of cryptocurrencies begins with Bitcoin, a pioneering digital asset that introduced the world to the concept of decentralized finance and blockchain technology. The emergence of Bitcoin in 2008, amid the chaos of the global financial crisis, marked a paradigm shift that has had significant implications for traditional finance and beyond.

Since Bitcoin's inception, the cryptocurrency market has seen explosive growth, leading to the emergence of a new digital economy. Thousands of cryptocurrencies now exist, each with its unique characteristics and purposes. This surge of digital currencies has paved the way for a new financial landscape where decentralization, peer-to-peer transactions, and digital assets become a norm. The impact of cryptocurrencies on the financial landscape has been profound. By offering faster, cheaper, and more transparent transactions, they pose a significant challenge to traditional banking and financial systems. The promise of financial inclusion, privacy, and control over one's assets has attracted millions of users worldwide, prompting a lively discussion about the future of finance.

The rise of cryptocurrencies has also brought significant challenges, particularly in terms of regulation. As cryptocurrencies operate outside traditional financial systems, they pose a range of issues concerning consumer protection, financial stability, and legal jurisdiction, among others. Striking a balance between innovation and regulation has thus become a crucial issue for policymakers.

Looking into the future, cryptocurrencies represent a dynamic and promising field, albeit one filled with uncertainty. Whether cryptocurrencies will fully integrate into our financial system or remain a fringe element is still unknown, but their rise undeniably marks a significant chapter in our financial history.

14.1 Birth of Bitcoin

The genesis of Bitcoin can be traced back to a nine-page document known as the "Bitcoin: A Peer-to-Peer Electronic Cash System" white paper, published by an unknown person or group of people using the pseudonym Satoshi Nakamoto in October 2008. This white paper laid the foundation for a revolutionary new technology that proposed a system for electronic transactions without relying on trust or the need for a financial institution acting as an intermediary. Bitcoin was designed as a decentralized system, underpinned by a public ledger known as the blockchain. Blockchain technology allowed for transactions to be verified by a network of computers (or nodes) rather than a central authority, solving the double-spending problem that had previously hampered other attempts at creating digital money. This innovative technology ensured that every single transaction made with Bitcoin is recorded and verified, ensuring its security and transparency.

Bitcoin's operation relies on miners, who use powerful computers to solve complex mathematical problems. These problems are essentially the locks that secure each block of transactions in the blockchain. Miners compete to solve these problems, and the first to succeed is rewarded with a set amount of Bitcoin, incentivizing the maintenance and security of the system. This process also introduces new Bitcoins into the system, mimicking the process of mining for gold, hence the term "mining." Bitcoin was more than just a technological innovation; it was a reaction to the traditional financial system and the control it wielded. The timing of Bitcoin's emergence, amid the 2008 financial crisis, is no coincidence. Many perceived Bitcoin as an alternative to the mainstream financial system that had failed them. It was an answer to the problem of centralized control and trust, which had led to the crisis in the first place. It's worth noting that in the early days of Bitcoin, it wasn't the valuable asset it is today.

In fact, the first real-world Bitcoin transaction was for a pizza purchase in May 2010, where a man in Florida paid 10,000 Bitcoins for two pizzas. This event is now celebrated in the cryptocurrency community as 'Bitcoin Pizza Day.' At the time, those Bitcoins were worth about $41. Today, they would be worth millions.

Early adopters and believers in the technology's potential started investing and trading in Bitcoin, leading to the emergence of the first cryptocurrency exchanges. The introduction of these exchanges facilitated a wider reach and acceptance of Bitcoin, driving its growth and influence. Bitcoin's popularity skyrocketed, and its price along with it. The idea of a decentralized currency, free from government control, had captivated the world, and Bitcoin was on its way to becoming a phenomenon in the financial industry. As Bitcoin began to grow in value and recognition, so too did the community around it. Software developers, cryptography enthusiasts, libertarians, and early tech adopters were among the first to engage with Bitcoin. They were attracted by its promise of decentralization, its technological innovation, or its potential for financial gain. The development of Bitcoin's underlying technology, blockchain, was driven by a dedicated open-source community. This community played a vital role in refining and improving the Bitcoin software, contributing to its stability and security.

A key event that helped galvanize the Bitcoin community was the establishment of the Bitcoin Foundation in 2012. The Foundation aimed to promote Bitcoin, drive its adoption, and shape the narrative around it. This helped create a more organized structure for the community and allowed for more concerted efforts to promote and improve Bitcoin. Despite its growth and popularity, Bitcoin faced numerous challenges during its initial years. One of the biggest of these was the infamous Mt. Gox incident. Mt. Gox, once the largest Bitcoin exchange in the world, filed for bankruptcy in 2014 after losing approximately 850,000 Bitcoins, valued at around $450 million at that time. This was due to a hack that exploited a flaw in the Mt. Gox security system. The Mt. Gox incident shook the Bitcoin community, leading to a severe drop in Bitcoin's price and casting doubt on the security and viability of Bitcoin.

Another challenge Bitcoin faced was its association with illicit activities. Due to its anonymous nature, Bitcoin became the preferred mode of transaction on the Dark Web, a part of the internet not indexed by traditional search engines and known for hosting illegal activities. The most infamous example was the Silk Road, an online marketplace primarily used for selling illegal drugs. Bitcoin was the currency of choice for transactions on the Silk Road, which drew the attention of law enforcement agencies and tarnished Bitcoin's image in the public eye.

Despite these setbacks, Bitcoin continued to grow and evolve. These challenges acted as catalysts, prompting the Bitcoin community to improve security measures, develop better trading platforms, and work towards enhancing the public perception of Bitcoin. Bitcoin's resilience in the face of adversity only underscored its potential to disrupt traditional financial systems and solidified its position as a groundbreaking technology. Today, Bitcoin has grown far beyond its humble beginnings and has set the stage for a new era of digital currencies.

14.2 Growth of Cryptocurrencies

Following Bitcoin's inception, the world of cryptocurrencies exploded into a landscape of innovation and diversity. Bitcoin had proven that it was possible to create a decentralized digital currency that operates independently of traditional financial institutions. This concept was then adopted and adapted by countless developers and innovators, giving birth to thousands of different cryptocurrencies, each with their own unique features and functions.

One of the first significant cryptocurrencies to emerge after Bitcoin was Litecoin. Created by Charlie Lee in 2011, Litecoin was designed to provide faster transaction confirmations and a different hashing algorithm. It was often described as silver to Bitcoin's gold. Although Litecoin was closely based on Bitcoin, it demonstrated that it was possible to create new cryptocurrencies by making small changes to Bitcoin's open-source code. This opened the floodgates for the creation of countless other cryptocurrencies. Another milestone in the growth of cryptocurrencies was the creation of Ethereum in 2015. While Bitcoin was created as a form of digital money, Ethereum expanded the potential uses of blockchain technology. It introduced the concept of smart contracts, which are self-executing contracts with the terms of the agreement directly written into lines of code. Ethereum also made it easier for developers to create their own decentralized applications (dApps) and even their own tokens, leading to the ICO (Initial Coin Offering) boom of 2017.

The ICO boom was a pivotal event in the growth of cryptocurrencies. It was during this period that thousands of new cryptocurrencies were created, as any project or company could now easily issue their own token to raise funds. While this led to an unprecedented surge in the number and value of cryptocurrencies, it also resulted in many scams and fraudulent projects. The ICO boom and subsequent crash served as a harsh lesson about the dangers of unregulated markets and the importance of investor protection.

It also led to increased attention from regulators and helped pave the way for more structured and regulated forms of token offerings, such as Security Token Offerings (STOs) and Initial Exchange Offerings (IEOs). Throughout this period, the value of cryptocurrencies fluctuated wildly, with periods of rapid growth followed by sharp crashes. For instance, the price of Bitcoin soared from around $1,000 at the beginning of 2017 to nearly $20,000 by the end of the same year, before falling back to around $3,000 in 2018. Despite these fluctuations, the overall trend has been one of significant growth. As of today, the total market capitalization of all cryptocurrencies combined is in the trillions of dollars, a far cry from the modest beginnings of Bitcoin. Despite the growing pains and volatile market fluctuations, the growth of cryptocurrencies represents a significant shift in the way individuals and organizations approach finance and investment.

As the sector matured, institutional investors began to take notice. The potential of blockchain technology's immutability, transparency, and efficiency became increasingly attractive to traditional financial institutions, which began to invest in and adopt blockchain-based solutions.

The meteoric rise of cryptocurrencies also prompted technological innovation. Many new projects emerged, each seeking to address perceived limitations in the design and functionality of earlier cryptocurrencies. For instance, cryptocurrencies like Monero and ZCash were created with a focus on enhanced privacy and anonymity, responding to criticisms that Bitcoin transactions could be traced by determined attackers. In contrast, others like Ripple targeted the realm of international financial transactions, aiming to streamline and expedite cross-border money transfers.

Another notable development in the cryptocurrency world was the birth of stablecoins - cryptocurrencies designed to minimize volatility. Stablecoins are typically pegged to a reserve of stable assets, such as fiat currencies like the US Dollar, or commodities like gold. Examples include Tether (USDT), which claims to be backed 1:1 by US dollars, and DAI, a decentralized stablecoin whose value is maintained through a system of smart contracts on the Ethereum blockchain. Stablecoins play a crucial role in the cryptocurrency ecosystem, providing a haven during periods of volatility and a medium of exchange for trading pairs on cryptocurrency exchanges. Additionally, the DeFi, or decentralized finance, movement represents one of the most exciting developments in the growth of cryptocurrencies. DeFi applications aim to recreate traditional financial systems, such as loans, insurance, and derivatives, in a decentralized manner, removing the need for intermediaries like banks. Built primarily on Ethereum, DeFi projects utilize the network's smart contract functionality to create automated, transparent financial services accessible to anyone in the world with an internet connection.

Through all these developments, it's evident that the growth of cryptocurrencies has far outpaced the simple creation of new digital assets. Cryptocurrencies have become an entirely new asset class, with a complex ecosystem of interconnected technologies and services. From being an esoteric interest for a small group of enthusiasts, cryptocurrencies have become a significant factor in global financial systems, impacting everything from personal finance to international money transfer and complex financial instruments.

Lastly, it's important to note that the growth of cryptocurrencies has not been confined to the realm of finance. The underlying blockchain technology has found uses in diverse sectors like supply chain management, healthcare, and digital identity verification. The growth of cryptocurrencies, therefore, represents not just a rise in new forms of digital money but an expansion of a groundbreaking technology into many different aspects of society.

14.3 Impact on Finance

Cryptocurrencies, as a radical innovation in the financial world, have brought significant disruptions to traditional finance. Bitcoin and other digital currencies have presented themselves not just as a new asset class, but also as a transformative force that challenges traditional notions of money, exchange, and financial intermediation. This transformation is manifested in various aspects of finance, which has led to a comprehensive rethinking of established systems and practices.

For one, cryptocurrencies have introduced an entirely new form of investment, with the promise of astronomical returns enticing both individual and institutional investors. Bitcoin's phenomenal rise in value over its relatively short life has created stories of "Bitcoin millionaires" who were early adopters of the cryptocurrency. The trend has seen even conservative investors devoting a portion of their portfolios to cryptocurrencies, aiming to cash in on the volatility and potential upside while hedging against risks in more traditional asset classes. This new investment avenue has widened the diversity of assets available to investors and added a new dimension to portfolio management. Additionally, cryptocurrencies and blockchain technology have stimulated the birth of a new financial system that operates in parallel to the traditional one - the world of decentralized finance, or DeFi. This system operates entirely on blockchain technology, offering services such as lending, borrowing, trading, yield farming, and more. DeFi platforms have the potential to democratize finance, allowing anyone with a smartphone and internet connection to participate in financial activities that were once the exclusive domain of banks and other financial institutions. This development is gradually pushing the financial sector towards a more inclusive and equitable form.

Cryptocurrencies have also posed a significant challenge to the global payments system. With Bitcoin and other cryptocurrencies, it's possible to send money across the globe in minutes, bypassing the traditional banking system with its associated fees and delays. The potential of cryptocurrencies for remittances and international money transfers has put significant pressure on banks and other financial institutions to innovate and improve their services. The introduction of Initial Coin Offerings (ICOs) as a new form of fundraising has also revolutionized the finance sector. Startups and projects can now raise funds by issuing their own tokens, circumventing traditional venture capital and crowdfunding channels. This method provides an avenue for projects to access global capital and for investors to participate in early-stage investment opportunities.

The lack of regulation has also led to numerous scams and failures, necessitating caution from investors and scrutiny from regulators.

While the scope of cryptocurrencies' impact on finance is extensive, it also warrants closer examination. The disruption caused by cryptocurrencies is not uniform; instead, it varies across different spheres and degrees of finance. First, on an individual level, cryptocurrencies have introduced an alternative to traditional banking, especially in regions with limited access to such services. They offer a unique way to store, manage, and transfer funds that's not reliant on traditional financial institutions. For instance, unbanked or underbanked individuals in developing countries can use Bitcoin and other digital currencies to participate in the global economy, bypassing the need for a conventional bank account. Furthermore, the ability of cryptocurrencies to preserve value in times of economic instability has made them particularly appealing in countries grappling with hyperinflation or economic crises.

In the realm of businesses and corporations, cryptocurrencies are increasingly being recognized as a legitimate form of payment. Several major companies around the world now accept Bitcoin and other digital currencies as a payment option, further solidifying their place in the financial landscape. This development is indicative of the shift in perception of cryptocurrencies from a speculative asset to a valid medium of exchange.

In the investment landscape, cryptocurrencies have created an entirely new asset class. With their distinct risk and return characteristics, cryptocurrencies offer diversification benefits in the context of an investment portfolio. Furthermore, the creation of various crypto-assets such as altcoins, stablecoins, and tokenized securities has opened new investment and trading opportunities, with potential for high returns albeit with a high degree of risk.

Beyond the realms of individual finance, business transactions, and investments, cryptocurrencies also promise profound changes in the financial infrastructure itself. Blockchain, the underlying technology of cryptocurrencies, offers prospects for unprecedented transparency, security, and efficiency in financial transactions. Its decentralized nature challenges the current paradigm of a centralized financial system, suggesting possibilities for a more inclusive and democratic financial landscape.

Despite their transformative potential, cryptocurrencies have also invited a fair share of criticism and skepticism. Concerns around their volatility, their use in illicit activities, the environmental impact of mining activities, and their potential to destabilize the financial system have cast a shadow over their promise. These challenges necessitate careful consideration and balanced perspectives when assessing the impact of cryptocurrencies on finance.

The vast and varied impact of cryptocurrencies on finance is undeniable. It spans across different spheres of finance, altering the way we conceive of and interact with money and financial services.

14.4 Regulatory Challenges

As the world grapples with the unprecedented changes brought about by cryptocurrencies, one of the most pressing issues is the challenge of regulation. Cryptocurrencies present a unique set of regulatory challenges due to their decentralized, anonymous, and transnational nature. Regulatory authorities around the world are attempting to strike a balance between facilitating innovation, protecting consumers and investors, and preventing illicit activities. The lack of a central governing body for cryptocurrencies complicates the development of regulatory frameworks. The decentralized nature of cryptocurrencies means that they operate outside of traditional banking and monetary systems, making them difficult to regulate using existing laws and regulations.

The anonymity provided by cryptocurrencies is another significant regulatory challenge. While privacy is one of the selling points of cryptocurrencies, it also allows for their use in illicit activities such as money laundering, terrorism financing, and tax evasion. As such, regulators are grappling with how to prevent the misuse of cryptocurrencies while respecting privacy rights. The transnational nature of cryptocurrencies poses jurisdictional challenges. Cryptocurrencies operate on a global scale, beyond the confines of national borders. This means that any effective regulatory framework would likely need international cooperation. Countries have divergent views and approaches to cryptocurrency regulation, ranging from outright bans to full acceptance.

The volatility and risk associated with cryptocurrencies add another layer to their regulatory challenges. Price swings can be severe, and the lack of investor protection mechanisms in the cryptocurrency market exposes investors to potential significant losses. Regulators must find ways to protect investors without stifling the innovation that cryptocurrencies bring to the financial sector.

Regulatory inconsistencies also pose a challenge. In the absence of uniform global regulation, regulatory arbitrage may occur, where entities choose to operate in jurisdictions with less stringent regulations. This could potentially lead to a "race to the bottom," where countries lower their regulatory standards to attract cryptocurrency businesses.

Given the recent development of this technology and the constant innovation in the field, it is a daunting task for regulators and policymakers to fully comprehend the intricacies of blockchain technology and the multitude of cryptocurrencies that exist today. This limited understanding hampers the ability of these bodies to create effective and appropriate regulatory frameworks.

Furthermore, the unique features of cryptocurrencies bring forth novel legal and regulatory questions. For instance, how should cryptocurrencies be classified for regulatory purposes? Are they currencies, commodities, securities, or a new asset class altogether? Different jurisdictions have given different answers to these questions. The U.S. Commodity Futures Trading Commission views Bitcoin as a commodity, while the U.S. Internal Revenue Service treats it as property for taxation purposes. Meanwhile, in the European Union, Bitcoin is recognized as a currency. This lack of uniformity in the classification of cryptocurrencies further complicates regulatory efforts.

Enforcement of regulations is yet another challenge. Even if regulatory frameworks are developed, enforcing them on a decentralized and anonymous system is a formidable task. Traditional enforcement mechanisms often rely on central intermediaries, such as banks, which can provide information about transactions and parties involved.

In a cryptocurrency system where transactions are peer-to-peer and parties can remain anonymous, these traditional enforcement methods are not effective. Regulators need to find new methods of enforcement that are suited to the decentralized and anonymous nature of cryptocurrencies. In addition, the rapid pace of innovation in the cryptocurrency space could potentially render regulations obsolete shortly after they are enacted. New developments such as Decentralized Finance (DeFi) platforms, Non-Fungible Tokens (NFTs), and the proliferation of new cryptocurrencies present new challenges that regulators must keep up with. This constant game of catch-up poses significant challenges to regulatory bodies attempting to create comprehensive and effective regulations.

Lastly, it's important to note the risk of over-regulation. While it is crucial to have regulations in place to prevent misuse and protect consumers and investors, over-regulation could potentially stifle innovation. Policymakers must be careful to strike the right balance between regulation and innovation. Overly stringent regulations could hinder the development of new technologies and services in the cryptocurrency space, depriving society of their potential benefits.

Despite these myriad challenges, the importance of effective cryptocurrency regulation cannot be understated. The potential of cryptocurrencies to revolutionize finance and commerce makes it crucial for regulatory bodies to rise to the challenge and create thoughtful, effective, and adaptable regulations that can protect consumers and investors while still fostering innovation.

14.5 Future of Cryptocurrencies

The rapid growth of cryptocurrencies and their increasing acceptance points to an environment where they may become an integral part of the global financial ecosystem.

The use of cryptocurrencies for everyday transactions is expected to increase as more businesses and service providers begin to accept them as payment. Already, large corporations like Microsoft and Tesla have made headlines for their acceptance of Bitcoin, and many small and medium-sized businesses are following suit. With the development of more efficient and user-friendly payment processing systems for cryptocurrencies, it is likely that the trend of increased acceptance will continue.

Cryptocurrencies could also play a crucial role in remittances and cross-border transactions. As it stands, sending money across borders can be a costly and time-consuming process. Cryptocurrencies could revolutionize this process by providing a faster, cheaper, and more efficient means of transferring money across borders. Remittance services using cryptocurrencies have already begun to emerge and have seen significant success, particularly in regions like Sub-Saharan Africa where traditional banking services are less prevalent. We may also see increased integration of cryptocurrencies into traditional financial systems. As cryptocurrencies gain acceptance, traditional financial institutions may begin to offer cryptocurrency-related services. This could include things like cryptocurrency checking and savings accounts, loans in cryptocurrency, or even cryptocurrency credit cards. Some major banks have already begun to explore these services. This integration could go a long way in enhancing the credibility of cryptocurrencies and fostering their widespread adoption.

In terms of investment, cryptocurrencies are likely to continue to attract attention as a speculative asset due to their volatility. As more people become aware of cryptocurrencies, it is expected that a larger pool of investors will be interested in investing in them. With the development of more sophisticated cryptocurrency investment products, such as cryptocurrency ETFs and mutual funds, investing in cryptocurrencies may become more accessible to the general public.

As cryptocurrencies continue to grow and develop, it is likely that they will face increased regulatory scrutiny. As previously discussed, regulating cryptocurrencies is a complex task due to their decentralized and often anonymous nature.

The potential for misuse of cryptocurrencies for illicit activities like money laundering and fraud makes it likely that regulators will continue to strive to develop effective regulatory frameworks for cryptocurrencies. It remains to be seen how these regulatory efforts will shape the future of cryptocurrencies.

It is important to note that while the future of cryptocurrencies appears promising, it is also uncertain. Cryptocurrencies are a relatively new phenomenon, and the market is highly volatile. Future growth will depend on a variety of factors, including technological advancements, regulatory decisions, and market demand.

15 Wall Street and Silicon Valley

The rapid advances in technology over the past few decades have reshaped many aspects of our lives, including the way we interact with financial systems. In particular, two giants of the American economy, Wall Street and Silicon Valley, find themselves at a fascinating intersection. These two entities, one representing the financial capital of the world and the other the hub of technological innovation, are increasingly converging in unexpected ways, fostering a unique and dynamic relationship. Wall Street, the traditional powerhouse of finance, is increasingly relying on the innovation and technological prowess of Silicon Valley to maintain competitiveness and achieve growth. Conversely, Silicon Valley, the epicenter of global tech innovation, has been seeking the vast capital and regulatory experience of Wall Street to streamline the highly regulated and complex world of finance.

As these two titans continue to intertwine, there are bound to be collaborative endeavors and conflicts. We will witness instances of brilliant cooperation where technology and finance merge seamlessly to create better financial products and services. Simultaneously, tensions may surface as two different cultures with distinct perspectives grapple with diverging interests and visions about the future of finance. The interactions between Wall Street and Silicon Valley have significant implications for the global financial landscape. The blend of technology and finance, often referred to as "fintech," is a booming field with a potential to revolutionize traditional banking and financial services. This trend is ushering in an era of robo-advisors, algorithmic trading, mobile banking, peer-to-peer lending platforms, and blockchain applications, all altering the face of finance.

This fusion of technology and finance offers both opportunities and challenges. We are presented with the prospect of greater efficiency, accessibility, and personalization in financial services. Yet, there are also potential pitfalls, including new kinds of risks and disruptions, not to mention the complications arising from regulation and oversight.

15.1 Interactions

At the intersection of Wall Street and Silicon Valley lies a tapestry of intricate interactions that has altered the traditional financial ecosystem. Each has its strengths; Wall Street has its roots in robust financial systems and deep expertise, while Silicon Valley is synonymous with technological innovation and disruption. It's through these combined strengths that the landscape of the financial industry is being radically reshaped.

The relationship between Wall Street and Silicon Valley, initially built on investments in technology companies, has become increasingly complex over time. In the early days, Wall Street, the monolith of the global financial system, viewed technology as an auxiliary tool to streamline operations and facilitate transactions. Investment banks, brokerage firms, and financial service companies sought the services of technology firms to improve their trading systems, data management, and customer interfaces. This early interaction planted the seeds for more profound and symbiotic relationships. As technology advanced, Silicon Valley started to develop financial products of its own, thus venturing into what was once Wall Street's exclusive domain. The birth of fintech companies like PayPal marked the beginning of this transformation. PayPal's success in creating an online payments system sent a clear message: technology could not only assist traditional financial services but could also invent entirely new ones.

On the flip side, Wall Street began to recognize the value of integrating technology into its core operations beyond just using it as a supportive tool. The rise of algorithmic trading, high-frequency trading, and robo-advisors provided Wall Street firms with an edge that was hard to ignore. These advances helped firms analyze vast amounts of data at lightning speed, execute trades more efficiently, and offer personalized financial advice at a lower cost.

This intricate dance between Wall Street and Silicon Valley extended beyond the operational aspect of finance. Venture capital investments from Wall Street into tech startups began to increase, and Silicon Valley began to see Wall Street as not just a customer or competitor, but also a vital funding source. The Initial Public Offering (IPO) of tech companies became a common trend, further cementing the ties between Wall Street's financial might and Silicon Valley's technological prowess. Today, the interaction between Wall Street and Silicon Valley is more profound than ever. Both sectors have started to realize the importance of each other's role in the modern financial landscape. While they operate in different spheres, their shared interests in leveraging technology and capital have created a compelling dynamic that is reshaping the financial world. This convergence is likely to intensify in the years to come as technology continues to disrupt traditional financial models and as Wall Street seeks to harness this disruption to its advantage.

Technological innovation has emerged as an undeniable driving force within the financial sector. From the days of ticker tapes and telephones to the current age of algorithmic trading and blockchain technology, the march of progress has been relentless. Wall Street, with its long history and ingrained systems, initially faced difficulty in adapting to these changes. In contrast, Silicon Valley, the cradle of these innovative technologies, was quick to embrace and leverage these developments. This dynamic has led to a fascinating exchange of ideas and methodologies between the two sectors. Wall Street's rigorous regulatory environment and risk-averse nature have inspired a more cautious approach to technological innovation within the financial industry. Silicon Valley, known for its "move fast and break things" philosophy, has had to learn to consider the intricate and regulated world of finance. This has resulted in a certain level of restraint and maturity in Silicon Valley's approach towards financial technology innovation.

In return, Silicon Valley's relentless drive towards innovation has pushed Wall Street to step out of its comfort zone. Traditional financial institutions have had to rethink their operations to stay competitive in the face of disruptive technologies. This need for change was further accelerated by the financial crisis of 2008, which shook public trust in traditional financial institutions and opened the door for tech-based alternatives to banking and financial services. As these traditional financial institutions began to invest more heavily in technology, we witnessed a surge in the demand for tech talent within Wall Street. Firms started recruiting from technology companies and prestigious computer science programs to bolster their technological capabilities. Meanwhile, Silicon Valley companies began to tap into the expertise of financial professionals to streamline the complex and heavily regulated world of finance.

The widespread adoption of machine learning and artificial intelligence in financial analytics is a prime example of this blend of Wall Street and Silicon Valley cultures. Algorithmic trading, credit risk modeling, fraud detection, and customer service automation are just a few areas where these technologies have made significant inroads.

The emergence of blockchain technology and cryptocurrencies, predominantly a Silicon Valley innovation, has been another transformative force within the financial industry. Wall Street has been exploring the potential applications of blockchain in areas like clearing and settlement processes, trade finance, and identity verification.

In essence, the interactions between Wall Street and Silicon Valley have extended well beyond mere transactions or competition. The two are now deeply intertwined, with each shaping the other's future. This interplay of finance and technology promises to push the boundaries of innovation and drive the financial industry towards a more efficient, inclusive, and resilient future.

15.2 Collaborations

Transitioning from interactions, it is also crucial to illuminate the pivotal role of collaborations between Wall Street and Silicon Valley. These collaborations have birthed new avenues for growth, improved customer experience, and led to significant technological advancements in the financial industry.

In an age where technology and finance have become inseparable, collaborations are a necessity, not a luxury. As financial institutions seek to embrace the digital revolution, they often turn to tech companies for their expertise and innovative solutions. Similarly, tech companies entering the finance industry often collaborate with established financial institutions to understand the complexities of financial regulations and gain customer trust.

One of the early and successful examples of such collaboration was the partnership between Apple Inc. and Goldman Sachs. This alliance led to the birth of the Apple Card, a credit card that symbolized a major shift in the banking sector. It represented an amalgamation of the cutting-edge technology provided by Apple and the banking expertise of Goldman Sachs. The Apple Card's simplistic application process, real-time fraud protection, and visual spending summaries were a fresh departure from traditional credit card offerings, reflecting Silicon Valley's user-centric design philosophy. Collaborations in the realm of fintech have also led to the rise of robo-advisors, which have significantly democratized access to investment advisory services. Companies like Betterment and Wealthfront, working closely with Wall Street, have utilized machine learning algorithms to offer personalized investment advice at a fraction of the traditional cost. This collaborative venture marked an important step towards the goal of financial inclusion.

The payments sector has seen a similar influx of collaborations, perhaps the most notable one being between J.P. Morgan and PayPal.

The partnership allowed Chase customers to add their credit and debit cards to their PayPal accounts, essentially integrating a banking giant with a leader in digital payments.

Another collaborative stride has been in the field of blockchain technology. Wall Street firms have been teaming up with tech companies to explore the potential of blockchain in improving efficiency and transparency. The creation of R3, a consortium of over 200 financial institutions, and tech companies is an excellent example of collaborative efforts to design and apply blockchain technology across the financial industry.

Not all collaborations have been between large organizations. Wall Street firms have also been collaborating with fintech startups to boost their digital offerings. In return, these startups gain a reputable partner, access to a vast customer base, and the expertise to deal with regulatory hurdles. This symbiotic relationship is a driving force for innovation in the financial industry.

In essence, collaborations between Wall Street and Silicon Valley have become a cornerstone of the evolving financial landscape. These partnerships are shaping a future where finance and technology are even more seamlessly intertwined, delivering superior customer experiences, and ushering in a new era of financial services. The exploration of these collaborations indeed warrants a closer look, as it provides a window into the future of the financial world.

15.3 Conflicts

Though collaborations between Wall Street and Silicon Valley have yielded many successful ventures, the relationship between these two powerful sectors is not without its frictions and conflicts. Despite the obvious synergies and mutual benefits, a number of clashes have emerged, as these two realms, with their distinct cultures, regulatory landscapes, and business models, try to find common ground.

One of the most notable conflicts is rooted in the difference in pace and approach to innovation. Wall Street, due to its regulatory constraints and conservative nature, is often cautious and slow in adopting new technologies. Silicon Valley, on the other hand, is renowned for its rapid innovation and disruptive mindset - encapsulated in the mantra "move fast and break things." This difference in philosophy often leads to tensions when these sectors attempt to work together.

The tensions are also exacerbated by the competition for talent. Silicon Valley's reputation for innovation, along with the promise of substantial rewards in successful startups, has made it a magnet for top talent. Wall Street, with its more traditional and formal work environment, has often struggled to attract the same caliber of technologists, data scientists, and engineers. The battle for talent is an ongoing source of conflict between these two worlds.

Regulation has been another focal point of contention. The financial sector is one of the most heavily regulated industries in the world, and for good reason, given the potential for systemic risks.

Tech companies have often chafed against these regulations, viewing them as impediments to innovation and growth. Regulatory arbitrage has emerged as tech firms find ways to offer financial services while avoiding the full scope of financial regulations - a practice that has provoked the ire of traditional financial institutions.

A notable example of such conflict was the standoff between Facebook and financial regulators worldwide over the proposed launch of its cryptocurrency, Libra. While Facebook viewed Libra as an innovative way to enable global financial inclusion, regulators and financial institutions saw it as a potential threat to monetary stability and a way for the tech giant to avoid financial regulation. Further, the two sectors often find themselves at odds over issues of privacy and data security. Tech companies have thrived on the commoditization of user data, utilizing it to drive their advertising models and personalize their services. In contrast, financial institutions have been under stricter regulations about data handling due to the sensitive nature of financial information. The European Union's General Data Protection Regulation (GDPR) and the California Consumer Privacy Act (CCPA) have added further complexity to this issue, making the reconciliation of data practices between the two sectors more difficult.

These conflicts don't just exist in the realm of theory; they have real-world consequences. Uber's clash with New York over driver benefits, Google's ongoing battles with antitrust authorities, and Wall Street's pushback against fintechs' banking charters all underscore the importance of understanding and managing these conflicts.

It's important to note that these conflicts also present opportunities. Regulatory scrutiny may lead to more robust and responsible products. Competition for talent might spur improved working conditions and benefits. The pressure to reconcile different approaches to innovation can result in better services for customers. Indeed, as we move forward, understanding these conflicts will be crucial to shaping a future where Wall Street and Silicon Valley can coexist, collaborate, and innovate to the benefit of all.

15.4 Future Outlook

Even with these conflicts, the intersection of finance and technology holds great promise. The interplay between these sectors is evolving and will continue to shape the future of finance, technology, and the global economy.

The fusion of tech's innovative prowess with the financial acumen of Wall Street has the potential to create robust solutions that address some of the world's most pressing financial challenges. From increasing financial inclusion through fintech solutions, to leveraging big data for improved financial services, the symbiosis of these sectors can drive significant progress. The growth of fintech and the increasing integration of technology in finance suggest that the trend of collaboration and interaction between Wall Street and Silicon Valley is likely to accelerate. The advent of technologies like artificial intelligence, blockchain, and cloud computing will continue to revolutionize the financial sector, leading to the creation of more efficient, secure, and inclusive financial systems.

Yet, along with these opportunities come challenges that need to be addressed. The pace of technological change and the relentless push for innovation must be balanced with the need for security, privacy, and financial stability. There will be an increasing need for a regulatory framework that can accommodate innovation while safeguarding the integrity of the financial system. As technology becomes more ingrained in our financial systems, the need for digital literacy and understanding of complex financial products will also become crucial. There is a risk that as financial services become more complex and technologically driven, they could become less accessible to the average person, thus widening the financial literacy gap. Efforts must be made to ensure that the benefits of this fusion reach all strata of society, not just the technologically savvy or financially literate.

As the world becomes more interconnected, the challenges we face become more global in nature. It is crucial that Wall Street and Silicon Valley work together with policymakers around the world to create global solutions. This includes not just cooperation on regulatory and policy matters but also a commitment to addressing global challenges like financial inequality and climate change.

In conclusion, the relationship between Wall Street and Silicon Valley will continue to shape the financial landscape. The conflicts and collaborations between them will evolve as they find the balance between innovation and regulation, competition and cooperation, risk and reward. While there are certainly challenges to be faced, the potential benefits - from greater financial inclusion and efficiency to innovative financial products and services - make this a future full of promise. The key to realizing this potential lies in finding a balanced approach that can harness the strengths of both sectors while mitigating their weaknesses and conflicts.

16 Environmental, Social and Governance Investing

A rapidly emerging trend commands our attention. This is the realm of Environmental, Social, and Governance investing, often abbreviated as ESG. This innovative investment approach has fundamentally reshaped the landscape of global finance and has significant implications for investors, businesses, and society at large.

In recent years, there has been an increasing acknowledgment of the critical role that financial markets can play in addressing some of the world's most pressing challenges. From climate change and environmental sustainability to social justice and ethical governance, the influence of financial markets extends well beyond pure economics. The incorporation of ESG factors into investment decisions is a reflection of this changing paradigm. ESG investing represents a shift away from traditional investing concepts, which focused solely on financial returns. Instead, it encourages investors to consider broader impacts and integrate ESG factors into their decision-making processes. This includes considerations about how a company operates in the world, how it treats its employees, how ethically it behaves, and what environmental impact it has.

The impact of this ESG movement on finance is profound and wide-ranging. It is reshaping the ways in which businesses operate, forcing them to reconsider their roles and responsibilities towards all stakeholders, not just shareholders. It's prompting governments to reassess their regulatory frameworks and encouraging financial institutions to design new financial products and services that meet the growing demand for ESG-compatible investments.

Despite the promising growth and potential of ESG investing, it is not without its challenges. There are issues related to transparency, standardization, and the potential for 'greenwashing.'

The realignment of investment strategies towards ESG principles poses questions about performance and returns.

Regardless, the future of ESG investing is undeniably promising, as investors increasingly seek to align their financial goals with their values.

16.1 Definition

Environmental, Social, and Governance (ESG) investing, also known as sustainable investing, is an investment discipline that considers environmental, social, and governance factors alongside financial factors in the investment decision-making process. This growing approach recognizes that ESG factors can have a significant impact on the financial performance and long-term viability of companies, and hence, on the return of investments.

Environmental considerations in ESG investing focus on how a company's operations affect the natural world. These might include the company's carbon footprint, waste management, water usage, pollution levels, and its strategy towards reducing its environmental impact. These elements provide insights into a company's environmental stewardship and its potential liabilities related to environmental issues. For instance, a company with poor environmental practices may face regulatory fines, reputational damage, and a higher cost of doing business due to inefficiencies or clean-up requirements. On the other hand, companies with strong environmental practices may benefit from cost savings, access to new markets, and enhanced reputation. Therefore, for an investor, understanding a company's environmental practices can provide important insight into its risk profile and growth potential.

Social factors in ESG investing relate to people and relationships – that is, how a company manages relationships with its employees, suppliers, customers, and the communities where it operates. Social factors could include labor practices, human rights, diversity and inclusion, customer satisfaction, data protection and privacy, and community relations.

A company with fair labor practices, good community relations, and high customer satisfaction may benefit from a motivated workforce, customer loyalty, and a good reputation, leading to stronger financial performance. Conversely, poor social practices can result in high employee turnover, customer boycotts, and reputational damage, potentially hurting financial performance.

Finally, governance refers to a company's leadership, executive pay, audits and internal controls, shareholder rights, and transparency. These factors can provide investors with an understanding of a company's management structure, its conflicts of interest, and how well it is run. Good governance can help ensure that a company is managed in the shareholders' best interest and can mitigate risks associated with unethical behavior or corruption.

These definitions illustrate how ESG factors are related to a company's long-term health and financial performance, and hence, can be of interest to investors.

It is important to note that ESG investing is not one-size-fits-all – different investors may prioritize different ESG factors based on their investment goals, risk tolerance, and personal values. Therefore, ESG investing represents a broad spectrum of investment approaches, strategies, and techniques. From negative screening and exclusion of certain sectors or companies, to positive screening for companies with strong ESG practices, to impact investing with the explicit goal to create positive social or environmental impacts alongside financial returns, ESG investing provides a range of options to investors seeking to align their investment decisions with their values and goals.

16.2 Growth of ESG Investing

ESG investing has experienced significant growth over the past few decades. This surge can be attributed to a confluence of factors, including increasing awareness about social and environmental issues, regulatory changes, investor demand, and a growing recognition of the financial materiality of ESG factors.

Environmental crises such as climate change, deforestation, and water scarcity have become front-page news, leading to heightened public concern and awareness. Many individuals and institutions want their investment practices to reflect their values and beliefs, and to contribute to a more sustainable world. This growing awareness of environmental and social issues has been a significant driver of the growth of ESG investing. For instance, the devastating impacts of climate change have been increasingly recognized, and many investors want to ensure that their investments are part of the solution rather than the problem. As a result, there is growing interest in investments in renewable energy, energy-efficient technologies, and companies with strong climate strategies.

Regulatory changes have also played a significant role in the growth of ESG investing. Around the world, governments and regulatory bodies have been implementing policies and regulations that encourage or require the consideration of ESG factors in investment decisions. These include policies to promote transparency and disclosure, as well as financial incentives for sustainable investments. Such regulatory changes have helped to mainstream ESG investing and have made it an increasingly important part of the investment landscape.

Another important driver of the growth of ESG investing has been the increasing recognition by investors and other market participants that ESG factors can be financially material. There is a growing body of research indicating that companies with strong

ESG practices may outperform their peers in the long run. These companies can often operate more efficiently, face fewer legal and regulatory risks, have better employee morale and productivity, and enjoy stronger customer loyalty. It has been observed that during periods of market volatility and economic downturns, ESG-focused portfolios tend to be more resilient. This resilience can be attributed to the fact that companies with strong ESG practices often have robust risk management processes in place, are better positioned to adapt to changing market conditions, and are more likely to have loyal customers and motivated employees, all of which can contribute to long-term financial stability and growth.

Investor demand has also been a key driver of the growth of ESG investing. More and more investors, both individuals and institutions, are demanding investment products and strategies that consider ESG factors. This demand is driven by a desire to align investments with personal or institutional values, as well as a recognition of the potential financial benefits of ESG investing. To meet this demand, investment firms have been developing a wide range of ESG investment products and strategies, including ESG-focused mutual funds and exchange-traded funds (ETFs), impact investment funds, and green bonds. This has further contributed to the growth of ESG investing by providing investors with more options to incorporate ESG factors into their investment decisions.

In conclusion, the growth of ESG investing can be attributed to a variety of factors, including increasing social and environmental awareness, regulatory changes, investor demand, and a growing recognition of the financial materiality of ESG factors. These trends indicate that ESG investing is likely to continue growing in the future, becoming an increasingly important part of the global investment landscape.

16.3 Impact on Finance

ESG investing has experienced significant growth over the past few decades. This surge can be attributed to a confluence of factors, including increasing awareness about social and environmental issues, regulatory changes, investor demand, and a growing recognition of the financial materiality of ESG factors.

Environmental crises such as climate change, deforestation, and water scarcity have become front-page news, leading to heightened public concern and awareness. Many individuals and institutions want their investment practices to reflect their values and beliefs, and to contribute to a more sustainable world. This growing awareness of environmental and social issues has been a significant driver of the growth of ESG investing.

For instance, the devastating impacts of climate change have been increasingly recognized, and many investors want to ensure that their investments are part of the solution rather than the problem. As a result, there is growing interest in investments in renewable energy, energy-efficient technologies, and companies with strong climate strategies.

Regulatory changes have also played a significant role in the growth of ESG investing. Around the world, governments and regulatory bodies have been implementing policies and regulations that encourage or require the consideration of ESG factors in investment decisions. These include policies to promote transparency and disclosure, as well as financial incentives for sustainable investments. Such regulatory changes have helped to mainstream ESG investing and have made it an increasingly important part of the investment landscape.

Another important driver of the growth of ESG investing has been the increasing recognition by investors and other market participants that ESG factors can be financially material. There is a growing body of research indicating that companies with strong ESG practices may outperform their peers in the long run. These companies can often operate more efficiently, face fewer legal and regulatory risks, have better employee morale and productivity, and enjoy stronger customer loyalty.

It has been observed that during periods of market volatility and economic downturns, ESG-focused portfolios tend to be more resilient. This resilience can be attributed to the fact that companies with strong ESG practices often have robust risk management processes in place, are better positioned to adapt to changing market conditions, and are more likely to have loyal customers and motivated employees, all of which can contribute to long-term financial stability and growth.

Investor demand has also been a key driver of the growth of ESG investing. More and more investors, both individuals and institutions, are demanding investment products and strategies that consider ESG factors. This demand is driven by a desire to align investments with personal or institutional values, as well as a recognition of the potential financial benefits of ESG investing. To meet this demand, investment firms have been developing a wide range of ESG investment products and strategies, including ESG-focused mutual funds and exchange-traded funds (ETFs), impact investment funds, and green bonds. This has further contributed to the growth of ESG investing by providing investors with more options to incorporate ESG factors into their investment decisions. ESG investing has also spurred advancements in financial technology and data analytics. With the growing demand for ESG investing, the need for comprehensive and accurate ESG data has become increasingly critical. This has led to the rise of numerous ESG data providers and fintech startups that leverage advanced technologies such as artificial intelligence and machine learning to analyze vast amounts of ESG data and generate actionable insights.

These developments have not only made ESG investing more accessible but have also contributed to greater transparency and efficiency in the financial market.

The rise of ESG investing has also affected risk management within the financial industry. ESG factors have become an important component of risk assessment. For instance, environmental considerations can have direct implications for physical assets owned by companies, as in the case of real estate companies facing risks related to climate change. The shift towards more sustainable practices and renewable energy can also affect the valuation of companies in industries such as fossil fuels. Therefore, understanding and integrating ESG risks have become crucial for comprehensive risk management.

At the same time, ESG investing has also opened up new channels for capital flows. As more investors look to align their portfolios with their values, there has been a marked increase in capital being directed towards companies and projects that are seen as contributing to positive social and environmental outcomes. This has enabled innovative green technologies, renewable energy projects, and social enterprises to attract much-needed funding. The result has been the growth of sectors that may be critical to addressing some of the major challenges our society faces, from climate change to social inequality.

ESG investing is shaping the dynamics between different market participants. Institutional investors such as pension funds and insurance companies, who are traditionally risk-averse, have been leading proponents of ESG investing. This is because good ESG practices are often indicative of effective management and long-term sustainability, which aligns with their investment horizons. At the same time, individual investors are increasingly factoring in ESG considerations into their investment decisions, creating a consumer-driven push for ESG investing.

Despite the clear benefits and impacts, the road to integrating ESG factors into the broader finance landscape hasn't been without obstacles. The challenges range from the lack of standardized ESG metrics and reporting frameworks to greenwashing, where companies overstate their environmental credentials to attract investors. The path to overcoming these challenges will shape the future direction of ESG investing.

16.4 Challenges

It's essential to understand that the challenges faced are not insurmountable. Instead, they represent areas of growth and improvement, and the evolution of ESG investing is inextricably tied to the progressive resolution of these challenges.

One way to confront the problem of greenwashing is by enhancing disclosure standards and increasing transparency. To this end, standard-setting bodies around the world are striving to formulate common frameworks for ESG disclosure. For instance, there are efforts to harmonize different ESG reporting standards into a globally accepted one, akin to what we have for financial reporting. This would make it easier for investors to compare ESG metrics across different companies and industries, thereby mitigating the issue of greenwashing.

To address the issue of data accuracy and reliability, technological advancements can play a significant role. The rise of big data and artificial intelligence offers promising prospects for sophisticated data collection and analysis. Automated ESG data collection and advanced algorithms can enable more accurate measurement of a company's ESG performance. Moreover, blockchain technology could be utilized to ensure data integrity and prevent tampering, further enhancing the reliability of ESG data. Addressing the challenge of balancing the three pillars of ESG — environment, social, and governance — requires a nuanced approach that takes into account the unique circumstances of each business. Fostering open communication between investors and companies can lead to a better understanding of the difficulties faced by companies in achieving optimal ESG performance. It may also encourage the creation of customized ESG strategies that reflect both the investor's ESG expectations and the company's operational realities.

Mitigating these challenges will necessitate the involvement of all stakeholders in the financial ecosystem. Regulators will need to ensure appropriate oversight, standard-setting bodies will need to refine and consolidate ESG metrics, and companies will need to commit to transparency and ethical behavior. Investors, for their part, will need to remain diligent and informed, critically examining ESG information instead of passively accepting it.

The future of ESG investing will significantly depend on how effectively these challenges are addressed. And while the journey might be fraught with complexities, it holds immense potential to reshape the world of finance in a manner that aligns economic growth with sustainable and equitable practices. As we continue to move forward, we must remember that ESG investing is more than just a trend—it represents a shift in how we conceive of value and growth, an evolution that takes into account the wider repercussions of financial activity on society and the planet. The discussions surrounding these challenges and their solutions will be essential to shaping the path we take as we continue to explore the vast landscape of ESG investing.

16.5 Future of ESG Investing

The future of ESG investing looks promising, though it isn't without challenges. As we've explored in the previous sections, ESG investing has come a long way from being a niche investment approach to becoming a mainstream investing strategy. It's more than just a buzzword - it's increasingly shaping the investing landscape across the globe, shifting paradigms and influencing business models. However, it's crucial to understand that the path forward for ESG investing isn't linear but dynamic and evolving.

The potential future of ESG investing is expected to continue its growth trajectory. Many industry experts predict an exponential rise in ESG investments over the next decade. This is fueled by a myriad of factors such as increasing awareness about the significance of sustainable practices, shifting societal attitudes towards climate change and social justice, and the evolution of regulatory frameworks promoting transparency and accountability. Furthermore, the younger generation of investors - the millennials and Gen Z - who are known for their preference for sustainability and ethical business practices, are also anticipated to drive ESG investing's future growth.

The rising trend of ESG investing is likely to bring about transformative changes in corporate strategies. As companies realize that robust ESG performance can attract investment, reduce risk, enhance reputation, and potentially increase profitability, they may integrate ESG considerations more deeply into their business models and decision-making processes. Companies may move towards greater transparency and more robust reporting of their ESG activities. This, in turn, could lead to the development of more sophisticated ESG metrics and benchmarks that better reflect a company's true ESG performance. In addition to this, there's a growing understanding that ESG factors can materially affect a company's financial performance. This is likely to lead to a greater integration of ESG factors into traditional financial analysis, further reinforcing the significance of ESG investing. As a result, ESG investing might not remain as a separate investing approach, but it could become a fundamental aspect of all investing.

The future of ESG investing could also witness the emergence of innovative financial products and services designed around ESG principles. There might be an increase in ESG-themed funds, bonds, and indices. Furthermore, the rise of technology might enable the development of platforms that allow investors to customize their portfolios based on their individual ESG preferences.

The future of ESG investing is not devoid of uncertainty. It will likely depend on how effectively the challenges associated with ESG investing are addressed. These challenges include enhancing data reliability and accuracy, preventing greenwashing, and achieving a balanced approach to managing environmental, social, and governance issues. As we've discussed earlier, addressing these challenges will require concerted efforts from various stakeholders, including investors, companies, regulators, and standard-setting bodies. The role of technological advancements in overcoming these challenges also cannot be overstated.

The evolving future of ESG investing is expected to herald a new era of financial stewardship that emphasizes long-term, sustainable growth. While the prospects look bright, they are intertwined with the challenges that still persist in the realm of ESG investing. Overcoming these challenges would be essential to fully realize the potential of ESG investing and to ensure its benefits are optimally harnessed.

As we explore the potential trajectory of ESG investing, it's essential to underscore the role of technology. Technology, particularly advancements in data analytics, artificial intelligence (AI), and machine learning, is poised to reshape ESG investing.

These technological tools can aid in addressing one of the significant challenges faced by ESG investing: data quality and reliability. AI and machine learning can be employed to assess vast quantities of data more effectively, uncover new insights, and improve the accuracy of ESG ratings and scores. Technology can also help in streamlining the reporting and disclosure process, enabling companies to provide more transparent and consistent ESG information.

On another front, the use of blockchain technology might be instrumental in enhancing transparency and reducing fraud. For instance, blockchain could be used to track and verify a company's ESG claims, thereby preventing greenwashing. Additionally, technological innovation could lead to new ESG investment products. For instance, robo-advisors with ESG capabilities can offer personalized ESG investing options, catering to the diverse preferences of investors. Furthermore, the evolution of ESG investing would be largely influenced by regulatory developments. While there has been significant progress in recent years, more consistent and harmonized regulations are needed. Regulatory measures might involve mandating ESG disclosures, standardizing ESG metrics, and ensuring accountability for greenwashing. Regulatory support can significantly enhance investor confidence in ESG investing and contribute to its growth.

Investor education and awareness is another area that is likely to see increased focus in the future. As ESG investing becomes mainstream, there is a growing need to educate investors about the nuances of ESG investing. This could involve understanding the various ESG strategies, interpreting ESG ratings and scores, and recognizing the impact of ESG factors on investment performance.

Investor demand, particularly from millennials and Gen Z, is expected to play a significant role in propelling the future growth of ESG investing. These younger generations are known for their commitment to sustainability and their desire to make a positive impact on society. They might not only increase their allocations to ESG investments but also demand greater transparency and accountability from companies regarding their ESG performance.

While we've spoken about the growth of ESG investing, it's important to note that the nature of ESG investing itself could evolve. Currently, the approach is primarily about mitigating ESG risks and aligning investments with ethical values. However, in the future, ESG investing might shift towards capitalizing on ESG opportunities. Investors could increasingly seek out companies that not only have robust ESG practices but also provide innovative solutions to environmental and social challenges. This approach, often termed as "impact investing," could represent the next frontier of ESG investing.

In the final analysis, the future of ESG investing will likely be shaped by a combination of factors – technological advancements, regulatory developments, investor preferences, and market dynamics. It's a future that holds immense promise, but also significant challenges. As we move forward, it's crucial to approach this future with a sense of optimism, coupled with a realistic understanding of the challenges. Only by doing so can we ensure that ESG investing reaches its full potential and contributes to a more sustainable and inclusive financial system.

17 The Future of American Finance

The vast universe of American finance has always been subject to the forces of evolution, marked by ebbs and flows, booms and busts. At its core, it remains a dynamic system, constantly reinventing itself in response to shifting market trends, policy changes, technological advancements, and the evolving needs of society. Now, as we stand on the brink of a new era, it becomes crucial to explore the future of American finance, to trace the trajectory it might follow in the years to come.

In the preceding chapters, we have traced the journey of American finance from its origins to the modern-day, through moments of crisis and recovery, the rise of new financial products and technologies, shifts in regulatory paradigms, and changing societal attitudes. Each of these historical moments has contributed to molding American finance into its current form and will continue to inform its future direction.

The ongoing evolution in finance is driven by numerous factors, some evident today, and others that may emerge unexpectedly tomorrow. These include potential trends, impending challenges, and the future prospects of banking and financial markets. Each represents a piece of a larger puzzle that, when put together, provides a glimpse into the future landscape of American finance.

Looking ahead, the future holds numerous possibilities. Will it be a future shaped by the rise of new technologies, the impact of climate change, the proliferation of ESG investing, and changing societal attitudes towards finance? Or will it be a future marked by growing financial inequalities, increased market volatility, and the threat of new financial crises? It's likely to be a blend of both, offering opportunities for growth and innovation, as well as posing significant challenges that need to be effectively addressed.

As we delve into the intricacies of this complex topic, it is essential to recognize that the future of American finance will not be a predetermined path, but a journey marked by continuous adaptation, transformation, and occasional reinvention. The decisions we make today, the trends we embrace, the challenges we overcome, and the visions we dare to envisage will play a crucial role in shaping this journey.

Ultimately, the future of American finance will be a reflection of our collective aspirations for a financial system that is not only robust, resilient, and efficient but also equitable, inclusive, and sustainable. As we embark on this exploration of the future, let's keep this vision at the forefront, guiding our perspectives and shaping our discourse.

17.1 Potential Trends

As we navigate into the future of American finance, several potential trends loom large on the horizon, each one carrying the potential to disrupt established norms and bring about significant change.

Firstly, let's explore the role of technology, which has already started to redefine the landscape of American finance. Emerging technologies such as Artificial Intelligence (AI), blockchain, and big data analytics have the potential to revolutionize all aspects of the financial industry, from banking and investment management to insurance and real estate. Artificial intelligence and machine learning have begun to automate many aspects of finance, from credit scoring and loan approvals to high-frequency trading and fraud detection. Big data analytics and predictive modeling offer unprecedented insights into market trends, customer behavior, and risk management. Blockchain technology, the underlying technology for cryptocurrencies, promises a new era of transparency, security, and decentralization in financial transactions.

In the world of investment, the rise of Environmental, Social, and Governance (ESG) investing is another trend to watch. As society becomes more conscious of the environmental and social impacts of business activities, more investors are seeking to align their investment choices with their values. The growing demand for ESG-compliant investments has the potential to drive significant capital flows towards sustainable and socially responsible businesses. This trend could fundamentally reshape the investment landscape, forcing businesses to pay more attention to their ESG performance, and influencing the development of new financial products and services. Another transformative trend is the democratization of finance. New technologies and business models are making financial services more accessible and affordable to the masses. Digital platforms, robo-advisors, and neobanks are breaking down barriers to financial inclusion, enabling more people to participate in the financial system. This trend could not only expand the customer base for financial services but also foster financial literacy and empowerment among traditionally underserved populations.

Meanwhile, the ongoing evolution of regulatory frameworks presents another significant trend. The financial crisis of 2008 has highlighted the importance of robust and effective financial regulation in maintaining financial stability and protecting consumers. In the years to come, we are likely to see further refinements in financial regulation, influenced by factors such as technological advances, changing market structures, and lessons from past crises. However, striking a balance between promoting innovation and protecting consumers will be a key challenge. The global interconnectivity of financial markets is yet another trend that is set to increase. The growth of international trade and investment, coupled with the proliferation of digital technologies, has made financial markets more interconnected than ever. This trend can bring both opportunities and risks. On the one hand, it can enhance market efficiency, diversification, and risk sharing. On the other hand, it can amplify financial shocks and make crisis management more complex.

Lastly, the impact of socio-economic factors, such as demographic changes, income inequality, and social mobility, cannot be ignored. These factors can influence the demand for financial services, affect financial stability, and shape public attitudes towards finance. In particular, the aging population in the U.S. will have far-reaching implications for retirement planning, healthcare financing, and estate planning. Income inequality and social mobility can impact the distribution of wealth, access to financial services, and the stability of the financial system.

In conclusion, the future of American finance is likely to be marked by significant trends that can reshape the industry in profound ways. Embracing these trends, understanding their implications, and adapting to the changes they bring about will be key to navigating the future landscape of American finance. However, as with any trend, the path ahead is fraught with uncertainties, and success will hinge on the ability to anticipate, adapt, and innovate.

17.2 Impending Challenges

While the future of American finance promises new opportunities and advancements, it also presents a series of impending challenges that could pose significant hurdles in its evolution. These challenges span across a range of areas, including technology, regulation, economic and social issues, and global influences.

Among these, perhaps the most pressing challenge lies in the integration and regulation of new technologies. Emerging tech trends like artificial intelligence, machine learning, big data, blockchain, and fintech innovations are creating a tectonic shift in the financial industry. While these technologies promise significant improvements in efficiency, accessibility, and transparency, they also introduce new risks and vulnerabilities. Cybersecurity is a prime concern, as more financial transactions become digital and are stored on cloud servers, the risk of data breaches, identity theft, and cyber-attacks grows. The industry faces the dual challenge of harnessing the potential of these technologies while safeguarding against their inherent risks.

In parallel, the challenge of regulatory adaptation is crucial. The speed at which new financial technologies are emerging presents a challenge for regulatory bodies to keep pace. Regulators are confronted with the task of creating frameworks that protect consumers and maintain the stability of the financial system, while also fostering innovation. This challenge is magnified by the global nature of these technologies, which often operate beyond the confines of national jurisdictions.

On the economic front, the potential for economic volatility and financial crises remains a significant challenge. As the memory of the 2008 financial crisis lingers, there is heightened awareness of the potential for systemic risk within the financial system. Despite efforts to strengthen financial regulation and supervision, the risk of future crises cannot be eliminated completely. Factors such as high levels of corporate and public debt, economic imbalances, and uncertainties in the global economy could potentially trigger financial instability.

Socioeconomic disparities and financial inequality present another challenge. Despite the progress in financial inclusion, significant segments of the American population still lack access to basic financial services. Income inequality and wealth concentration can fuel social tensions and create distortions in the financial system. In this context, ensuring that the benefits of financial innovation reach all segments of society and contribute to equitable growth is a significant challenge. Climate change and sustainability issues also pose considerable challenges for the financial industry. As the impacts of climate change become increasingly evident, there is growing recognition of the financial risks associated with environmental degradation and the transition to a low-carbon economy. These risks include physical risks from climate-related disasters, transition risks from changes in policy and technology, and liability risks from lawsuits. Managing these risks and integrating sustainability considerations into financial decision-making is a complex and urgent challenge.

Finally, the changing demographics of America pose a challenge for the financial sector. The aging population implies a shift in financial needs, with a greater emphasis on retirement planning, long-term care insurance, and estate planning. At the same time, younger generations have different attitudes and expectations towards finance, driven by their experiences and technological advancements. Catering to the diverse and evolving needs of these different population segments will be a significant challenge.

In essence, the path to the future of American finance is fraught with challenges. Navigating these challenges will require foresight, adaptability, and a balanced approach that recognizes the trade-offs between risk and reward. The ultimate test will lie in the ability of the American financial industry to turn these challenges into opportunities for innovation, growth, and greater financial stability.

17.3 Future of Banking

As we look towards the future of banking in America, it's essential to consider several evolving trends and their potential to reshape the financial landscape. Traditional banking as we know it is undergoing a transformation, driven by emerging technologies, changing customer expectations, and shifting regulatory environments. In terms of technology, we can anticipate that the digitization of banking will continue to accelerate. Mobile banking and online platforms have already made it easier for customers to manage their finances from the comfort of their own homes. These technological advancements will likely continue to grow, with AI and machine learning playing increasingly significant roles. These technologies will aid in everything from risk assessment to customer service, where chatbots will become more refined, capable of handling complex queries and providing personalized assistance.

The emergence of fintech companies and their successful incursion into traditional banking domains also implies a future where collaboration and competition will exist in tandem. Banks may partner with fintech firms to leverage their innovative technologies and service models, effectively boosting their digital transformation efforts. However, these collaborations will not diminish the competitive threat fintech poses, particularly as these companies continue to innovate and challenge the established norms.

Moreover, the future of banking will be influenced by evolving consumer behavior and expectations. Millennials and Gen Z, in particular, are showing different banking behaviors compared to older generations. They are more inclined to use digital channels, value seamless user experiences, and show a greater openness to non-traditional financial service providers. Catering to the needs and preferences of these digitally savvy generations will be a key focus for banks in the future. In the realm of products and services, we may see banks moving away from a transaction-based model to a more advisory-based approach. As simple transactions become increasingly automated, the human element of banking could become more centered on providing financial advice and personalized services. Banks will likely leverage data analytics to gain deep insights into customer behavior, enabling them to offer tailored financial solutions.

Regulatory changes and their implications will also significantly shape the future of banking. As seen in the aftermath of the financial crisis of 2008, regulatory changes can greatly influence the structure and operations of banks. Furthermore, the growing emphasis on sustainable finance means banks will likely face increased scrutiny of their roles in addressing social and environmental issues. Banks may need to adjust their strategies and operations to meet evolving regulatory requirements, particularly concerning transparency, data protection, and sustainability.

Finally, the area of cybersecurity will continue to be of paramount importance. As banking services become increasingly digital, the potential for cyber threats grows. Future banking will require robust security measures, state-of-the-art systems, and a continuous focus on mitigating risks associated with cyber threats.

Looking forward, the future of banking in America is likely to be vastly different from what it is today. The shift towards a more digital, customer-centric, and sustainable model seems inevitable, and it's up to the banks to navigate this transition effectively while ensuring they remain profitable and meet the diverse needs of their customers. The challenges are plentiful, but so too are the opportunities for innovation and evolution.

17.4 Future of Financial Markets

As we peer into the future of American financial markets, we need to recognize that they are currently at an inflection point. The rapid pace of technological advancement, changing regulations, and evolving societal expectations are converging to reshape these markets fundamentally. This metamorphosis promises to be as unpredictable as it is transformative, bringing forth new challenges and opportunities.

Technological advancements stand at the forefront of this transformation. High-frequency trading algorithms, predictive analysis tools, and decentralized finance are only a few of the elements contributing to this new financial landscape. Automation and artificial intelligence will continue to permeate financial markets, performing tasks ranging from basic data processing to complex portfolio management. The advent of blockchain technology and the proliferation of cryptocurrencies are already challenging conventional understandings of financial markets. These digital assets provide a decentralized and transparent alternative to traditional finance, disrupting established market structures. We anticipate a growing presence and acceptance of these technologies in mainstream financial markets.

Further, big data and AI have started revolutionizing investment strategies and risk assessment methodologies. For instance, AI-driven hedge funds use machine learning algorithms to predict market trends and make investment decisions. As these technologies advance and become more accessible, we may see an even greater shift towards such predictive analytics and algorithm-driven investment strategies. Beyond technology, evolving regulations also hold a crucial role in shaping the future of financial markets. The changing regulatory landscape, driven by the need for greater transparency, customer protection, and risk mitigation, will likely redefine market structures. For instance, the increasing focus on ESG (Environmental, Social, and Governance) factors will push companies to be more transparent about their ESG risks and performance, changing the dynamics of investment decision-making.

In this new regulatory environment, the importance of compliance will be amplified. Firms will have to invest in robust compliance structures and procedures, and adapt their operations to a more transparent and risk-averse market environment. Additionally, societal and demographic shifts will impact the future of financial markets. The rise of a more conscious investor, concerned not only with financial returns but also with the societal and environmental impact of their investments, will drive a shift in investment strategies. As more investors prioritize ESG-compliant investments, companies and financial markets will need to align themselves with these principles to stay relevant.

Lastly, the democratization of finance, partly driven by the rise of fintech and digital platforms, will influence the future market dynamics. These platforms lower the barrier to entry for retail investors, contributing to a more diverse and inclusive financial market. However, this also poses new challenges related to investor protection and market stability, as the recent GameStop episode demonstrated.

In conclusion, the future of American financial markets is poised to be highly dynamic, increasingly inclusive, and more tech-driven. The balance between innovation and regulation will be critical in ensuring these markets remain effective conduits for capital allocation while also preserving market integrity and stability. These changes promise a future where financial markets will look very different from their present form, but the ultimate shape of these transformations remains to be seen.

17.5 Outlook

In the final analysis, the outlook for the future of American finance is optimistic yet complex, presenting an intricate web of evolving trends, challenges, and opportunities. With the accelerating pace of technology, regulatory changes, the rise of ESG investing, and an evolving customer landscape, American finance is on the cusp of a transformation that will likely redefine its operational and strategic contours. Technological advancements are poised to bring about a paradigm shift. Artificial intelligence, machine learning, big data analytics, blockchain, and an array of FinTech innovations are expected to create a more efficient, accessible, and inclusive financial landscape. From robo-advisors offering personalized financial advice to blockchain's potential to revolutionize transaction mechanisms, the future is digital.

While these developments offer substantial opportunities, they also pose challenges. As technology becomes deeply integrated into financial operations, concerns surrounding data security, privacy, and ethical AI usage become more pressing. Similarly, the decentralization associated with blockchain and cryptocurrencies will pose regulatory and stability challenges. The future of finance will thus necessitate effective regulation that safeguards consumers and maintains market stability without stifling innovation. Regulatory changes are also set to reshape the financial industry, particularly in the realm of ESG investing. As societal pressure mounts for businesses to align with ESG goals, and as regulatory bodies move towards mandating ESG disclosure, sustainable finance will likely take center stage. However, challenges such as ESG rating standardization and greenwashing will need addressing.

The future will also be significantly influenced by demographic and societal changes. The rise of a new, conscious investor looking beyond financial returns, the growing importance of financial inclusion, and a customer base that values digital experiences will require financial institutions to rethink their strategies and business models.

Despite these challenges, the future of American finance seems promising. As the industry navigates through these changes, it is set to emerge more resilient, inclusive, and in tune with the demands of the digital age. The road ahead is fraught with disruption and uncertainty, but also abundant with opportunities for those willing to adapt, innovate, and lead.

In essence, the future of American finance will be marked by dynamic change and evolution. The financial sector has always been at the heart of American capitalism, and as we look to the future, it seems poised to continue in this role, albeit in a much-transformed avatar. From Wall Street to Silicon Valley, from the local bank branch to the global investor, the wheels of American finance continue to turn, driving not just the US but also the global economy towards a future of immense possibility.